CONGESTION CONTROL IN COMPUTER NETWORKS: THEORY, PROTOCOLS AND APPLICATIONS

DISTRIBUTED, CLUSTER AND GRID COMPUTING
YI PAN - SERIES EDITOR

Advanced Parallel and Distributed Computing: Evaluation, Improvement and Practice (Volume 2 in Distributed, Cluster and Grid Computing)
Yi Pan and Rajeev Raje (Editors)
2006. ISBN: 1-60021-202-6

Parallel and Distributed Systems: Evaluation and Improvement (Volume 2 in Distributed, Cluster and Grid Computing)
Yuanshun Dai, Yi Pan and Rajeev R. Raje (Editors)
2006. ISBN: 1-60021-276-X

Performance Evaluation of Parallel, Distributed and Emergent System (Volume 1 in Distributed, Cluster and Grid Computing)
Mohamed Ould-Kahona and Geyong Min (Editors)
2007. ISBN: 1-59454-817-X

From Problem Toward Solution: Wireless Sensor Networks Security
Zhen Jiang and Yi Pan (Editors)
2009. ISBN: 978-1-60456-457-0

Congestion Control in Computer Networks: Theory, Protocols and Applications
Jiaxin Wing
2010. ISBN: 978-1-61728-698-8
2010. ISBN: 978-1-61761-149-0 (E-book)

CONGESTION CONTROL IN COMPUTER NETWORKS: THEORY, PROTOCOLS AND APPLICATIONS

JIANXIN WANG

Nova Science Publishers, Inc.
New York

For permission to use material from this book please contact us:
Telephone 631-231-7269; Fax 631-231-8175
Web Site: http://www.novapublishers.com

NOTICE TO THE READER

The Publisher has taken reasonable care in the preparation of this book, but makes no expressed or implied warranty of any kind and assumes no responsibility for any errors or omissions. No liability is assumed for incidental or consequential damages in connection with or arising out of information contained in this book. The Publisher shall not be liable for any special, consequential, or exemplary damages resulting, in whole or in part, from the readers' use of, or reliance upon, this material. Any parts of this book based on government reports are so indicated and copyright is claimed for those parts to the extent applicable to compilations of such works.

Independent verification should be sought for any data, advice or recommendations contained in this book. In addition, no responsibility is assumed by the publisher for any injury and/or damage to persons or property arising from any methods, products, instructions, ideas or otherwise contained in this publication.

This publication is designed to provide accurate and authoritative information with regard to the subject matter covered herein. It is sold with the clear understanding that the Publisher is not engaged in rendering legal or any other professional services. If legal or any other expert assistance is required, the services of a competent person should be sought. FROM A DECLARATION OF PARTICIPANTS JOINTLY ADOPTED BY A COMMITTEE OF THE AMERICAN BAR ASSOCIATION AND A COMMITTEE OF PUBLISHERS.

Additional color graphics may be available in the e-book version of this book.

LIBRARY OF CONGRESS CATALOGING-IN-PUBLICATION DATA
Wang, Jianxin, 1969-
Congestion control in computer networks : theory, protocols, and applications / author, Jianxin Wang.
p. cm.
Includes bibliographical references and index.
ISBN 978-1-61728-698-8 (hardcover)
1. Routing (Computer network management) 2. Local area networks (Computer networks)--Traffic. I. Title.
TK5105.543.W36 2010
004.6'8--dc22
2010026082

Published by Nova Science Publishers, Inc. ✦ *New York*

CONTENTS

Forward   vii
Preface   ix

Part I. Introduction and Performance Evaluation   1

Chapter 1   Introduction   3
Chapter 2   Analysis and Comparison of Congestion Control Protocols in High
                 Bandwidth-Delay Product Networks   19
Chapter 3   Performance Analysis of Congestion Control Protocols in Different
                 Network Environments   33
Chapter 4   Survey on Router Buffer Sizing in High Bandwidth-Delay Network   51

Part II. Active Queue Management   67

Chapter 5   A Robust Proportional Controller for AQM Based on Optimized
                 Second-Order System Model   69
Chapter 6   Design of a Stabilizing Second-Order Congestion Controller for
                 Large-Delay Networks   91
Chapter 7   PFED: A Prediction-based Fair Active Queue
                 Management Algorithm   107
Chapter 8   Downlink Temporal Fairness in 802.11 WLAN Based on Virtual
                 Queue Management   119
Chapter 9   An Adaptive Loss Differentiation Algorithm Based on Queue
                 Management   129
Chapter 10   A Prediction-Based AQM Algorithm for Diffserv Networks   139

PART III. TCP in High Speed Network   151

Chapter 11   ARROW-TCP: Accelerating Transmission toward Efficiency and
                 Fairness for High-Speed Networks   153

Chapter 12   TCP Congestion Control Protocol based on Cooperation Mode in
                 High Bandwidth-Delay Product Networks   **175**

Part IV. TCP in Mixed Wired and Wireless Network   **189**

Chapter 13   A Cross-Layer TCP for Providing Fairness in Wireless Mesh
                 Networks   **191**
Chapter 14   An ECN-Based Congestion Control Algorithm for TCP
                 Enhancement in Wireless Local Area Networks   **205**
Chapter 15   A Channel-Aware Scheduling Algorithm for Improving
                 TCP Fairness   **217**
Chapter 16   An Improved TCP with Cross-layer Congestion Notification Over
                 Wired/Wireless Hybrid Networks   **227**
Chapter 17   A Prediction Method for Congestion Probability Based on ECN
                 Over Wired-Wireless Hybrid Networks   **237**
References   **253**
Index   **271**

FOREWORD

When the resource demands exceed a network's capacity, the network gets congested and its performance degrades. Network traffic congestion control concerns controlling traffic entry into a network as to avoid congestive collapse by attempting to avoid oversubscription of aeny of the processing or link capabilities of the network nodes and links. For example, we can take resource reducing steps such as sending fewer packets into a network to achieve this goal. Congestion control is different from flow control. While congestion control prevents too much traffic into a network, flow control prevents the sender from overwhelming the receiver.

For a number of years, I have believed that traffic congestion control plays an important role in the Internet's success and is a tough problem to solve. With the emergence of wireless networks and mobile computing and the tremendous increase in the number of Internet users, the Internet is becoming more sophisticated and many new issues in congestion control arise and need special attentions. In addition, congestion control becomes even more important and tougher to solve due to the changes in network environments. For example, TCP in mixed wired and wireless networks is a new research problem, which requires special solution since current policies overlook many issues in this mixed environment. Thus, new congestion control algorithms and protocols which adapt this new wired/wireless environment need to be designed, developed, evaluated and implemented.

The aim of this book is to provide a comprehensive overview of current congestion control policies used in computer networks, especially for the Internet, and to give an update on the state-of-the-art in congestion control research. This book systematically describes the idea, concepts and principals of congestion control in different environments and presents the performance evaluation and comparisons of various algorithms and protocols through rigorous analysis and extensive simulation. A lot of examples and figures are used in the book to illustrate the concepts and methods as well their uses in different environments, which makes the book easy to read and understand. In fact, reading the book is a fun. I firmly believe that students and scientists working in networks will find this book valuable and accessible.

The modern theory of congestion control was pioneered by Frank Kelly, a professor from University of Cambridge, who applied microeconomic theory and convex optimization theory to describe how individuals controlling their own rates can interact to achieve an "optimal" network-wide rate allocation. Since his theory is introduced to computer networks, a lot of papers have been published. In fact, each year many workshops, special sessions or special journal issues have been dedicated to this topic, an indication of how important this topic is. Several books in the similar areas have also been published. However, this book is unique in that it presents cutting edge research topics and methodologies in the area of congestion control, especially in the new wireless network environments. It summarizes the most recent research results from a young research team from China. Many results presented in this book have just or never been published in the literature and represent the most advanced technologies in this exciting area. It also provides a comprehensive and balanced blend of theoretical algorithms and practical case studies. I firmly believe that this book will further promote research in this exciting area.

Dr. Jianxin Wang is a rising star in the area of algorithm design for both computer networks and biological networks. He is leading a research team at Central South University, China, and his team has achieved a lot of novel results in these areas. His vision of creating such a book to summarize their most recent research results in congestion control in a timely manner deserves our loud applause. This book is ideally suited both as a reference and as a text for a graduate course on computer networks. This book can also serve as a repository of significant reference materials as the list of references cited in each chapter will serve as a useful source for further study in this area. The author, Dr. Jianxin Wang and the publisher, the Nova Science Publishers, deserve a loud applause for producing such a book that is a major contribution not only to congestion control, but more generally, to the development of the Internet.

I highly recommend this timely and valuable book to the reader. I believe that it will benefit many readers and make a significant contribution to the further development of the Internet and its applications, especially in the wireless and multimedia environments.

Dr. Yi Pan
Chair and Professor
Department of Computer Science
Georgia State University, USA

Changjiang Chair Professor
Department of Computer Science
Central South University, China

PREFACE

Computer networks play an important role on connecting resources and people. The tremendous growth of the Internet and the advances of computer technology have been pushing forward computer networks for high speed and broad bandwidth. At the same time, with the emergence of wireless technologies, such as IEEE 802.11 and Bluetooth, mobile users are enabled to connect to each other wirelessly.

As the Internet becomes increasingly heterogeneous, the issue of congestion control becomes ever more important. The large increase in traffic demands and the relentless demand for network capacity have produced a need for new flexible types of congestion control. Further more, with the widespread adoption of wireless networks, congestion control is becoming more complicated due to traffic contention among neighboring links and heterogeneity in their transmission speeds in wireless channels.

In this book, the author firstly reviews the background and concepts of Internet congestion control and gives an overview of the state-of-the-art in congestion control research, in an accessible and easily comprehensible format. This book also reports the innovative algorithms and protocols for congestion control and the use of analytical, simulation-based modeling and evaluation. Consequently, this book will provide academics and researchers in computer science, electrical engineering and communications networking, as well as students with advanced networking and Internet courses, with a thorough understanding of the current state and future evolution of Internet congestion control.

This book contains 17 chapters and is basically divided into four main parts, notably introduction and performance evaluation, active queue management, TCP in high speed network, TCP in mixed wired and wireless network The author believes all of these chapters not only provide novel ideas, new analytical models, simulation results and handful experience in this field, but also provide very interesting ideas to stimulate further original research activities in the area.

ORGANIZATION AND OUTLINE

This book is organized into four parts, which are briefly described in the sequel.

Part I: Introduction and Performance Evaluation

Chapter 1 reviews the research area of congestion control and avoidance approaches. The research area is divided into three hierarchical layers: congestion control modeling, link algorithm and source algorithm. According to their order, the important advances in each layer are introduced. In this chapter, some important concepts, such as the traffic model and protocol model, scheduling algorithm, AQM algorithm, and TCP protocol, are clarified, analyzed and summarized. Finally, the difficulty and evaluation of congestion Control are presented based on this review.

Chapter 2 firstly categorizes high-speed TCP protocols to loss-based, delay-based and ECN based three groups and describes all these protocols. Based on this study, the influence of RTT, router buffer size and AQM algorithm to the performance of congestion control protocol are emphatically analyzed. Lastly a general performance comparisons and analysis result of most representative protocols are given using ns2 simulator. Subsequently, the chapter summarizes the current existing open issues, and provides some further interesting research directions.

Chapter 3 firstly makes performance comparison for a variety of proposed congestion control protocols under different network environments by simulations. Then the analysis of the advantages and disadvantages of them is given. The results show that, there is no one with optimal performance in all kinds of network environments among these proposed congestion control protocols. At the end of this chapter, it is concluded that future research work can focus on the design of congestion control mechanism with strong adaptability to different environments.

Chapter 4 reviews the researches of buffer sizing in routers, and then focuses on five typical buffer sizing methods based on the model of TCP protocol. Meanwhile, several primary factors which influence buffer requirement are analyzed. Simulation results showed that: (1) buffer sizing methods based on different assumptions should be adapted to different network environments. (2) When high-speed TCP protocols are used in the high bandwidth-delay network, buffer size could be reduced greatly.

Part II: Active Queue Management

Chapter 5 proposes a novel AQM algorithm which is based, for the first time, on the optimized second-order system model, called Adaptive Optimized Proportional Controller (AOPC). AOPC measures the latest packet loss ratio, and uses it as a complement to queue length in order to dynamically adjust packet drop probability. Through using TCP throughput model, AOPC is capable of detaching from the number of TCP sessions and insensitive to various network conditions. The parameter tuning rule is in compliance with the optimized second-order system model which has a small overshoot and fast convergence speed. Simulation results demonstrate that AOPC is more responsive to time-varying network conditions than other algorithms, and obtains the best tradeoff between utilization and delay.

Chapter 6 addresses the problem of the stability of congestion control for networks with large round-trip communication delays. The drastic queue oscillations in large delay networks of PI, REM and DC-AQM decrease the link utilization and introduce the avoidable delay jitter. To address this problem, a robust IMC-PID congestion controller based on internal model control principle is developed to restrict the negative impact on the stability caused by the large delay. Simulation results demonstrate that the integrated performance of proposed scheme outperforms others as communication delay increases, and achieves high link utilization and small delay jitter.

Chapter 7 proposes a novel active queue management algorithm PFED, which is based on network traffic prediction. The main properties of PFED are: (1) stabilizing queue length at a desirable level with consideration of future traffic, and using a MMSE (Minimum Mean Square Error) predictor to predict future network traffic; (2) imposing effective punishment upon misbehaving flow with a full stateless method; (3) maintaining queue arrival rate bounded by queue service rate through more reasonable calculation of packet drop probability. Simulation results show that PFED outperforms RED and CHOKe in stabling instantaneous queue length and in fairness. It is also shown that PFED enables the link capacity to be fully utilized by stabilizing the queue length at a desirable level, while not incurring excessive packet loss ratio.

Chapter 8 proposes a temporal fair AQM－TFRED (Temporal Fair RED) on AP (Access Point) in multi-rate 802.11 WLAN. Taking into account the transmission rate of each flow, TFRED sets different drop probability for each flow going through the AP to guarantee equal channel usage time for each wireless node. Analysis and simulation results show that, compared with throughput fair AQM algorithms, TFRED achieves temporal fairness, per-flow throughput protection, and great increase in total throughput.

Chapter 9 points out that BQM discriminator cannot be fit to different network states and proposes an adaptive BQM, whose key idea is to adjust the primary parameters according to network events and to track the dropping pattern on routers. The simulation results show that the accuracy of A_BQM discriminator is higher than that of BQM in different network states and A_BQM can adjust itself adaptively according to network states.

Chapter 10 proposes a new active queue management algorithm-PIO based on the prediction of the arrival rate in DiffServ networks. In PIO, the average arrival rate for IN packets and all packets in the next interval are predicted firstly. The PIO algorithm decides whether or not to drop the arriving packet according to the queue length for IN packets, the total queue length for all packets, the predicted arrival rate for IN packets and all packets in the next interval. Through the simulation, this chapter analyzes the PIO performances with respect to the stabilization of the queue, packet loss ratio and attainable throughput under the different subscription ratio and the different number of connections. The simulation results indicate that RIO improves the stabilization of queue and reduces packet loss ratio efficiently whether the network is under-subscribed or over-subscribed, while providing statistical assurance for the bandwidth.

Part III: TCP in High Speed Network

Chapter 11 proposes a novel congestion control protocol, ARROW-TCP, to address the issues of stability and convergence in existing transmission control protocols. Theoretical analysis shows that ARROW-TCP is globally stable and achieves exponential convergence to efficiency and fairness in a constant time. Meanwhile, ARROW-TCP obtains ideal performance of zero queuing delay, free packet loss by converging monotonically to the fair allocation and avoiding overshooting link capacity. Moreover, the price mechanism leverages ARROW-TCP into max-min rate allocation in hybrid multi-bottleneck scenarios. Finally, extensive simulations are conducted to verify our theoretical analysis and the simulation results demonstrate that ARROWTCP outperforms other transmission control protocols in terms of stability, convergence, and packet loss rate.

Chapter 12 proposes a novel TCP congestion control protocol based on cooperation mode (CCP), which uses 1 bit routers' explicit feedback predicted information and round-trip times (RTT) delay signals to adjust the congestion windows appropriately. NS2 simulations show the efficiency, TCP-friendliness and fairness of CCP in High Bandwidth-Delay Product (BDP) Networks.

Part IV: TCP in Mixed Wired and Wireless Network

Chapter 13 investigates the "Counter Starvation" problem among TCP flows with different hops away from the BS in wireless mesh network. Existing solutions mainly focus on the policies at MAC layer or network layer. But how these policies affect the congestion mechanism of TCP has been overlooked. This chapter proposes a priority-based congestion control by using "Counter Cross-Layer ECN" Analysis and simulation results demonstrate that this scheme can improve the fairness of TCP flows while ensuring the network efficiency.

Chapter 14 proposes an ECN-based access point congestion control algorithm called APCC (AP congestion control). The main properties of APCC are: (1) Using both wireless channel load and buffer queue length as congestion indicators, APCC ensures low packet loss rate, low queue delay, and high goodput; (2) APCC guarantees the up/down TCP fairness by marking the ECN bit in TCP DATA and ACK packets; (3) Taking into account the wireless channel rate of each TCP flow, APCC sets different ECN marking probability for each flow to achieve the time fairness and high network efficiency.

Chapter 15 proposes the Up/Down Time Fair LAS (UDTFLAS) scheduling algorithm to achieve the wireless channel usage time fairness between the uplink and downlink TCP flows. Taking into account the transmission rate and the direction of each TCP flow, UDTFLAS gives the higher transmission probability to the TCP flows with the higher wireless data rate, as well as in the downlink direction. Analysis and simulation results show that UDTFLAS achieves the up/down time fairness, per-flow throughput protection, and great increase in total network throughput.

Chapter 16 proposes a cross-layer ECN scheme that TCP sender will trigger congestion control by ECN if RTS count in its receiving packet exceeds a given thresh. This cross-layer design is an efficient enhancement to congestion control based on ECN, by which forms a model coupling existing TCP over wired/wireless networks. To verify this new TCP model, WLAN including multi TCP flow and multi-hop wireless/wired hybrid networks are designed in NS2. Simulation results show that it can improve network performance and can be easily extended to other TCP variants.

Finally, Chapter 17 focuses on congestion control mechanism based on ECN. It has been deeply considered that in what manner the sender should have response to ECN feedback, which has been overlooked in existing TCP variants. And the proposed method, CPECN (Congestion Probability based on Explicit Congestion Notification) is to control TCP behavior based on the calculating of Congestion Probability when loss events occurring. Then CPECN is applied into two TCP protocols, Reno and Westwood. Simulation results demonstrate that TCP variants coupled with CPECN method can improve the network performance.

ACKNOWLEDGMENTS

My sincere thanks to my own graduate students from the Networks Research Group for their considerable assistance; to the many faculty and researchers who have offered useful advice and from whom I have learned so much; I would like to thank my students Dr Jiawei Huang, Jin Ye, Liang Rong, Hao Gong, Wenyu Gao, Jie Chen, Chunquan Li, Donglei Chen, for their contributions to many chapters in this book. Dr. Jiawei Huang, Mingming Lu, Murtada Khalafallah, Yao Liu, Jie Chen and Hui Liu helped me edit the book. I would like to express my deep thanks to the Editor-in-Chief, Professor Yi Pan, for giving me with the opportunity to write this book in Nova Science Book Series on Wireless Networks and Mobile Computing. I also deeply thank him for the guidance and support he has provided us throughout the different phases of preparing this book. Finally, we gratefully acknowledge the support of the entire production team at Nova Science Publishers.

Jianxin Wang
Central South University
Email: jxwang@mail.csu.edu.cn

PART I. INTRODUCTION AND PERFORMANCE EVALUATION

Chapter 1

INTRODUCTION

1.1. WHAT IS CONGESTION?

In computer networks, when resource demand exceeds network capacity, network performance will degrade. This phenomenon is called network congestion. Congestion is the result of the statistical multiplexing principle [1, 2] upon which Internet is based, with the objective of maximizing resource utilization. Under statistical multiplexing principle, the available bandwidth of link, the computing and storage capacity of nodes are shared by all users. When a node's input rate exceeds its output rate, the excessive traffic accumulates in the node's buffer. The node is said to be congested; that is, the node's output link becomes a bottleneck link. If the buffer queue is filled, the node will drop any incoming packets. Furthermore, the packet loss will induce retransmission and bring about more traffic. The persistent congestion causes packet loss and retransmission, and thus the total throughput of network is reduced.

The Internet firstly experienced the congestion problem in the 1980s. One of the earliest documents that mention the term "congestion collapse" is written by Van Jacobson [3] at the Lawrence Berkeley National Laboratory (LBNL). In October 1986, the data rate between the University of California at Berkeley and LBNL (sites separated by 400 yards and two IMP hops) collapsed from 32 Kbit/s to just 40 bit/s. From then on, with the rapid development of Internet and the fast increase of terminal devices, the congestion problem has become one of the most critical issues in network research.

Essentially, a network link is said to be congested if contention for it causes queues to build up and packets to start getting dropped. In such a case, the increasing overload causes long packet queues and results in end-to-end delays, as well as increases packet loss rate.

Figure 1-1 shows a schematic view of throughput as a function of the offered load on the network. Initially, at low levels of offered load, throughput is roughly proportional to offered load, because the network is under-utilized. Then, throughput plateaus at a value "knee" equal to the bottleneck link bandwidth because packets start getting queued. When offered load is increased even further, the throughput shows a "cliff" effect, starting to decrease and eventually go to zero and this is the point where the network will suffer congestion collapse.

Congestion is a fundamental problem in network because sharing network infrastructure is the way to achieve cost-effective and scalable networks. Therefore the critical problem is how to manage congestion carefully.

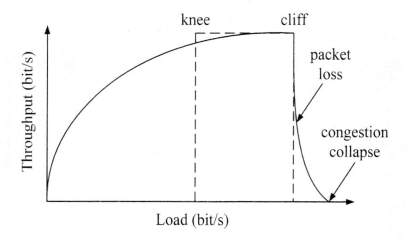

Figure 1-1. Schematic view of throughput vs. offered load.

1.2. HOW TO MANAGE CONGESTION?

Internet uses the TCP/IP model as the framework protocols with the property of best-effort [4]. In this model, each packet is processed and forwarded through a node along one of the several possible output links, at a rate determined by the bandwidth of that link. In the meantime, more packets, which in general could belong to any other flow, could arrive to the same node. The node tries to accommodate the packets in its buffer and process them. If there isn't enough space in the buffer, some of the arriving packets may be dropped.

The above discussion makes it clear that congestion occurs when the demand is greater than the available capacity. Therefore, it is a common choice to improve the network capacity to solve congestion in a method called overprovisioning. This leads to the following beliefs: (1) Congestion caused by the shortage of buffer space could be solved when larger memories are used. (2) Congestion due to the small bandwidth could be solved if more high-speed links become available.

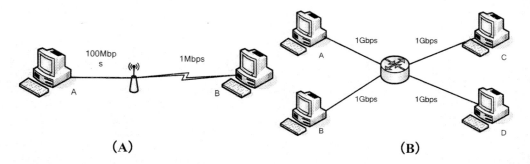

Figure 1-2. Typical network congestion.

However, without proper protocol redesign, the congestion problem cannot be resolved by overprovisioning [5]. Figure 1-2(a) shows a typical wireless LAN connecting to the Internet. The bandwidth of wired link is 100Mbps, and the bandwidth of the wireless link is 1 Mbps. When flow is sent form wired node A to wireless node B, congestion will occur on the access point (AP). It is obvious that too much traffic (form wired node A to wireless node B) will lead to buffer overflow and packet loss on the AP. If infinite-buffer is used on AP, however, the queue and delay could get so long that by the time the packets come out of the queue, most of them will be already timed out and have been retransmitted by higher layer. In fact, too much buffer space is harmful since duplicates of the same packets have to be dropped after they have wasted precious network resources.

On the other hand, since the network traffic is dynamic, congestion cannot be solved only by the high-speed links. In Figure 1-2(b), the links with the high bandwidth value of 1Gbps are also susceptible to congestion. A simultaneous transfer of two flows from nodes A and B to node C can lead to a total input rate of 2Gbps at the router while the output rate is only 1Gbps. Thereby congestion occurs. Furthermore, increased link speeds increase the mismatch between the fastest and the slowest links in a network, which increase the chance of causing congestion at the interconnection nodes from high-speed to low-speed parts of the network.

1.3. CONGESTION CONTROL

Based on the above analysis, the effective way of congestion management is to control the congestion by adjusting the transmission rate of a data source to the available bandwidth at the bottleneck link along the routing path. The goal of congestion control is to maximize network throughput while maintaining a low loss ratio and small delay.

From the view of the control theory, congestion control can be broadly classified into open-loop and closed-loop [6]. Open-loop control is suitable for connections whose traffic characteristics and performance requirements can be precisely specified in advance. Open-loop connections will specify their requirements to the network elements which will reserve, if available, the necessary resources. Without any feedback, open-loop congestion is handled by combining admission control [7, 8, 9], policing [10, 11, 12], and scheduling mechanisms [13, 14, 15]. However, neglecting feedback is clearly not a good choice when it comes to dissolving network congestion, where the dynamics of the system – the presence or absence of other flows – dictate the ideal behavior.

Closed-loop control is more appropriate for networks where resource reservation is not possible or when the traffic behavior cannot be formally specified. Thus, closed-loop is the main scheme used by congestion control in Internet. In closed-loop congestion control, the sources continuously probe the network state and adjust their transmission rates based on feedback received from it.

In this closed-loop procession, congestion control should address three fundamental questions: (1) How to detect congestion? (2) How to feedback the congestion information to the sources of congestion? (3) How to determine the available capacity for a flow at any point of time? To answer these questions, congestion control model, source algorithm and link algorithm have become the important research issues. Figure 1-3 shows the related research areas in congestion control.

One important research area is congestion-control modeling, including mechanistic models and traffic models. Mechanistic models, such as TCP model [16], TCP/AQM fluid model [17] and TCP/AQM duality model [18], are developed to understand the properties of congestion control protocols and algorithms. While mechanistic models focus on specific congestion-control protocols or algorithms, traffic models are developed to obtain a better understanding of the characteristics of the network traffic. The typical traffic models include Poisson processes [19] and self-similarity [20]. The interest towards such models is two-fold: (1) these models are needed as input in network simulations; (2) these models can help design congestion-control algorithms.

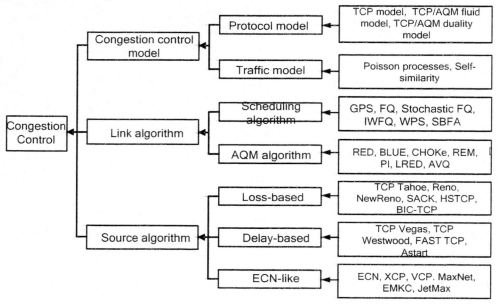

Figure 1-3. Research topics on congestion control.

The essence of congestion-control scheme is that a source adjusts its transmission rate according to the congestion measure of the underlying networks. Two approaches exist to accomplish this: one is source algorithm that dynamically adjusts the transmission rate in response to the congestion along its routing path; the other is link algorithm that controls the congestion right at the location where congestion occurs. In the current Internet, the source algorithm is carried out by TCP [21], and the link algorithm is carried out by active queue management (AQM) [22] and scheduling algorithm [23] at intermediate nodes.

In link algorithms, apart from forwarding the packets, the intermediate nodes are responsible for controlling the congestion by managing the queue in buffer. The link algorithms focus on two main concepts, namely active queue management and scheduling algorithms. Active Queue management algorithms manage the length of packet queues by dropping or marking packets whenever necessary whereas scheduling algorithms determine which packets to be sent next.

Traditionally, packets are dropped only when the queue is full. This Drop-Tail policy may keep queues at or near to maximum occupancy and cause unfair resource usage. Different with the drop-tail policy, active queue management, such as RED [24], BLUE [25],

CHOKe [26], REM [27], PI [28], LRED [29] and AVQ [30], which drops packets before a queue becomes full, can avoid these problems. The goal of scheduling algorithm is primarily to control queuing delay and bandwidth sharing. There are varieties of scheduling algorithms, such as GPS [31], FQ [32], Stochastic FQ [33], IWFQ [34], WPS [35], SBFA [36].

When congestion control takes place only at the end systems, it is termed source algorithm. As the most commonly used transport-layer protocol today, TCP is a typical source algorithm to control congestion. According to the type of congestion feedback, the congestion control algorithms of TCP protocol can be broadly classified into three categories:

1) Loss-based TCP protocol. In this category, the source detects congestion by the feedback of packet loss. The famous loss-based TCP protocols include TCP Tahoe, Reno [37], NewReno [38], SACK [39], HSTCP [40] and BIC-TCP [41].

2) Delay-based TCP protocol. In delay-based TCP protocols, a source interprets the Round Trip Time (RTT) as the indication of network congestion. TCP Vegas [42], TCP Westwood [43], FAST TCP [44] and Astart [45] belong to this category.

3) ECN-like TCP protocol. In such a case, the intermediate nodes are responsible for generating and forwarding the explicit congestion feedback to the source. Then these protocols, such as ECN [46], XCP [47], VCP [48], MaxNet [49], EMKC [50] and JetMax [51], can get more accurate congestion information by getting help from the intermediate nodes.

1.3.1. Congestion-Control Model

In the congestion-control study, the function of the congestion control model is to analyze the network performance, predict the trend of traffic change and provide a theoretical basis for the congestion feedback. Current congestion-control models can be divided into traffic model and mechanistic model. The traffic model takes the network traffic as the state variables, whereas the impact of other network parameters is aggregated for the process noise. The mechanistic model is usually established for various specific protocols and algorithms, and thus has strong pertinence.

Traffic model is the theoretical foundation for understanding and predicting network behavior, analyzing network performance and designing the network. The main idea is to extract the essential random properties from network traffic. Although Poisson model has achieved great success in telecommunication networks, its applicability to computer networks is still controversial [52]. Self-similarity in network traffic has been proposed and evaluated with the relevant data analysis [53]. Based on the self-similar model, long-range dependence model, wavelets model and multi-fractal traffic model are proposed [54-56]. However, since the self-similar models have a poor analytical property and high computational complexity, its application is still limited.

The mechanistic models (mainly for the TCP protocol and AQM algorithm) are proposed to analyze the network performance such as throughput, loss rate, delay and queue length. The major mechanistic models include the TCP steady-state throughput model, TCP/AQM-fluid model and TCP/AQM dual model. TCP steady-state throughput model gives a simple analytic characterization of the steady state throughput, as a function of loss rate and round trip time. TCP/AQM-fluid model uses differential equations to model the interactions of a set of TCP flows and AQM routers. Based on optimization theory, S.H. Low proposed TCP/AQM dual model [18], which models TCP congestion control and AQM as a distributed optimal rate allocation problem with certain utility function.

Since the current Internet is very complex and dynamic, intuitive or heuristic methodology becomes infeasible in network research. Thus, the congestion-control model will play a role with increasing importance in analyzing, understanding and designing various network congestion control algorithms.

1.3.2. Scheduling

As one of the key technologies to ensure quality of network service, scheduling algorithms determine the order of packets to accept services. The main function of scheduling is to allocate network resources through scheduling policy. Scheduling algorithm may have different applications in different environments. For example, to assure quality of service, the scheduling algorithm could be used to isolate malicious traffic flow to the normal business flow. The scheduling algorithm may also be used to allow users to share the available bandwidth fairly, or implement classified link sharing among different users.

Depending on the service rules, the queue scheduling algorithm can be divided into First Come First Served (FCFS), Round Robin Scheduling (RR) [57], Generalized Processor Sharing (GPS) and random scheduling algorithm. According to the applicable environments, queue scheduling algorithm can be divided into wired and wireless network scheduling algorithms. According to the scheduling object, scheduling algorithm can be divided into rate-based and delay-based. According to the working state, it can be divided into persistent work algorithms and non-persistent work algorithm. A brief introduction about several classical types of queue scheduling algorithms is as follows.

(1) Round-Robin-based Scheduling

A router that provides round-robin scheduling has a separate queue for every flow, where a flow may be identified by its source and destination address. The algorithm lets every active data flow (that has data packets in the queue) to take turns in transferring packets on a shared channel in a periodically repeated order.

However, the traditional Round-Robin (Round Robin, RR) algorithm does not identify different queues (traffic flows) distinctly. Thus, if different queues have different packet lengths, longer packets may receive more service time than shorter ones, which incurs unfairness. Moreover, this algorithm cannot provide delay guarantee to the business flow. In order to overcome these drawbacks of the RR algorithm, several improvements, such as Weighted Round Robin (WRR) [58], Deficit Round Robin (DRR) [59], Smooth Round Robin (SRR) [60], and Stratified RR [61], have been proposed. These improved algorithms try to maintain the simplicity of RR algorithm, and improve the delay and fairness performances at the same time.

(2) GPS-based Scheduling

In [31], A. K. Parekh proposed a new scheduling scheme - Generalized Processor Sharing (GPS). A GPS scheduler is a rate-based scheduler, which can guarantee link bandwidth for a flow. GPS is an ideal model, concerning about flows. However, in the real network, the smallest transmission unit is packet. Therefore, the authors named GPS in the real network as PGPS (Packet GPS). Since PGPS scheduling algorithms guarantee the rate of each flow, which is coupled with the delay, these algorithms can achieve the bound of end-to-end delay of the flow. The GPS-based algorithms mainly include FFQ [62], VC [63], CSVC [64], TSFQ [65], and LAS [66].

(3) Random Scheduling

Random-based scheduling algorithm is based on a random queuing selection, that is, a scheduler randomly selects the next packet from all waiting queues. Random-based scheduling algorithms include random priority queuing approaches [67, 68] and random fair queuing approaches [69-71]. Compared with other scheduling algorithms, random-based scheduling algorithms have better scalability and thus are easier to be deployed in large networks. Its drawback is that these algorithms only provide statistical (not deterministic) QoS guarantees.

1.3.3. Active Queue Management

Drop-tail, as the simplest and most commonly used algorithm in the current Internet routers, drops the packets from the tail of a completely full buffer of queue. Drop-Tail has two important drawbacks: Lock-Out and Full Queues [22]. In some situations Drop-Tail allows a single flow or a few flows to monopolize the queue, preventing other flows from getting space in the queue. Since Drop-Tail signals congestion only when the queue has become full, the queue usually maintains a full status for long periods of time. It becomes important to reduce the steady-state queue size and this is perhaps the most important goal of queue management.

Active Queue Management denotes a class of schemes designed to provide improved queuing mechanisms for the intermediate nodes. Research in this area was inspired by the original RED in 1993. These schemes are called active because they dynamically signal congestion information to sources; either explicitly, by marking packets (e.g. Explicit Congestion Notification) or implicitly, by dropping packets. This is in contrast to traditional passive Drop-Tail policy: packets are dropped if and only if the queue is full. The Internet Engineering Task Force (IETF) recommended the deployment of AQM in Internet routers in 1998.

According to the metrics used to measure congestion, AQM schemes can be classified into three categories: queue-based, rate-based, and mixed schemes that combining queue and rate metrics. In queue-based schemes, congestion is observed by average or instantaneous queue length and the control aim is to stabilize the queue length. Rate-based schemes accurately predict the utilization of the link, determine congestion, and react based on the packet arrival rate. Rate-based schemes can provide early feedback for congestion. Other AQM schemes deploy a combination of queue length and input rate to measure congestion and achieve a tradeoff between queue stability and responsiveness.

(1) Queue-based AQM

Queue-based AQM algorithms compute a dropping probability based on some function of the queue length. When the queue is not full, the intermediate node may drop packet. In this way, the node alleviates congestion by detecting incipient congestion early and delivering congestion notification to the end source before overflow occurs.

The Random Early Detection algorithm (RED) was first proposed by Floyd and Jacobson. In the RED algorithm, average queue size is determined for each packet arrival using an Exponential Weighted Moving Average (EWMA) window. The EWMA queue length *avg* is compared with a minimum and a maximum threshold, to determine the next action of the router.

A RED capable router is configured with three parameters, the minimum threshold q_{min}, the maximum threshold q_{max}, and the maximum marking probability p_{max}. When a packet arrives at the router, if the average queue length is below q_{min}, the router will not drop the packet. If the average queue length exceeds q_{min} but is below q_{max}, the router will drop the packet with probability $p=((avg-q_{min})/(q_{max}-q_{min}))p_{max}$. If the average queue length is above q_{max}, the packet is dropped with probability 1. Therefore, the dropping probability at the router increases linearly as the average queue length builds up from the minimum threshold to the maximum threshold. The dropping function of RED is shown in Figure 1-4.

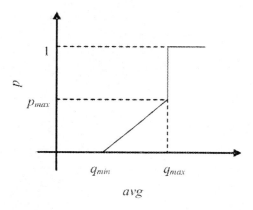

Figure 1-4. Dropping function of RED.

Since RED acts in anticipation of congestion, it does not suffer from the "Lock-Out" and "Full Queues" problems inherent in the drop-tail mechanism. By keeping the average queue size small, RED reduces the delays experienced by most flows. The main disadvantage of RED algorithm is that its performance is very sensitive to the parameters settings and a badly configured RED router will not do better than a drop-tail router. To solve these problems, some other queue-based AQM algorithms such as Adaptive RED [72], DRED [73] and SRED [74] have been proposed to modify RED. However, since the queue length is a cumulative difference value of rate mismatch between en-queue and de-queue, the queue length is insensitive to current queue arrival and drain rates. This incurs the conservative or aggressive packet dropping behavior when the queue length is small or large in queue-based AQM algorithms.

(2) Rate-based AQM

Rate-based AQM algorithms determine congestion and take actions based on packet arrival rate. The goals of the rate-based AQM algorithms are to alleviate the rate difference between en-queue and de-queue, and achieve low loss, low delay and high link utilization.

One of the famous rate-based AQM algorithms is Adaptive Virtual Queue algorithm (AVQ), which maintains a virtual queue whose capacity is less than the actual capacity of the link. When a packet arrives in a real queue, virtual queue is also updated to reflect the new arrival. Packets in the real queue are dropped when the virtual buffer overflows.

BLUE uses packet loss and link idle events to manage congestion. BLUE maintains a dropping probability. If the queue is continually dropping packets due to buffer overflow, BLUE increases the dropping probability, thus increasing the rate at which it sends back the congestion notification. Conversely, if the queue becomes empty or if the link is idle, BLUE decreases its dropping probability. The most important consequence of using BLUE is that congestion control can be performed with a minimal amount of buffer space. This can reduce end-to-end delay over the network.

Other typical rate-based AQM algorithms include AFD [75], CSFQ [76] and GREEN [77]. Although these rate-based AQM schemes can obtain good transient performance because of its fast responsiveness, large queue length jitter may occur by the reason of no explicit control mechanism of queue size under dynamic network scenarios. Thus, although the rate information speeds up the response, it must be carefully used to avoid instability.

(3) Queue/rate-based AQM

To take advantage of the responsiveness of queue-based AQM and stability of rate-based AQM, some mixed queue/rate-based AQM algorithms are proposed, which can control the queuing delay and accurately anticipate congestion in its initial stage. REM, PFED [78], VRC[79], AOPC[80] and IMC-PID[81] belong to this category.

REM is an active queue management mechanism that aims to achieve both high utilization and negligible loss and delay in a simple and scalable manner. The key idea is to decouple congestion measure from performance measure such as loss, queue length or delay. Another algorithm called RaQ [82] uses the input rate and current queue length to calculate the packet dropping probability. From the point of view of control theory, RaQ can be seen as dual loop feedback control. The inner loop is rate feedback control and outer loop is queue length feedback control. Since the rate feedback control enables RaQ to respond congestion quickly, it can decrease the packet loss due to buffer overflow. At the same time, since the queue-length-feedback control stabilizes RaQ's queue length around the expected queue length, it can achieve predictable queuing delay and lower delay jitter.

1.3.4. Explicit Congestion Notification

AQM mechanisms detect congestion before the queue overflows, and provide an indication of this congestion to the end nodes. Thus, AQM can reduce unnecessary queuing delay for all traffic sharing that queue. However, AQM algorithms use packet dropping as the mechanism for congestion indication. This increases the latency caused by the retransmission, and will harm the performance of interactive flows (such as remote logins) and transactional protocols (such as HTTP requests, the conversational phase of SMTP, or SQL requests).

To reduce the impact of loss on latency-sensitive flows, S. Floyd proposed the Explicit Congestion Notification (ECN) scheme. Combined with AQM algorithm, ECN uses the Congestion Experienced (CE) bit in a packet header as an indication of congestion. When a router recognizes that its buffer is getting close to congestion, it sets the CE bit in packets (marks the packet) flowing through the buffer. When the destination nodes receive the packets with the CE bit, these nodes copy the CE bits into the ECN-Echo bit in ACK packets. On receiving an ECN-Echo bit that has been set (=1), the source reacts in exactly the same way a TCP source reacts to loss of a packet. Thus, the source is informed of congestion through ECN scheme and avoids the potential for excessive delays due to retransmissions after packet losses.

Since ECN is effective only when it is combined with AQM, the benefits of ECN depend on the precise AQM being used. Moreover, the use of ECN has been found to be detrimental to performance on highly congested networks when using AQM algorithms that never drop packets [275].

1.3.5. Transmission Control Protocol

TCP is the core element of the original Internet (then ARPANET) protocol suite that provides reliable data transmission between two peers across an unreliable IP-based communication channel. In 1974, Vint Cerf and Bob Kahn, firstly described an internetworking protocol model for sharing resources using packet-switching among the nodes. A central control component of this model was the Transmission Control Protocol that incorporated both connection-oriented links and datagram services between hosts [83].

In the early days, TCP used window-based control to avoid losses at the destination: the window size at the source may not be larger than the amount of buffer available at the receiver. In order to control congestion, a second window called congestion window (cwnd) was introduced later, so that the amount of data a source can transmit is limited by the minimum of the receiver's advertised window and the congestion window. In 1988, Van Jacobson added congestion control functionality to TCP. The congestion control algorithms include four intertwined congestion window adjustment schemes: *slow start*, *congestion avoidance*, *fast retransmit*, and *fast recovery*. The dynamics of the congestion window are graphically illustrated in Figure 1-5.

At startup, a TCP connection begins with a window size of one packet. In the absence of losses, the window size is increased by one for each ACK received until it exceeds a threshold referred to as slow-start threshold (*ssthresh*). This increasing method results in doubling the size of the congestion window every RTT. In this way, during the *slow start* phase a connection can grow its window rapidly and thus claim very quickly any available bandwidth.

Once the congestion window exceeds *ssthresh*, the window size increases by $1/cwnd$ for each ACK received, which results in Additive Increase (AI) of approximately one packet per RTT. The window increase phase during which the window size increases linearly is called *congestion avoidance*. The justification behind this phase is that, during the congestion avoidance phase, a connection probes slowly for extra bandwidth without causing congestion to the network.

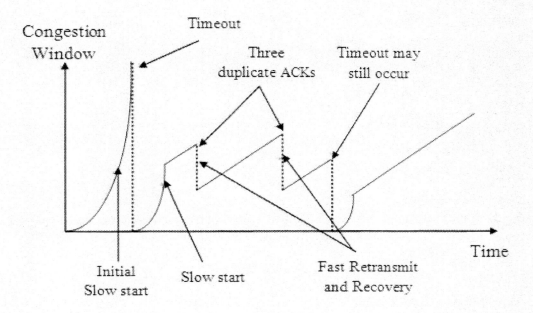

Figure 1-5. The dynamics of the congestion window.

TCP interprets a packet loss as an indication of network congestion. Packet loss causes TCP to shrink the congestion window and retransmit the lost packet. Packet loss is detected either from timeouts or from three duplicate ACKs. When a loss is detected from a timeout, the *ssthresh* value is set to half the current window size and the window size is set to one packet.

However, the receipt of multiple duplicate ACKs is interpreted as an indication of transient rather than persistent congestion. Returning ACKs is an indication of packets flowing through the network. When a duplicate ACK is received, the sender will not know if it is because a packet was lost or simply that a packet was delayed and received out of order at the receiver. Typically, less than three duplicate ACKs should be received when simple out of order conditions exist. If however more than two duplicate ACKs are received by the sender, it is a strong indication that at least one packet has been lost. Thus, when three duplicate ACKs are received, the retransmit for the missing packet occurs immediately without waiting for a time out. This behavior is defined as *fast retransmit*. After fast retransmission, the sender enters into *fast recovery* phase.

Since the fast retransmit algorithm is applied to the case, where at least three duplicate ACKs have been received, the TCP sender has implicit knowledge that there is packet still flowing to the receiver. The reason is that the duplicate ACKs can only be generated when a packet is received. This is an indication that serious network congestion may not exist and that the lost segment was a rare event. Thus, the *ssthresh* value is set to half of the current window size and the congestion window size is set to *ssthresh*+3 packets (Multiplicative-Decrease, MD). For each additional duplicate ACK the congestion window is increased by one packet until the ACK for the retransmitted packet arrives. At that time, the congestion window is set to *ssthresh* and the system enters the congestion avoidance phase. In this way, fast recovery resumes transmission with a larger window, incrementing as if in *congestion avoidance* mode. This allows for higher throughput under the condition of moderate congestion.

Because of its popularity, significant effort has gone into devising new techniques or enhancing existing ones in order to improve TCP performance. Based on the type of congestion feedback, these new TCP protocols can be classified into three categories: Loss-based TCP, Delay-based TCP and ECN-like TCP.

(1) Loss-based TCP

Jacobson's original TCP congestion control is the canonical example of Loss-based TCP: packet loss indicates network congestion, and so a TCP sender should decrease its window size accordingly. The drawback is that a TCP sender keeps increasing its window until it causes buffer overflows. These "self-induced" packet drops cause increased loss rate, decreased throughput, and significant delay. Improvements such as TCP NewReno and TCP SACK were designed to enhance the efficiency of TCP's loss recovery. HSTCP and BIC-TCP were proposed to improve the efficiency in high-speed link. While these algorithms can improve TCP performance, they still rely on packet loss as an implicit congestion signal.

(2) Delay-based TCP

An alternative congestion control technique for TCP, is delay-based TCP. This technique is preventive rather than reactive. The basic idea is that if the congestion window large enough to saturate the available bandwidth, the transfer will cause increasing queuing at the bottleneck link, and thus increasing RTTs. Thus, the sender should decrease the send's congestion window when the RTTs start increasing.

A typical delay-based TCP is TCP Vegas, designed by Jain. TCP Vegas monitors RTTs and reacts to increases in RTT in a manner that network congestion will be avoided before it becomes significant. In this way, TCP Vegas increases throughput by reducing the frequency of packet loss and timeouts. Inspired by TCP Vegas, the networking research community considered several other ways to improve TCP, including TCP Westwood, FAST TCP and Astart. However, measurement studies have shown that there is little correlation between increased delays (or RTTs) and congestive losses [84, 85, 86]. This experimental observation raises major doubts on whether delay-based TCP algorithms would be effective in practice.

(3) ECN-based TCP

Both loss-based and delay-based TCPs treat the network as a black box and infer congestion via implicit signals such as loss and delay. Research studies have shown that using only packet loss or delay as a signal of congestion poses fundamental limitations in achieving high utilization and fairness while maintaining low bottleneck queue and near-zero packet drop rate.

In the light of TCP's scalability issues in high-speed networks, ECN-based TCP has gained interest in the last several years. These algorithms rely on routers to provide congestion feedback by modifying the congestion window [47], packet loss [50], single-bit congestion indication [87, 88, 46], queuing delay [44, 89, 49], or link prices [90, 30, 91]. This helps flows converge their sending rates to some social optimum and achieve a certain optimization objective.

XCP uses explicit window adjustment for a flow to increase or decrease its congestion window. Each packet carries a congestion header that contains three fields: the sender's current congestion window size: *cwnd*, the estimated round trip time: *rtt*, and the router feedback field: *feedback*. Each sender fills its current *cwnd* and *rtt* values in the congestion header on packet departures, and initializes the feedback field to its desired window size.

The core control mechanism of XCP is implemented at routers. Each router has two logical controllers: efficiency controller and fairness controller. In each control interval, the efficiency controller computes available bandwidth. The fairness controller is responsible for fairly allocating bandwidth to each flow. In each control interval, if the spare bandwidth is positive, each flow gets an equal amount of additive increment of rate. If the spare bandwidth is negative, each flow gets a rate decrement proportional to its current rate. A router writes the network window adjustment (the increment minus the decrement) information in the feedback field of a packet. A more congested downstream router may overwrite this field with a smaller increment or a larger decrement. The receiver echoes back the feedback to the sender, and the sender adjusts its window size accordingly.

In this way, XCP and other ECN-based TCP schemes, such as VCP, MLCP [92], MaxNet and RCP [93], use explicit feedback from the routers to aid end-hosts in taking decisions. Such protocols have been shown to perform better than their counterparts with implicit feedback. However, ECN-based TCP schemes are likely to induce more overhead on routers. Moreover, such schemes require significant changes in the routers and end-hosts which make their deployment difficult.

1.4. DIFFICULTY AND EVALUATION OF CONGESTION CONTROL

The research of congestion control has been well advanced for thirty years. Though many protocols and algorithms have been proposed, there are still a lot of requirements for these themes.

1) The congestion control scheme must work in different network environments, such as high-speed networks, wireless networks and hybrid networks. Compared with traditional networks, these networks have different and dynamic characteristics, such as large bandwidth-delay product of high-speed link, high loss rate and time variety of wireless channel. This requires the congestion control to be applicable to various environments.

2) During congestion, when the available resources are less than the demand, it is important to allocate the available resources fairly. However, no common definition of fairness has been accepted by all researchers. For example, some researchers define fairness as a scheme, where all users get a nonzero share of resources. Others argue that all users should get equal resources. Moreover, the definition of user is not clear. Some researchers treat each sender-receiver pair as a user, while others only treat each connection (each sender-receiver pair may has many connections) as a user.

3) One important objective of congestion control is to ensure that the resource demand does not exceed the network capacity. Since the available network capacity is dynamic, the congestion control scheme should match the demand dynamically to the available capacity. It should ask users to increase the demand when additional capacity becomes available and to decrease it if the demand exceeds the capacity. Thus, the congestion control scheme should be responsive.

4) Because the control decisions depend on the congestion feedback, the overhead of the feedback should be minimized. In particular, it should not increase traffic during congestion. This is one of the reasons why explicit feedback is considered undesirable. However, research studies have shown that using only packet loss or delay as a signal of congestion poses fundamental limitations in achieving high utilization and fairness while maintaining low bottleneck queue and near-zero packet drop rate.

To evaluate the congestion control scheme, the researchers proposed a class of evaluation criterions, which focus on two core properties as efficiency and fairness.

Resource efficiency can be expressed in terms of Power function [94, 95]. The power of a resource is defined as the ratio of its throughput to its response time. Maximizing the power is the objective in networks. This optimization criterion tries to allocate resource at a load where the throughput is high while its response time (queuing delay) has not increased significantly as a result of the high utilization.

A commonly used definition of fairness is called max-min fairness [96]. Informally, a max-min fair allocation is the one that maximizes the share of connections whose demand is not fully satisfied. Connections whose requests are not fully satisfied are allocated the same amount under a max-min fair allocation. A max-min allocation maximizes the utilization of the bottlenecked resource (usually link or buffer). However, it is only an ideal objective, while the degree of fairness can not be described.

One way to measure fairness is via a fairness index, which is a function of the mean and variance of the throughputs achieved by different flows [97]. If x_1, x_2, ..., and x_n are the throughputs of n competing flows, the fairness index f is defined as

$$f = \frac{\left(\sum_{i=1}^{n} x_n\right)^2}{n\sum_{i=1}^{n} (x_n)^2} \tag{1-1}$$

Clearly, $1/n \leq f \leq 1$, and a smaller value of f signifies a larger degree of unfairness in allocations.

In addition to efficiency and fairness, a congestion control approach must scale well with increasing link speeds and distances and with increasing number of users. Its implementation must be simple in order to keep up with increasing rates while at the same time its execution should be independent of the number of network users. At the same time, some congestion control methods allow for fine tuning by providing a set of tunable parameters. The control method in use must be resilient to parameter mis-tuning. Furthermore, because of the inherently distributed nature of the congestion control, each node only has incomplete knowledge of the traffic in the network. Thus, another important goal of a practical scheme is that it must not display large oscillatory behavior, and must try to converge towards high efficiency and fairness.

Chapter 2

ANALYSIS AND COMPARISON OF CONGESTION CONTROL PROTOCOLS IN HIGH BANDWIDTH-DELAY PRODUCT NETWORKS

2.1. INTRODUCTION

TCP has been considered to be a very effective network transfer protocol since it was proposed in 1980s [98]. However, with the development of the gigabit networks, wireless networks, wireless sensor networks and satellite networks, the traditional TCP congestion-control protocol faces a lot of new challenges. With the rapid development of network technology, the next generation Internet has been gradually formed [99, 100]. More and more researchers have begun to conduct scientific research which uses the 10Gbps ~ 1Tbps high-speed network to transmit data, such as the massive data research of quantum physics, earth observation science and radio astronomy, etc. The backbone of Internet has begun to show a new obvious characteristic: high bandwidth-delay product (BDP) [40]. In this network environment, researchers find that the traditional TCP protocol itself becomes the bottleneck of network performance in the following aspects:

1) Traditional TCP manages its congestion window by Additive Increase and Multiplicative Decrease (AIMD) mechanism. However, AIMD restricts the efficiency of TCP in high BDP networks [40, 101, 41, 44, 45]. For example, over 83,333/2 RTTs are required for TCP to increase its window from half utilization to full utilization of 10Gbps with 1500-byte packets, which is approximately 1 hour with 100ms RTT. This requires that no packet to be lost within 1 hour. In other words, the number of lost packets cannot be more than 1 per 2,600,000,000 packets, which is less than the theoretical limit of the network's bit error rates. Once a packet is lost, due to the conservative nature of the AI mechanism, it takes more than 1 hour to recover from the congestion avoidance phase to the steady state of high network efficiency [40], which is unacceptable in the real networks.
2) The increase of RTT aggravates the RTT unfairness problem. The RTT unfairness among different TCP flows in the traditional TCP protocols becomes worse in high BDP networks [41].

3) With the increasing of BDP, networks become more unstable. It has been proved that high BDP causes TCP flows to jitter frequently, which incurs the instability of queues in routers in term of queue length [102, 47, 103]. It has also been pointed out that active queue management (AQM) mechanism cannot maintain queue stability in high BDP networks and the performance of TCP will be degraded as bandwidth or delay increases [47].

Therefore, numerous congestion-control protocols for high BDP networks have been proposed to solve the problems mentioned above. Based on the thorough examination of the congestion-control protocols mentioned above, this chapter analyzes the impact of RTT, the buffer of the bottleneck router and active queue management algorithms to the congestion-control protocols. It also makes a comprehensive comparison, analysis and evaluation of the performance of various protocols in different network environments through simulations.

Section 2.2 summarizes the current congestion-control protocols in high BDP networks. In Section 2.3, the performances of various protocols are evaluated in different network environments through NS2, and the simulation results are thoroughly analyzed. Then, the open problems and further research directions are discussed in Section 2.4. Section 2.5 concludes this chapter.

2.2. BACKGROUND AND RELATED WORK

Since TCP was proposed in 1980s, numerous congestion-control protocols have been proposed to improve the performance of TCP [104, 105]. Most of these enhancements focus on the management mechanism of the congestion window. According to the type of congestion feedback utilized by the congestion window, these TCP protocols can be broadly classified into three categories: LCA (Loss-based Congestion Avoidance algorithms), DCA (Delay-based Congestion Avoidance algorithms) and ECN-based algorithms.

2.2.1. Loss-based Congestion Avoidance Algorithms

TCP Tahoe is the first LCA-based TCP enhancement. It uses the packet-loss information piggybacked through ACK to adjust the congestion window at the source side. Similarly, TCP Reno [38], New Reno [106] and Sack [39] also use the packet-loss information to improve the traditional TCP. Recently, with the emerging of high BDP networks, a lot of new LCA-based protocols, including HSTCP [40], STCP [101], BIC-TCP [41], CUBIC [107] and H-TCP [108], were proposed to improve the utilization of link bandwidth.

HSTCP adjusts the growth mode of its congestion window to adapt the data transfer in high BDP networks. It uses an adaptive function to adjust the congestion window dynamically. It defines two incremental functions $f(x)$ and $g(x)$ corresponding to ACK signal and packet-loss signal, respectively. A corresponding relation exists between these incremental functions and the packet-loss rate. TCP sender dynamically adjusts the incremental functions based on the expected packet-loss rate. Meanwhile, to be compatible with traditional TCP, the growth mode of HSTCP reduces to that of the traditional TCP when the size of the congestion window becomes less than 38 data packets.

STCP is also a simple sender-side enhancement to the congestion-window adjustment algorithm. In order to meet the requirement of high BDP networks, it replaces the AIMD mode with the multiplicative increase multiplicative decrease (MIMD) mode, which can swiftly adjust the congestion window. Similar to HSTCP, the growth mode of STCP also reduces to that of the traditional TCP when the size of the congestion window is less than 32.

BIC-TCP proposes a new window adjustment mechanism, which regards the congestion control as a search process to determine the existence of the packet-loss event in an interconnected network system. The search process consists of binary-search increase and linear increase. The basic idea of binary-search increase is similar to the classical binary search algorithm. When it detects an event of packet loss, BIC-TCP reduces its window by a multiplicative factor. BIC-TCP has two important parameters for adjusting the window size, one is W_{max} which is the window size just before the reduction and the other is W_{min} which is the window size just after the reduction. BIC-TCP performs a binary search by jumping to the midpoint between W_{max} and W_{min}. Since packet losses have occurred at W_{max}, the window size that the network can currently handle without loss must be somewhere between W_{max} and W_{min}. However, jumping to the midpoint could be too much increase within one RTT. So if the distance between the midpoint and the current minimum is larger than a fixed constant, called S_{max}, BIC-TCP increases the current window size by S_{max} (linear increase). If BIC-TCP does not get packet losses at the updated window size, the window size becomes the new minimum. If it gets a packet loss, the window size becomes the new maximum. This process continues until the window increment is less than some small constant, called S_{min}, at which point, the window is set to the current maximum. In this way, BIC-TCP controls the sending rate to achieve the best utilization and the stable transmission state. In order to maintain backward compatibility and TCP friendliness, BIC-TCP sets a minimum threshold value of the window and still uses the traditional TCP growth strategy when the congestion window is less than the minimum threshold.

Although BIC achieves pretty good scalability, fairness, and stability during the current high speed environments, the BIC's growth function can still be too aggressive for TCP, especially under short RTT or low speed networks. Furthermore, several different phases of window control add a lot of complexity in analyzing the protocol [41].

CUBIC is an enhanced version of BIC-TCP. It simplifies the window control of BIC-TCP and improves the TCP friendliness and RTT fairness. In CUBIC, a cubic function replaces the growth function in BIC-TCP, to achieve better scalability and stability.

The origin is set to be W_{max}. So after a window reduction, the window grows very fast, but as it gets closer to W_{max}, it slows down its growth. At W_{max}, its increment becomes zero. After that, the window grows slowly, accelerating its growth as it moves away from W_{max}. It has the same plateau as in BIC's window curve, but its growth rate accelerates much more slowly than BIC's. This slow growth significantly contributes to the improved TCP friendliness of the protocol. Furthermore, the function extremely simplifies the window control since there is only one function to use and no multiple phases.

H-TCP uses the time interval t between two successive events of packet loss as the feedback. If the time interval t is small, the congestion may be heavy; otherwise, it might be just light congestion. Since the time interval t is a new congestion metric, there is few relevant evaluation and research on this metric. So the performance of H-TCP needs further evaluation.

Generally speaking, loss-based congestion avoidance algorithms are passive congestion-control mechanisms, which estimate the network congestion based on the events of packet loss. As long as packet loss does not occur, these protocols will not decrease its sending rate regardless of the actual network load. This type of protocols maximizes the utilization of the remaining bandwidth and reveals its aggressiveness when network status is near the network saturation point. On one hand, it greatly increases the network-bandwidth utilization; on the other hand, the fast increase of the network utilization also implies that the next packet-loss event is not far away. Therefore, while these protocols improve network bandwidth utilization, it also indirectly enlarges packet-loss rate and intensifies throughput oscillation.

2.2.2. Delay-based Congestion Avoidance Algorithms

TCP Vegas [42] is the first delay-based congestion-control algorithm. It adjusts the congestion window based on variation of the RTT delay. If RTT becomes larger, it believes that congestion occurs and reduces the congestion window accordingly. If RTT becomes smaller, it is no longer congested and the congestion window should be increased. Otherwise, the congestion window remains the same. Compared with the packet-loss signal, RTT signal is more sensitive and timely reflects the congestion of the network. Therefore, the delay-based algorithms can estimate the available bandwidth more accurately. A series of delay-based protocols for high BDP networks are also proposed. FAST TCP [44], Astart [109], and TCP Africa [110] are typical examples.

FAST TCP: Similar to TCP Vegas, FAST TCP uses the queuing delay as the feedback factor, and utilizes the observed variation of ACK delay to adjust the congestion window. FAST TCP detects the congestion by considering both delay and packet loss. The congestion window w of FAST TCP is periodically updated based on the average RTT as follows:

$$w(k+1) = \frac{1}{2}(\frac{w(k-1) * baseRTT}{RTT} + \alpha + w(k)) \qquad (2-1)$$

where $baseRTT$ is the minimum RTT among all observed RTT samples, α is a parameter that controls fairness and the number of buffered packets in each flow. The best thing of Fast TCP is that it adjusts the sending window based on the actual congestion degree of the network. The adjustments are very small after the congestion window reaches the balanced point. When the congestion window is far from the balanced point, the adjustments are quite large. This speeds up the convergence of FAST TCP.

Astart is derived from TCP Westwood [43] to adapt to the high BDP networks. The basic idea is that it estimates the bandwidth by measuring the changes of RTT. It uses an Eligible Rate Estimate (ERE) algorithm to measure the available bandwidth. Astart adjusts the congestion window $cwnd$ and slow start threshold $ssthresh$ based on the measured bandwidth after the congestion occurs.

TCP Africa makes use of the RTT-delay detection of Vegas to determine the existence of congestion. It combines two different congestion window growth modes to adjust the send window adaptively. When there is no congestion, the protocol enters into the fast-growth model of HSTCP, which can proactively increase the congestion window to obtain the remaining bandwidth quickly. When approaching the congestion point, TCP Africa enters into the slow-growth mode of the traditional TCP to avoid large number of lost packets.

Compared with the delay incurred by packet-loss feedback, RTT delay reflects the congestion status more quickly. Therefore, a large number of delay-based congestion-control protocols have been proposed to improve the throughput of network. When the network is close to saturation point, these protocols show a certain degree of conservative, and avoid to loss packet frequently at the saturation point. However, recent studies have shown that there is no direct connection between the increasing delay and packet loss. This is because of the variability of the buffer size and the dependence of the delay sampling rate. The noise occurring in the network at any time will interfere with delay sampling. Thus, the delay-based protocols cannot control the congestion window accurately and effectively in real networks [117, 85]. Moreover, delay-based protocols show serious weakness when coexisting with loss-based protocols.

2.2.3. ECN-based Algorithms

Apart from the implicit signals such as loss and delay, TCP also uses explicit signals, such as ECN (Explicit Congestion Notification) [46], to detect congestion. In this mechanism, the router detects congestion status and directly sends the congestion feedback to the sender. AECN [88], Quick-Start [111], XCP [47], VCP [48] and the C3P [112] are all based on this explicit feedback mechanism.

In high BDP networks, both AECN and Quick-Start use an explicit self-feedback mechanism to adjust the TCP congestion window dynamically. Contrary to traditional ECN, these two protocols explicitly notify the sender to increase the congestion window when available bandwidth is big enough.

Inspired by the design of ABR mechanism in ATM, XCP protocol uses more bits to store congestion related information, which provide more congestion feedback information to the sender. The contribution of XCP lies in separating the efficiency and fairness policies of congestion control, which enables routers to quickly make use of available bandwidth while managing the allocation of bandwidth to flows conservatively. XCP packets carry a congestion header through which the sender requests a desired throughput. Routers make a fair per-flow bandwidth allocation without maintaining any per-flow state. Thus, the sender learns of the bottleneck router's allocation in a single round trip.

Yong Xia et al. [48] proposed VCP in 2005. Compared with XCP, VCP uses only two ECN bits for congestion feedback. With VCP, each router computes a load factor and uses this factor to classify the level of congestion into three regions: low-load, high-load and overload. Only two ECN bits are used to encode the congestion feedback information. Based on this information, the source selects the appropriate strategies. VCP is able to approximate the XCP's performance, such as high efficiency, low persistent bottleneck queue and negligible congestion-caused packet loss. However, the fairness convergence speed of VCP is slow.

C3P is a congestion-control protocol integrating two feedback mechanisms. C3P uses one ECN bit and RTT delay to adjust the congestion windows. In this way, C3P provides a new congestion-control mode in which the end-system and router are combined. Compared to other ECN-based protocols, C3P uses less cost to obtain more feedback information, and classifies the congestion into more status.

ECN-based protocols are more agile than the end-to-end congestion-control protocols, and thus can control congestion more accurately. This is because the majority of congestion occurs in the intermediate nodes rather than end nodes. The proactive feedback of the intermediate nodes can be sent quickly and accurately to end nodes. However, intermediate nodes are involved in the congestion detection process, which will bring much more burden and complexity overhead to the network. Moreover, the ECN-based protocols require massive modification to existing protocols, for example, changing the IP header.

2.3. SIMULATION COMPARISON OF CONGESTION CONTROL PROTOCOL

In recent years, several works have been proposed to evaluate the enhanced congestion control protocols for high BDP networks, from the macro or micro points of view [105, 113]. This section gives a comprehensive comparison and analysis of the performances of the enhanced congestion control protocols for high BDP networks. The simulation comparison focuses on the effect of RTT delay, buffer size and queue management mechanism.

Simulation experiments use the typical dumbbell topology, which illustrates the characteristics of the real network environment [41]. In high BDP networks, most of the congestion occurs in the core of the network rather than the edge. The core link can easily become the bottleneck when large number of flows aggregate. The Poisson distributed UDP flows act as the background flows, whose peak value of throughput is equal to 5% of the bottleneck bandwidth. In the simulation, the parameters of the protocols are shown in Table 2-1.

Table 2-1. Protocol Parameters Settings

Protocol	Parameters Settings
BIC-TCP	$Smax=32$, $Smin=0.01$, $beta=0.125$
HSTCP	$LowWindow=38$
STCP	$LowWindow=16$
FAST	$alpha=312$, $mithresh=0.75$
XCP	$tcp\_xcp\_on=1$, $thresh=0.6*buffer$, $maxthresh=0.8*buffer$
VCP	$alpha=1$, $beta=0.875$, $k=0.25$, $t_p=200$
C3P	$alpha=3$, $beta=0.8$, $k=1.01$, $t_p=200$

2.3.1. RTT Fairness

TCP is known that bandwidth fairness problems exist among flows with different RTT. In high BDP network environment, the RTT fairness problem is aggravated with the increasing of RTT.

Table 2-2. Throughput ratio of protocols with different RTTs

Inverse RTT Ratio	1	3	6
Reno	1.116590	8.476595	16.015658
BIC-TCP	1.033434	9.696173	30.431101
HSTCP	0.942102	92.844748	384.833044
STCP	1.014234	125.54751	404.451871
FAST	1.125487	1.009883	19.543154
Astart	1.117415	5.152478	10.845742
XCP	0.973584	8.153879	14.548451
VCP	1.024814	2.036879	5.899970
C3P	1.014521	2.012452	8.445621

This section describes the following experiments: two flows with different RTT shares the same bottleneck link with 622Mbps bandwidth and 5ms delay. In the experiment, the RTT of one flow is set to 30ms, and the RTT of the other flow is set to 30ms, 90ms and 180ms, respectively. Table 2-2 shows the throughput ratio of two flows with different RTT.

In Table 2-2, for all protocols, with the increasing of inverse RTT ratio, the throughput ratio also increases. The flow with small RTT delay consumes more network bandwidth resources. Thus, the flow with large RTT cannot obtain its fair bandwidth.

The RTT unfairness of loss-based protocols is the worst because such protocols use the packet loss event to determine the existence of congestion. If there is no packet loss, the protocol will keep increasing its sending rate. Thus, the flow with small RTT obtains more growth in congestion window and can easily occupy the available bandwidth. Delay-based protocols, such as FAST and Astart, use relatively smooth congestion window adjustment mechanism when the network nears congestion. The flow with smaller RTT has the fast growth rate at the beginning. However, as the sending rate increasing, the congestion window of the flow with smaller RTT enters into the conservative growth mode firstly. In same time, the flow with larger RTT is still increasing the congestion window quickly. Thus, compared with loss-based protocols, the throughput ratios of FAST and Astart maintain at smaller value. ECN-based protocols show excellent RTT fairness because the fairness factor is used as an adjustable parameter in the explicit feedback.

2.3.2. Bottleneck Buffer Size

The router's buffer size has direct impact on the overall performance of congestion control protocols. The buffer size is usually set to a large value, such as 1500 packets [113, 115] in the CISCO's routers, to accommodate all "flight" packets. However, in [116], the authors point out that this "rule-of-thumb" is completely unnecessary in a real network. Such a large buffer not only wastes the network resources, but also increases the delay oscillation. This section uses a series of simulations to study the effect of bottleneck buffer size.

(1) The Utilization of Bandwidth and Buffer

This experiment gives the comparison and analysis of the utilization of bandwidth and queue when there is only one protocol flow through the bottleneck. The bottleneck bandwidth is set to 622Mbps and RTT delay is set to 60ms. The experiment runs for 150 seconds with Drop-tail queue policy. In the experiment, the bottleneck buffer is changed from 10 packets to 10,000 packets.

Figure 2-1 shows the bandwidth utilization of different protocols. When the buffer size is 10 packets, all protocols obtain low bandwidth utilization. When the buffer becomes larger, the throughputs of all protocol flows increase. The bandwidth utilization of loss-based protocol increases very quickly. The reason is that larger buffer can accommodate more packets and decrease the loss rate. As for the delay-based protocols, the increase of bandwidth utilization is not very obvious when the buffer is larger than 1000 packets. It is worth mentioning that FAST TCP shows poor performance under different buffer sizes. As mentioned in Section 2.2, FAST TCP has a controlling parameter α, which represents the number of buffered packets in equilibrium state. When the buffer size is smaller than α, FAST TCP cannot reach its stable equilibrium state and shows poor performance. For ECN-based protocols, since they can adjust their sending rate according to the load of bottleneck, the bandwidth utilization is relatively stable. This experiment also shows the performance of TCP Reno. No matter how much the buffer size is, TCP Reno cannot obtain high bandwidth utilization.

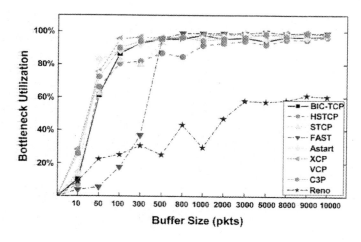

Figure 2-1. Link utilization of protocols with buffer size ranging from 10packets to 10000 packets.

Figure 2-2 shows the queue utilization of the bottleneck. The queue utilization directly reflects the RTT delay. In Figure 2-2, the loss-based protocols increase the queue utilization gradually with the increase of buffer size. The reason is that the loss-based protocols use the packet loss to detect congestion. Thus, the congestion window and the queue utilization will keep increasing as long as there is no packet loss. On the contrary, the delay-based protocols and the ECN-based protocols maintain relatively stable queue utilization. Since the window management mechanism is too conservative, TCP Reno is still unable to fully utilize the buffer to improve the bandwidth utilization even if the buffer space is very large.

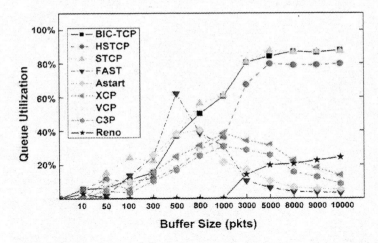

Figure 2-2. Queue utilization of protocols with buffer size ranging from 10 packets to 10000 packets.

(2) TCP Friendliness

In this section, TCP friendliness of different protocols is investigated. The TCP friendliness indicates the flow bandwidth allocation between high-speed TCP and TCP Reno. In this experiment, one high-speed protocol flow and one traditional TCP Reno flow share the bottleneck link of 622Mbps bandwidth and 80ms propagation delay. The buffer size of bottleneck router is set to 100, 1000 and 10,000 packets respectively.

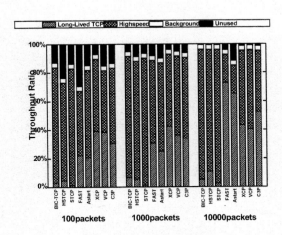

Figure 2-3. TCP-Friendliness of protocols with different bottleneck buffer.

In Figure 2-3, BIC-TCP, HSTCP and STCP consume much more bandwidth than TCP Reno. The reason of this TCP unfriendliness performance is that the aggressive congestion window management mechanism of the loss-based protocols is used there. When there is no packet loss, these protocols constantly increase their sending rates. Their sending rates show a concave trend from the macro view. The sending rate increases more quickly when closer to the maximum available bandwidth. This aggressive mechanism not only leads to high loss rate, but also occupies the unfair bandwidth. In contrast to loss-based protocols, Astart and TCP Reno have received fair bandwidth allocation, and their throughput ratio is about 2:1. Because of the sensitivity of its parameter α, the performance of FAST TCP is poor when the buffer size is less than α. Since the delay-based protocols use the delay instead of packet loss to detect congestion, the sending rate shows a convex trend from the macro view. The delay-based protocols do not excessively occupy the fair bandwidth of other flows, and thus show the TCP friendliness. Three ECN-based protocols also show excellent performance in the TCP friendliness. In Figure 2-3, the throughput ratio of XCP、 VCP and C3P to TCP Reno is about 1.5:1. Because of the explicit feedback mechanism, these protocols can achieve the fair bandwidth allocation when coexisting with TCP Reno flows.

To investigate the impact of buffer size on the protocols, the buffer size of bottleneck is set to 100, 1000 and 10,000 packets respectively. In Figure 2-3, when the bottleneck router buffer space is only 100 packets, the eight high-speed network protocols achieve low network utilization, and only occupy no more than 10% of the bandwidth. When the buffer size increases to 10,000 packets, the utilization rate of each protocol reaches to almost 100%. However, the throughput ratio of FAST and Astart to TCP Reno is 1:3. C3P also shows the similar problem and the throughput ratio is about 1:1.2. The reason is the weakness of delay-based protocols when delay-based and loss-based protocols coexist.

The experiment results show that the buffer size of bottleneck router has a big impact on the performance of high-speed protocols. When the number of flows increases in real network environment the impact will become more significant.

2.3.3. Queue Management Mechanism

In traditional networks, a number of Active Queue Management (AQM) mechanisms, such as RED [24], REM [27], PI [28] and LRED [29], are proposed to maintain the buffer queue stability and achieve low delay. However, some research results indicate that almost all the existing AQM mechanisms can not maintain the stability of queue in high BDP networks [102, 47, 114]. In order to adapt to the high BDP networks, whether the congestion-control protocol in end-systems can cooperate with the AQM mechanisms in intermediate nodes becomes a hot research issue.

In this section, extensive simulations are conducted to evaluate the performance of high-speed protocol with or without AQM mechanisms in high BDP networks. The bandwidth utilization, TCP friendliness and RTT fairness are chosen as the evaluation metrics. Since XCP, VCP and C3P use the explicit feedback from routers to adjust the sending rate, the performance of these explicit feedback protocols are referred.

The parameters of AQM are set as follows: *thresh*=500, *maxthresh*=750, *q_weight*=0.002, *linterm*=10 in RED. For PI algorithm, a=7.74e-011, b=7.66e-011, w=0.772.

(1) Bandwidth Utilization

To investigate whether high-speed protocol with different active queue management mechanisms can use the available bandwidth effectively, the bandwidth of bottleneck is set to 2.5Gbps. In each test, two high-speed flows of the same type and two long-lived TCP Reno flows coexist. Drop-tail, RED and PI are used as the active queue management mechanisms.

Table 2-3. Link utilization of protocols with different queue management

Protocol	Link Utilization		
	Drop-tail	RED	PI
BIC-TCP	97.0%	95.3%	96.2%
HSTCP	97.2%	92.1%	95.9%
STCP	98.0%	95.6%	96.9%
FAST	96.8%	95.1%	95.5%
Astart	96.1%	95.2%	95.4%
Protocol	Utilization		
XCP	97.8%		
VCP	97.1%		
C3P	97.2%		

Table 2-3 shows the link utilization of the high-speed protocols. The link utilization of each protocol is very close in Drop-tail and PI. The link utilization of delay-base and loss-based protocols decrease a little in RED. The reason is that RED drops packets before the queue becomes full, and thus decreases the link utilization.

(2) TCP Friendliness
In this section, the TCP friendliness of high-speed protocols under different queue management mechanisms is evaluated. The buffer size is set to 1000 packets in bottleneck routers. Other parameters in this scenario are the same as that in Section 2.2.2.

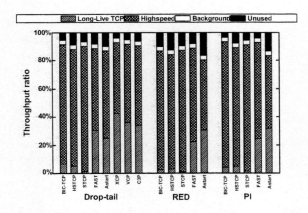

Figure 2-4. TCP-Friendliness of protocols with different queue management.

As shown in Figure 2-4, the TCP friendliness of high-speed protocols with AQM mechanisms do not obtain great improvement. It is obvious that AQM mechanisms bring little influence to TCP friendliness of these congestion control protocols in high BDP Networks.

The simulation results in Section 2.3.3 show that active queue management (AQM) mechanisms cannot bring large improvement to the performance of high-speed protocols.

AQM mechanisms are sensitive to network load and cannot achieve stability and convergence in high BDP Networks. Moreover, the performance of AQM will degrade with the increment of link bandwidth and delay. This will motivate researchers to develop new robust mechanisms with both stable control of buffer queue and fast convergence rate under different network scenarios. Due to the complexity of networks, the congestion control should not be an independent process but a joint behavior of TCP and AQM [47,112]. This will be an important rule in future research of congestion control.

2.4. Open Issues and Future Works

In the emerging high Bandwidth-Delay Product networks, the traditional TCP protocol itself becomes the bottleneck of the network performance. In traditional networks, TCP also has fairness problem when flows with different RTTs are competing over a shared link. But in high BDP networks, this problem becomes even worse and the RTT bias becomes larger. Various transport protocols for the high BDP networks have been proposed in recent years. In this chapter, extensive simulations are conducted to evaluate the performance of eight typical high-speed protocols. The simulation results show that there are still many open issues in congestion control for high BDP networks.

There is not adequate analysis on the effectiveness of various congestion control mechanisms in high BDP networks. Loss-based congestion control protocols were firstly proposed in this area. However, the simulation results show that the performance is improved only in bandwidth utilization, while serious problems still exist in the TCP friendliness, and RTT fairness. Delay-based congestion control protocols not only solve inefficient problem in high BDP networks, but also perform quite well in the TCP friendliness and RTT fairness. However, the simulation results also show the unfairness problems of delay-based protocols when coexisting with other types of protocols. Moreover, the studies in [117, 85] have shown that there is little correlation between delay and packets loss in networks. Thus, the reliability of delay-based protocols in nowadays Internet is still controversial. On the other hand, the performance of ECN-based congestion-control protocols can be greatly improved with the help of explicit feedback information. However, ECN-based congestion control protocols need the support of intermediate routers, which directly affects the scalability of these protocols. It will be a huge challenge to change the traditional end-to-end transmission service model of the Internet. It is a very interesting problem whether this type of mechanisms can be eventually used as the standard of next generation Internet protocol.

Recent studies have indicated that the existing active queue management (AQM) mechanism cannot be effectively applied to high BDP networks. The simulation results also show that the network performance has not been greatly improved by combining end-to-end congestion control mechanisms with the traditional active queue management algorithms. The performance of traditional AQM will even be degraded with the increment of link bandwidth and delay [47]. Lacking of information exchange between the end-to-end congestion control protocols and the intermediate routers is the main reason. ECN-based congestion control protocols could detect the congestion of networks with the support of intermediate routers. However, these protocols need too much feedback information and are hard to be deployed in nowadays Internet. Therefore, how to detect the congestion events quickly and effectively in high BDP networks is an important factor for TCP enhancement. Moreover, it is an important problem to find a simple and effective feedback mechanism between end nodes and intermediate nodes to establish relationship in the future study of congestion control.

Most of current works do not sufficiently emphasize the importance of the router buffer. The simulation results of this chapter show that the buffer size plays a decisive role in the performance improvement of congestion control mechanism, especially in delay-based protocols. How to set appropriate buffer size is one of the hot issues in recent years [116, 118]. Establishing the models of router buffer size and flow rate variation in the design of transmission protocol will bring unexpected inspiration in the research of this field.

If the algorithm evaluation relies on the typical simulation experiments alone, the conclusions are not very systematic, scientific and credible. Thus, theoretical analysis and proof is indispensable. The large-scale real network should be built to carry out effective evaluation and verification. The change from research work platforms to the real networks will be one of the primary goals.

2.5. CONCLUSION

In this chapter, a number of congestion control protocols in high Bandwidth-Delay Product networks are reviewed. The impact factors, such as RTT delay, the bottleneck router buffer and queue management algorithm, are also evaluated through NS2 simulation. In the end, based on the summary of open problems, future research directions are discussed and outlined.

Chapter 3

PERFORMANCE ANALYSIS OF CONGESTION CONTROL PROTOCOLS IN DIFFERENT NETWORK ENVIRONMENTS

3.1. INTRODUCTION

With the rapid development of computer networks, a growing number of Internet applications and users make the network congestion problems increasingly prominent, and degrade the performance of upper application system. To ensure the robustness of Internet, congestion control has become a hot area in computer network research [98]. At present, most of the data services, such as SMTP, TELNET, FTP, and HTTP, use TCP as the congestion control mechanism [3]. So TCP mechanism has a significant importance to detect and control network congestion. Due to the existing network congestion phenomenon, Jacobson put forward the original TCP congestion control algorithm in 1988. In recent years, a variety of new data transfer applications are emerging. These applications require different types of transmission networks, such as high-speed network to transmit massive data, wireless sensor networks to transfer environment monitoring and fire warning information, and satellite networks to send map and remote education data. In these new network environments, the traditional TCP congestion control protocol has to face enormous challenges. This chapter divides existing network environments into the following categories:

(1) Traditional Network Environment

The traditional network environment is characterized by small link capacity, high reliability of cable channel, and low link error rate. In such a network environment, the traditional TCP protocol is efficient because of its reasonable additive increase and multiplicative decrease (AIMD) window management strategy.

(2) High Bandwidth-Delay Network Environment

The backbone network of Internet today began to show the high bandwidth-delay characteristic [40]. In this network environment, researchers find that the network performance is degraded for these reasons [40, 41, 44, 45, 119, 120]:

1) Traditional AIMD mechanism of TCP leads to low bandwidth utilization.
2) The RTT difference increases the unfairness of throughput.
3) The frequent jitters of TCP flows make networks instable.

(3) Wireless Network Environment

In wireless networks, most of the packet loss is due to the high bit error rate, fading radio channel and unexpected disconnections. However, traditional TCP cannot distinguish and isolate wireless loss from congestion loss. As a consequence, TCP assumes all packet losses are due to congestion and reduces the congestion window unnecessarily.

(4) Satellite Network Environment

The satellite networks have large coverage, long transmission distance, and are able to transmit without geographical restrictions. However, the long delay of the link layer makes the satellite networks inefficient. Meanwhile, the satellite networks are more vulnerable to climate and other external environments, and thus the link bit errors cannot be negligible. The high link error rate makes TCP sender decrease transmission rates frequently, thereby reducing the overall performance.

To solve these problems, researchers have proposed numerous TCP variants. However, these protocols are generally designed for certain specific network environments. In real networks, the users may not be able to have priori knowledge of the type of network to be used. In this case, the protocol adapted to a specific network environment cannot guarantee the performance in other types of network environments. Therefore, the environmental adaptability of existing protocols becomes very important. This chapter classifies the TCP variants according to their adaptability to different network environments. The impacts of network environment on protocols performance are analyzed based on the comprehensive comparison and evaluation on performances of TCP variants.

The rest of this chapter is structured as follows. Section 3.2 summarizes the TCP variants in different network environments. The performance evaluations of various TCP variants in different network environments are presented in Section 3.3. The chapter is concluded in Section 3.4 with a summary of the results and highlights of the future works.

3.2. TCP CONGESTION CONTROL PROTOCOLS

Since the first TCP version was put forward, many improved TCP versions have been proposed for different network characteristics. The improvements mainly focus on the issues such as how to deal with the impact of high bandwidth or/and large propagation delay, and how to distinguish between wireless losses and congestion losses. Based on the suitable network environments, these protocols can be classified into traditional network protocol (T-protocol), high bandwidth-delay network protocol (H-protocol), wireless network protocol (W-protocol) and satellite network protocol (S-protocol).

3.2.1. TCP Protocols in Traditional Network

In the traditional wired networks, TCP controls the congestion by adjusting the congestion window (CWND). The traditional congestion control mechanism includes slow start, fast retransmit and congestion avoidance algorithm [38]. One class of TCPs are loss-based that use packet-loss as an indication of congestion. The typical proposals include TCP Reno [37] and Sack [39]. By contrast, another class of TCPs is delay-based, which make congestion decision based on Round Trip Time (RTT) variations, e.g., TCP Vegas [42].

TCP Reno is one of the most widely adopted TCP versions and is considered as the standard reference. TCP Reno uses the additive increase multiplicative decrease (AIMD) algorithm to adjust congestion window. The sender probes the available bandwidth by gradually increasing the CWND. When packet loss is detected by the reception of three duplicate acknowledgments or time out, the sender retransmits the lost packet and halves the size of CWND. By adding the Fast Recovery mechanism to the algorithm, TCP Reno improved the efficiency of congestion recovery.

TCP Vegas introduces an alternative congestion control policy, with the aim of preventing congestion losses by taking RTT delay as the congestion indicator. This TCP variant tries to detect changes of RTT. When the RTT is small and close to the minimum of all measured RTT, the network is not congested. When the RTT is larger than the minimum RTT, the buffer space is filling up and the network is approaching a congested state. Then TCP Vegas adjusts the CWND according to the RTT, and consequently stabilizes the CWND at an appropriate value.

3.2.2. TCP Protocols in High Bandwidth-Delay Networks

In the high bandwidth-delay networks, the top issue of congestion control is the under-utilization due to the slow growth of CWND. In the past few years, several TCP variants have been proposed to address this problem. Some typical proposals include loss-based HSTCP [40], HTCP [108], CUBIC [107], delay-based FAST [44], rate-based RAPID [121], and a series of proposals which use explicit network feedback [47, 48, 122, 123]. All these H-protocols try to overcome TCP's deficiencies in high bandwidth-delay networks. The proposals based on explicit feedback are more effective than end-to-end mechanism, but are hard to deploy in today's Internet as they require the assistance of routers. Thus, these proposals are excluded from the simulation comparison list. This chapter is specifically interested in the enhanced proposals that preserve the end-to-end semantics of TCP.

HSTCP behaves like the standard TCP and also uses packet drop to detect congestion. HSTCP modifies the TCP response function, making the increment of CWND more aggressive upon receiving an ACK and the decrement of CWND more gentle upon a loss event. To ensure compatibility with the standard TCP, HSTCP uses the standard TCP's default CWND response parameters when the CWND is less than a fixed threshold value (38 packets).

HTCP uses the time interval Δ between the successive packet drop events to indicate the congestion. The increasing factor of AIMD is a function of Δ. To mitigate unfairness between competing flows with different RTT, HTCP also scales the AIMD increasing factor. The AIMD decreasing factor is adjusted to improve link utilization based on the estimate of the queue size.

CUBIC is an enhanced version of BIC-TCP [41] with a goal of improving the TCP-friendliness and RTT-fairness. CUBIC adopts the cubic function $W_{cubic}=C(t-K)^3+W_{max}$ to decide the window increment in next round-trip time, where C is a constant used for scaling, t is the elapsed time from the last congestion event, W_{max} is the window size just before the last congestion event, and $K=(W_{max}\beta/C)^{1/3}$, where β is the multiplication decrease factor after the congestion event. The CWND grows very fast when it is far away from W_{max}, and it slows down its growth when it becomes closer to W_{max}. To improve the stability and the scalability of the algorithm, the congestion window increases in independence of round-trip time.

Fast TCP is based on Vegas TCP. Fast TCP reacts in both queuing delay and packet loss. The congestion CWND is updated every other RTT in the way
$$w \leftarrow \min \left\{ 2w, (1-\gamma)w + \gamma \left(\frac{baseRTT}{RTT}w + \alpha\right) \right\}$$,where $baseRTT$ is the minimum RTT value, $\gamma \in (0,1]$, α represents the number of packets that Fast TCP attempts to keep in the buffer along the path in stable state. When the packet loss is detected, Fast TCP quickly halves the CWND. When there is no packet drop, Fast TCP adjusts the CWND according to the RTT and α. The adjustment of CWND is very small at equilibrium, but is large when far away from the equilibrium, which makes Fast TCP converges rapidly to the equilibrium.

3.2.3. TCP Protocols in Wireless Networks

Due to high bit error rate (BER) in wireless networks, the core issue of improving wireless TCP performance is to isolate and distinguish wireless loss and congestion loss correctly. Recent works have addressed this issue. The solutions can be categorized into split connection, link layer approach and end-to-end approach. In the split-connection approaches [124, 125], the connection is divided into the wired part and wireless part, and the base station is responsible for the recovery of the wireless losses. Link layer solutions [126] mask losses from TCP through link layer retransmission, which increase the complexity of protocol implementation. Compared with these methods, end-to-end approach depends only on TCP senders and receivers to recover losses. Some typical proposals include TCP Veno [127], TCP-Bayes [128], TCP Westwood [43] and TIBET [129]. Among them, TCP Westwood is considered as a simple and effective solution.

TCP Westwood presents a bandwidth estimation algorithm which can discriminate the cause of packet loss. In Westwood, the sender estimates the current available bandwidth by continuously measuring the arriving rate of ACKs. After three duplicate acknowledgments or a timeout, unlike TCP Reno, Westwood sets the slow start threshold (*ssthresh*) and CWND according to the network available bandwidth. The CWND is calculated as $w \leftarrow \dfrac{RTT \times Bwe}{seg\_size}$, where B_{we} is the estimated bandwidth, RTT is the minimum round trip time and *seg_size* is the segment size. This approach can recover the CWND to an appropriate value which equals to the bandwidth used at the time packet loss is experienced. In this way, halving the CWND blindly after the packet loss is avoided. Westwood is shown to be more effective than Reno over wireless links, while achieving fairness and TCP-friendliness. Some studies show that, due to the clustering of packets, TCP Westwood may overestimate the available bandwidth [130]. The overestimate results in a large CWND, and thereby may lead to congestion.

3.2.4. TCP Protocols in Satellite Networks

The long propagation time and the random losses in satellite networks pose a big challenge to TCP. A number of TCP variants have been presented to solve the problems. The solutions can be classified in two categories. One class of approaches isolated the radio links from the wired network by "Performance Enhancing Proxies" [124]. Another class of approaches is end-to-end TCP enhancement which modifies the standard TCP algorithm. For example, TCP-Peach [131] uses the sudden start algorithm to replace the slow start algorithm in TCP.

TCP Hybla [132] is proposed with the primary aim of counteracting the impact of the long propagation time of satellite connections. To overcome this problem, Hybla removes the reliance on RTT by enabling the long RTT connections to transmit at the same instantaneous rate as that of the referred TCP connection with short RTT. This is accomplished by adjusting the CWND size to a normalized ratio ρ of the previous CWND size. The value of ρ is set as $\rho=RTT/RTT_0$, where RTT_0 is the round trip time of the referred TCP connection. In this way, Hybia improves the throughput of flow with long RTT. In addition, TCP Hybla includes other several important enhancements. The SACK option and timestamps is used to help alleviate the impact of packet losses. The bandwidth estimation is used in order to set the initial *ssthresh* appropriately. The packet spacing is adopted to counteract the burstiness due to Hybla's typical large CWND size.

3.3. PERFORMANCE EVALUATION OF TCP PROTOCOLS

The research community has been working intensively to analyze the performances of recently proposed TCPs [133, 134, 135]. However, most of existing works compare these TCPs in certain specific network environments instead of making comparison under different network conditions. In [135], the authors present the performances of high-speed protocols in satellite network and analyze the impact of different applications, while ignoring the situations in other network environments. In order to analyze the adaptability of these protocols to different network environments, this section compares and analyzes the performances of TCP variants in different network environments by considering the impact of bottleneck bandwidth, round trip time and random loss rate.

The NS2 simulation tools use a dumbbell topology with a single bottleneck link. To study the performances of protocols in the presence of variability and burstiness in flow arrivals, On/Off UDP traffic with different peak data rate(Type I, II, III occupies 0%, 10%, 50% of bandwidth respectively) is introduced into different network environments. The average burst time and idle time are both 1s, and the distribution follows an exponential On/Off model. In other simulations, Poison distributed UDP flows which occupy 5% of bandwidth are generated as background traffic. Two FTP connections share the bottleneck link and drop-tail policy is used in the bottleneck queue. The data packet size is 1460 bytes, while the ACK packet size is 40 bytes. All simulations are run for 150s. The capacity of non-bottleneck link is much larger than that of bottleneck link. The parameters of the simulations by default [136] are summarized in Table 3-1, where BDP represents bandwidth-delay product.

Table 3-1. Parameters Setting of Network Environments

	Bottleneck Bandwidth	RTT	Error Rate	Buffer Size
Traditional Network	10M	60ms	0	100 packets
High Bandwidth-Delay Product Network	622M	100ms	0	BDP
Wireless Network	10M	74ms	0.5%	100 packets
Satellite Network	10M	600ms	1%	BDP

Performance evaluation of the protocols is done mainly by measuring the goodput, packet loss rate, buffer occupancy and bandwidth utilization on the bottleneck link. Among them, goodput is the number of bits forwarded by the network within a certain time interval, excluding retransmitted data packets. It is an important metric in the network performance evaluation, and can reflect the impact of the network latency and packet loss on network performance.

3.3.1. Protocols Performance Analysis in Traditional Networks

In traditional network environments, traditional TCP variants have been shown to have better performances. However, for the protocols proposed for other network environments, their adaptability to the traditional networks is worthy of further study.

Figure 3-1 shows the performances of various protocols with different types of background traffic in the traditional network environments. In the absence of background flow, all protocols show good performances. Vegas achieves high throughput, while maintaining a low average queue length and negligible packet-loss rate. Due to taking RTT variances as congestion indicator, Vegas is able to predict congestion before the packet loss. Thus, Vegas can adjust the size of *CWND* earlier to avoid congestion, and reduce the number of lost packets. The window management of H-protocols is comparatively aggressive in high-speed networks. In low-speed networks, H-protocols also can adjust the window according to the network environment. HTCP takes time interval Δ of adjacent packet loss events as the congestion indicator. When Δ is less than threshold, the window growth mode uses the traditional mode of TCP. The mode of HSTCP is reduced to that of the traditional TCP when the size of *CWND* is less than 38 packets. The window adjustment of Fast TCP depends on the setting of parameter α, which is determined by the throughput mapping table. In low-speed networks, the small value of α makes the sending window converge to a smaller value. CUBIC uses real-time window growth policy, which does not change *CWND* with RTT. This method enables the window growth rate of CUBIC to be close to that of TCP Reno in low-latency network. However, the comparatively aggressive adjustments of the window introduce a higher packet-loss rate to H-protocols. S-protocol Hybla adjusts the window growth rate according to the RTT. When the RTT value as small as the reference RTT, its sending rate is the same as the traditional TCP. In addition, the adoption of the Hoe's end-to-end bandwidth estimation and packet spacing techniques effectively reduce the burstiness of the protocol. After On/Off UDP traffic are added to the simulation, theses protocols can still utilize available bandwidth effectively. However, the packet loss rates increased significantly with the increasing of burstiness, especially the loss rates of H-protocols and S-protocols. The increasing of burstiness also aggravates the queue jitter and decreases the average queue length.

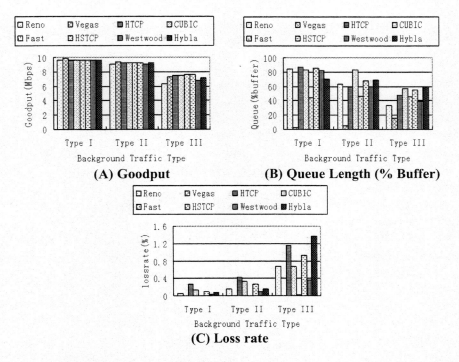

(A) Goodput   (B) Queue Length (% Buffer)

(C) Loss rate

Figure 3-1. Protocols performances in traditional networks.

Overall, the compatibility of H-protocols and S-protocols with traditional networks makes them effective in low bandwidth-delay networks, but the aggressive window growth rate makes their packet loss rate higher. The W-protocol Westwood has similar performance with T-protocols. Due to the link reliability, Westwood does not show its advantages.

3.3.2. Protocols Performance Analysis in High Bandwidth-Delay Network

In high bandwidth-delay networks, the greatest challenge to congestion control mechanism is the increasing capacity of bottleneck link. At first, the bottleneck capacity varying from 100Mb to 700Mb while leaving everything else fixed. Buffer size is set to 20% BDP.

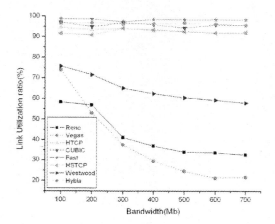

Figure 3-2. Link utilization with different bottleneck capacity.

Figure 3-2 shows that every H-protocol is able to maintain high utilization (≥90%). Since S-protocol Hybla speeds up the sending rate of the connection with high RTT, in this simulation, its *CWND* is multiplied 4 times. This fast increase of *CWND* enables Hybla to achieve a high utilization (≥90%). The link utilization of T-protocols Reno and Vegas declines significantly along with the increasing of bottleneck capacity, due to their conservative window-control strategy. Vegas has the lowest utilization because its congestion threshold is too small for high speed networks and reduces the *CWND* prematurely. W-protocol Westwood also achieves a low utilization due to its conservative window increase, but outperforms T-protocols because it recovers the *CWND* to an appropriate value in accordance with the available bandwidth after packet dropping.

Compared with traditional networks, the characteristics of high bandwidth-delay networks require more buffer space for the router. To study the effect of buffer size on protocol performance, a single connection is run with varying buffer size from 1% BDP to 100%BDP.

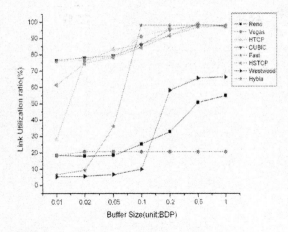

Figure 3-3. Link utilization with different buffer size.

Figure 3-3 shows the link utilization of the protocols with different buffer sizes. The link utilization of most protocols is growing along with the increase of the buffer size. The improvement of H-protocols is the highest because they can utilize the buffer space effectively to achieve the link capacity through the large growth of their $CWND$. When the buffer size is larger than 20%BDP, their utilization reaches to 90%. Among them, Fast TCP cannot work well when the buffer size is very small because each TCP Fast flow attempts to maintain α packets in the queue at the bottleneck link. When the buffer size is smaller than α, Fast TCP cannot reach the stable state and induces many packet losses. S-protocols can also achieve high throughput due to its large sending rate. T-protocols Reno and Vegas cannot make full use of buffer space to improve their throughput even when buffer size is large. W-protocol Westwood has a bad performance for adopting the conservative backoff method. When the buffer is small, the continuous growth of congestion window after backoff will lead to buffer overflow and performance degradation. As the buffer size increases, Westwood outperforms the T-protocols gradually.

To evaluate the impact of burstiness on the protocols, five TCP connections are simulated under different types of background traffic. In Figure 3-4, all H-protocols achieve higher goodput than T-protocols. Due to the effect of adopting queue delay as feedback, Fast TCP achieves the lowest queue length and packet loss rates compared with other H-protocols. HTCP achieves the lowest queue length in loss-based protocols, because of the adoption of adaptive window reduction, which can clear the buffer rapidly after the window reduction. This adaptive algorithm makes HTCP maintain high link utilization with a low persistent queue length. W-protocol Westwood also achieves high goodput while type I or type II traffic exists. But it has the largest packet loss rate. As mentioned before, Westwood may overestimate the available bandwidth, especially with multi-flows along the path. The overestimation produces a relatively small window reduction after each packet drop, which actually intensifies the congestion. Under type III traffic, since the background traffic occupied a lot of bandwidth, the performance of Westwood declines significantly and further aggravates the congestion. T-protocols cannot utilize the bandwidth effectively, thus they have low queue length and small packet loss rate. With the increasing of burstiness, the packet loss rates of all protocols increase modestly. The reason is that the effect of burstiness in high bandwidth-delay network is relatively small.

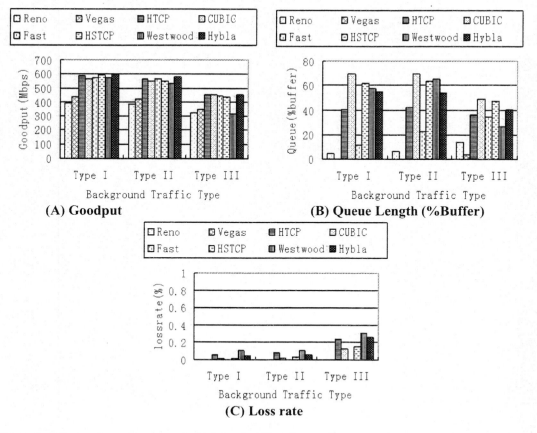

(A) Goodput   (B) Queue Length (%Buffer)

(C) Loss rate

Figure 3-4. Protocols performances in high bandwidth-delay product networks.

Based on the above analysis, T-protocols cannot adapt to the high bandwidth-delay networks, and thus shows poor performances. The S-protocol Hybla can trigger a fast window growth rate in large delay networks, and achieve a good performance. The W-protocol Westwood has some advantages compared with T-protocols due to its adaptive backoff mechanism.

3.3.3. Protocols Performance Analysis in Wireless Network

In order to assess the relation between throughput gain of protocols and the link error rate in wireless network, the protocols are evaluated with the BER varying from 0.01% to 5%.

In Figure 3-5, when the link error rate is less than 0.1%, all TCP proposals perform closely to each other. When the link error rate is larger than 0.1%, the goodputs of most proposals are higher than that of Reno. Hybla and Westwood have larger improvement around 0.1% to 1% error rate. When the error rate is larger than 1%, the performances of all protocols decline significantly. Among them, since Westwood can discriminate the cause of packet loss effectively and avoid reducing the *CWND* blindly, Westwood achieves a high goodput. The SACK option enables Hybla to quickly recover from multiple losses, and the fast window growth rate enables Hybla to occupy the available bandwidth quickly. These all lead to a higher goodput. Delay-based proposals, Vegas and Fast TCP, do not rely on packet loss to detect congestion and can avoid the impact of link error to a certain extent. Moreover, Fast TCP outperforms Vegas because of its rapid convergence to steady-state if α is set appropriately. The blind reduction of *CWND* after wireless loss causes a bad performance for TCP Reno. The protocol CUBIC adjusts the *CWND* according to the elapsed time since the last window reduction. Thus, in CUBIC, the increment and decrement of window all depend on packet loss feedback. As a consequence, CUBIC cannot deal with the impact of wireless loss, and thus has a lower goodput than Reno at the high error rate.

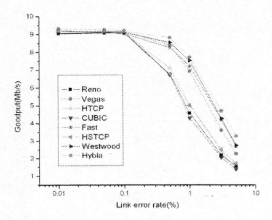

Figure 3-5. Goodput with different loss rate.

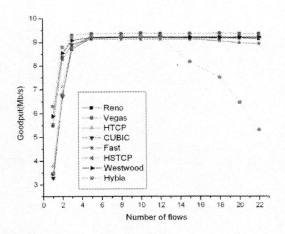

Figure 3-6. Goodput with different flow numbers.

To evaluate the protocols performances under the condition of network congestion, the goodput is measured with different number of flows (from 1 to 22). The link error rate is set to 0.5%. In Figure 3-6, if the number of flows is less than five, the protocols cannot utilize the bandwidth adequately, and have a great difference in goodput. However, as the number of the flows increases, the increased congestion can reduce the impact of link error and improve the goodput. Thus most of the protocols achieve high goodput. Due to the earlier reduction of *CWND*, Vegas has small packet loss rate, which leads to the highest goodput. For Fast TCP, the goodput decreases with the increasing of flow number, because the total buffer size, which the flows need to reach the equilibrium state, is larger than actual buffer size. When the number of flows is larger than 12, Hybla suffers from performance degradation because Hybla adjusts the sending rate based on the RTT. Only the decrease of RTT can make the CWND of Hybla grow slowly. The decrease of per-flow bandwidth share cannot make Hybla reduce its sending rate accordingly. With the increasing of flow number, the total sending rates of Hybla flows increase aggressively. This leads to the degradation in goodput.

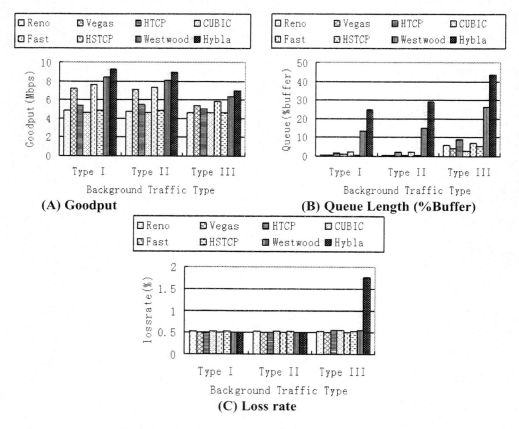

(A) Goodput   **(B) Queue Length (%Buffer)**

(C) Loss rate

Figure 3-7. Protocols performances in wireless network.

Next, the protocols are evaluated under different types of background traffic. Figure 3-7 shows the goodput of protocols with various types of background traffic. Under type I and type II traffic, Hybla, Westwood, Fast TCP and Vegas outperform other protocols. Except from the delay-based protocols, the proposals with high goodput also have a large queue size. The relatively poor performance of loss-based protocol results from the frequent backoff caused by the wireless loss. Under type III traffic, the protocols with high goodput under type I and type II traffic suffer from performance degradation. The other protocols have relatively low goodput because they cannot utilize the bandwidth effectively in wireless networks. Thus, the burstiness of On/Off traffic just has a little effect on the low-goodput protocols. It is noteworthy that Hybla achieves high goodput in all cases. However, the aggressive window management causes Hybla unable to response to the dynamic bandwidth quickly under large burst traffic. Thus, Hybla causes the serious congestion and leads to high packet loss rate.

As stated previously, the performances of protocols in wireless networks mainly depend on the ability of dealing with the link error. Usually, delay-based protocols and adaptive backoff protocols can avoid the irrational reduction of *CWND* brought by wireless loss. Moreover, the protocols with fast window growth rate can recover from loss rapidly.

3.3.4. Protocols Performance Analysis in Satellite Networks

One challenge faced by TCP in satellite networks is the slow response time caused by the long propagation time. To evaluate the adaptability to long latency, the protocols are evaluated under different RTTs.

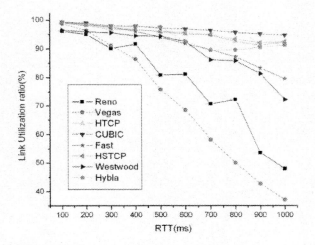

Figure 3-8. Link utilization with different RTTs (error rate =0).

Figure 3-8 shows the link utilization of protocols without wireless loss. For short RTTs (<200ms), all protocols provide high link utilization (>95%). With the increasing of RTT, the performances of T-protocols degrade significantly, while other protocols achieve high utilization (>90%) before RTT reaches 600ms. When RTT is larger than 600ms, the link utilization of some protocols show minor decline. The congestion control mechanism of S-protocol Hybla can avoid the impact of long RTT, and thus Hybla gets the same instantaneous sending rate as short-RTT connection. However with the increasing of RTT, too large *CWND* of Hybla flow makes the congestion worse and suffers from slight throughput decline. Except from Fast TCP, H-protocols maintain high performances with different RTT. CUBIC outperforms other protocols due to its independence on RTT. With the increasing of RTT, the performance of Fast TCP degrades because of the fixed parameter α, which is too small for long RTT and large buffer, cannot follow the change of RTT. Compared with T-protocols, Westwood utilizes the link capacity effectively due to its rational window adjustment.

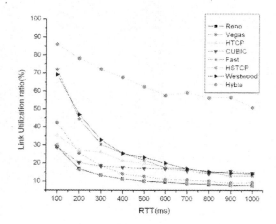

Figure 3-9. Link utilization with different RTTs (error rate=0).

The consequences may become severe in presence of wireless losses, because the interference of wireless losses on the congestion control mechanism causes detrimental *CWND* reductions. This is highlighted in Figure 3-9, which shows the link utilization of protocols with a uniformly distributed 1% loss rate. The presence of wireless losses makes all protocols suffer from performance decline compared with the situation in Figure 3-8. Hybla appears more effective than the other protocols in counteracting the high error rate. This is largely due to the SACK policy, which is important for a fast recover of multiple losses. H-protocols cannot show their advantages under the long RTT, because the frequent window backoff degrades their performances. Westwood's countermeasures against wireless losses are effective on shorter RTT channels, but show its limitation on long RTT channels.

After studying the impact of link error and RTT on the performance of the protocols, the simulations are run with varied background traffic. The performances of protocols are presented in Figure 3-10. In this case, most protocols show poor performances except Hybla. Compared with T-protocols, H-protocols (HTCP, CUBIC, and Fast TCP) achieve higher performance due to their fast sending rates, and W-protocol Westwood also shows advantages because of its bandwidth estimation algorithm. Under the combined influence of long RTT and high link error rate, HSTCP's *CWND* cannot exceed the threshold of mode switching. Thus, HSTCP acts in the same way as the TCP Reno. The under-utilization of link capacity leads the queue lengths and the packet-loss rates of protocols to be very small. Under the impact of background traffic, the performances of protocols are not affected by the burstiness since the network path is idle. Since Hybla is less aggressive under long RTT channels, it does not cause the large packet-loss rate.

In the satellite network environment, except for Hybla, most protocols cannot achieve good performance. The H-protocols and W-protocols are able to obtain higher goodput than T-protocols, but their improvement is slight.

Based on above analysis, it is clear that various protocols have distinct adaptability to different network environments. Each protocol has its own advantages and disadvantages, and cannot adapt well to all network environments.

The performance of all these protocols are summarized in Table 3-2, where the symbols represent the performance level of protocols: ***(excellent),**(good), * (average), Δ (poor).

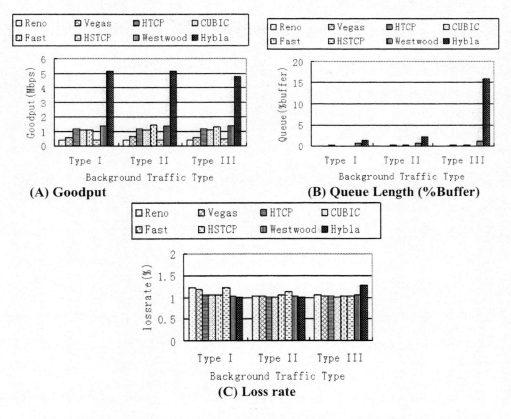

(A) Goodput

(B) Queue Length (%Buffer)

(C) Loss rate

Figure 3-10. Protocols performances in satellite networks.Table 3-2.Comparison of different protocols in different network environments

		Traditional Network		High Bandwidth-Delay Product Network		Wireless Network		Satellite Network	
		Reno	Vegas	HTCP	CUBIC	Fast	HSTCP	Westwood	Hybla
Traditional Network	Goodput	***	***	***	***	***	***	***	***
	Buffer Occupancy	*	***	*	*	**	*	*	*
	Loss rate	**	***	*	*	***	*	*	*
High Bandwidth-Delay Product Network	Goodput	△	△	***	***	***	***	*	***
	Buffer Occupancy	**	***	**	*	**	*	*	*
	Loss rate	***	***	*	**	***	**	*	*
Wireless Network	Goodput	△	**	△	△	**	△	***	***
	Buffer Occupancy	***	***	***	***	***	***	**	*
	Loss rate	***	***	***	***	***	***	***	△
Satellite Network	Goodput	△	△	△	△	△	△	△	***
	Buffer Occupancy	***	***	***	***	***	***	***	*
	Loss rate	**	**	***	***	**	***	***	**

3.4. CONCLUSION

This chapter presents a comprehensive performance evaluation of various TCP variants in different network environments. The chapter presents an overall analysis including throughput, queuing, and packet-loss rate with different type of background traffic. The causes of performance degradation of protocols are shown in different network environments. The analyses of typical protocols in different environments are summarized:

1) T-protocols, Reno and Vegas, can achieve high performance under traditional networks. However, the threshold settings of Vegas only fit to low bandwidth and short delay network. Due to the conservative AI and aggressive MD strategies, Reno cannot utilize the link capacity effectively in network environment with the characteristics of high bandwidth, long delay, or high packet-loss rate.

2) H-protocols have excellent performances under high bandwidth-delay networks. Under other network environments, due to its rapid convergent rate, Fast TCP has a strong adaptability to maintain a low queue length and negligible packet-loss rate. However, the performance of FAST TCP strongly depends on its parameters. In practice, it is difficult to get the appropriate value of parameters in real networks. HTCP shows its limitation in the network with high link error rate, because it uses the time interval between successive packets drops as indicator. On the other hand, HTCP's rational window reduction slightly reduces the impact of link errors, and maintains high link utilization with low transmission delay. The window management of CUBIC is independent on RTT, thus it can effectively deal with the long RTT. However, CUBIC is sensitive to packet loss, which limits its performance under some network environments. H-protocols show slightly better performances in wireless and satellite network compared with T-protocols.

3) W-protocol Westwood, which adopts more rational window reduction than Reno, has good performance in networks with high link error rate. Under high bandwidth-delay networks, the reasonable window reduction mechanism can reduce the recovery time. However, the bandwidth overestimation of Westwood may affect its performance with multi-flows. Under satellite networks, although Westwood can deal with high loss rate, frequent window backoff and slow growth make Westwood suffer from performance degradation in the case of long RTT.

4) S-protocol, Hybla, due to the RTT-adaptive window management, achieves efficiency in satellite networks, and shows adaptability to traditional networks and high bandwidth-delay networks. In wireless networks, Hybla achieves good performance by rapid sending rate and Sack policy. However, Hybla adjusts the *CWND* and *ssthresh* on RTT, and thus cannot fully learn the network state. Under the influence of bursty traffic, it is difficult for Hybla to adapt to the change of network status. In this case, the aggressiveness of Hybla causes large packet-loss rate. When multi-flows coexists, the aggressiveness also make Hybla degrade significantly due to the intensive congestion.

To sum up, no single protocol has an optimal performance in all network environments. There are still some open issues.

1) The emergence of the complex network applications, increased bandwidth, uncertain RTT, etc. are the reasons for performance decline of above protocols. How to choose a suitable congestion control mechanism without knowing the network environment is a problem. The ability to know the network environment plays a very important role in improving transmission performance. The changes of network environments can be learned by end-to-end delay, packet loss and other transmission characteristics. Then the questions, such as which parameters can effectively reflect the state of the network, how to obtain and feedback these information, and how to control the cost of perceiving environment, are the keys to the study.

2) Congestion control protocols should have the adaptability to different network environments. In order to improve reliability and efficiency, the congestion control protocol should have the ability to adjust the internal parameters and transmission strategies according to the external network environments. Thus, which parameters should be chosen and how to adjust transmission parameters to adapt to changes in the environment are worth further study.

3) Due to lack of unified model description, the existing protocols are static or quasi-static, and cannot rapidly track the dynamic network environment. The parameter selection of Fast TCP fully shows this flaw. For the adaptive transmission strategy, the model-based analysis is more conducive to an accurate judgment of the network status. The model-based analysis gives the algorithm good dynamic adaptability, and can finally optimize the transmission control. In future research, the mathematical analysis in control and optimization theory should be considered to analyze the stability of transmission control system and guide the optimal design of control parameters.

Chapter 4

SURVEY ON ROUTER BUFFER SIZING IN HIGH BANDWIDTH-DELAY NETWORK

4.1. INTRODUCTION

In Internet, routers play an important role in transferring packets. On one hand, router buffers could accommodate bursty traffic and decrease the packet loss rate. On the other hand, it could store superfluous packets temporarily during congestion until output link is idle, which can increase the link utilization. Therefore, buffer has great impact on enhancing the performance of routers and further improving the performance of the whole network as well. However, excessive buffers may cause queuing delay and delay jitter. Up to now, the studies of the demand of buffers have not drawn a consistent conclusion.

As a widely used rule, the rule-of-thumb [137] to set the buffer size is to let it equal to bandwidth-delay product. Although this rule is widely used because it is simple and easy to implement, as the network bandwidth and latency are continuously increasing, its defects have been exposed gradually.

1) When the network bandwidth and delay becomes larger, the buffer size also increases according to the rule of thumb. Excessive buffer size will cause some difficulties in designing routers, such as cooling, energy consuming, and the overhead of mother-board space, et al. In order to keep high-speed forwarding, the router needs to use high-speed memory chip. It takes huge cost to manufacture this type of chip based on the existing technology. Therefore, router buffers become the bottleneck of the networks.

2) Since the optical technology has been used in designing routers, the optical storage problem has not been resolved effectively. Under the existing technical condition, all-optical router could store only a few dozen packets, which is much smaller than the bandwidth-delay product.

3) Large buffers will increase end-to-end delay and delay jitter. It significantly affects the performance of real-time interactive transactions. Small buffers could decrease queuing delay and implementation complexity, but it will increase packet-loss rate and decrease throughput. Therefore, it is interesting to study how many packets that the router buffers should accommodate to achieve the optimal network performance.

Some recent works [116, 138, 139] challenge the rule of thumb theoretically. They consider that the size of buffer should decrease greatly. Meanwhile, the traffic data measured in real networks also challenge the rule of thumb. The queue length is difficult to exceed ten packets according to the measurement of Spring backbone router, because the utilization is always below 20%. In [157], the authors point out that buffer demands of backbone router are far less than the current settings through preliminary experiments in real network environment.

4.2. Theoretical Analysis of Router Buffer Sizing

The network model consists of two parts. The first part describes dynamics of TCP protocol. The second part describes dynamics of queue. This section presents the theoretical foundation for buffer issues from the following two aspects.

Firstly, a long TCP flow is considered. The packet loss rate is p, and the round-trip delay is RTT. According to the classical TCP's throughput equation, the average sending rate is:

$$x = \frac{0.87}{RTT\sqrt{p}} \tag{4-1}$$

If the loss rates of the queues along the routing path are q_1, ..., q_n, the end-to-end loss rate is $p=1-\prod(1-q_i)$. The drop probability in a queue with Poisson arrivals of rate y, service rate C and buffer size B, could be expressed as $q=L_B(y,C)$ [160], where $y=\sum x_i$. Combining the above equations together, it can simultaneously obtain throughputs x and drop probabilities p for each flow. This method is called as the fixed-point approach [162], the prerequisite of which is that TCP can always match the aggregated sending rate to the available bandwidth.

For a queue with given service rate and buffer size, Poisson distribution is usually adopted to fit the characteristic of the network traffic arriving at a queue. Firstly, the arrival process of the aggregated flow theoretically follows Poisson distribution in a shorter time scale, as the number of flows increases.

Secondly, the experience and measurement both show that traffic on the Internet approximately follow Poisson process in a short time scale. In this case, a negative exponential relationship exists between the overflow probability of queuing system and the buffer capacity. Drop probability decreases with the trend to approaching 0 as the buffer size increases. Thus, a buffer with the corresponding size could satisfy the requirement of pack-loss rate. Such an analysis scheme is a kind of open-loop analysis method that does not take into account network feedback from the input traffic. However, in real statistical multiplexing networks, packet arrival process has the properties of strong correlation and burstiness. Though network traffics follow Poisson distribution in short time scale, they are long-range dependent in long time scale. Further study is needed to extend existing mathematical models to real networks.

4.3. BUFFER SIZING SCHEMES

In recent years, a series of buffer sizing schemes are proposed in high bandwidth-delay networks. These schemes mainly include the Stanford model, Packet-Loss-Rate Based Rule, Buffer Sizing for Congested Link, Tiny Buffer Rule and Adaptive Drop-Tail algorithm. These classical schemes are presented in this section.

Traditional rule-of-thumb arises from the dynamics of TCP's congestion control algorithm, which assumes that a long TCP flow exists in the congested link and its window varies zigzag in its steady state. The largest size of congestion windows is $CT + B$ before packet loss occurs, where C is the bottlenecked bandwidth, T is round-trip time, and B is the buffer size of the bottlenecked link. Congestion window `size is reduced to $(CT + B)/2$ after the event of packet loss. Thus, this scheme requires the full utilization of the bottlenecked link, even when the congestion window is minimal, i.e., $(CT + B)/2 \geq CT$, namely $B \geq CT$. If multiple TCP flows synchronize with each other, the packet-loss events occur almost at the same time. In this case, the rule-of-thumb still holds. Thus, some works argue that buffer size could be significant decreased when flows are desynchronized [116, 152, 160].

The Stanford model [116] firstly improves rule-of-thumb. It focuses on a bottleneck link that carries N long TCP flows. When N is sufficiently large, there exists desynchronization among different flows. (Only a small number of flows experience packets dropped for each congestion event). Based on the central limit theorem, the aggregated window size and the queue size will follow the Normal distribution. The out link can achieve full utilization when buffer size is the bandwidth-delay product divided by the square root of the number of flows N, namely

$$B = \frac{RTT \times C}{\sqrt{N}} \tag{4-2}$$

In [116], the authors argue that buffer requirement of short flow depends on the link load and busty arrival traffic. When link carries a mix of both short and long TCP flows, buffer size is determined by the number of long flows. Short flows do not have a significant effect on the required buffer size. This scheme is only applicable to backbone routers, which have a great number of TCP flows, because the authors consider that the number of synchronized flows decreases as the number of flows increases. In fact, the relationship between the number of flows and synchronization should be studied further. In [142], the author also argue that the Stanford model can lead to high loss rate up to 5%-15% for achieving high link utilization.

FPQ (Flow Proportional Queuing) rule [140] is another improvement of the rule-of-thumb. Since the Stanford model tends to increase packet-loss rate significantly, it has serious impact on router performance and network stability. Morris considers the impact of packet-loss rate on heavy load for the first time. When a bottlenecked link is shared by multiple TCP flows, the packet-loss rate is proportional to the square of the number of TCP flows, namely

$$l = 0.76 \frac{N^2}{S^2} \tag{4-3}$$

where S is the sum of TCPs' sending window sizes. In order to avoid frequent timeout retransmission and throughput jitter caused by the small buffer space, the bottleneck link should assign enough buffer space for each TCP connection. FPQ monitors the number of active TCP flows and assigns the available queue space based on that number. In [140] it validates that it could avoid retransmission for timeout when each flow is assigned with 6 packets buffer space. However, this scheme could not fully utilize the bottleneck-link bandwidth when the number of flows is few. Moreover, what kind of flow should be counted in the number of flows N is not mentioned.

BSCL (Buffer Sizing for Congested Internet Links) [138] is a buffer sizing scheme for congested links. It manages to keep the bottlenecked link saturated without allowing the packet-loss rate to exceed a given upper bound. It assumes that most of the traffics (80%~90%) are generated by long TCP flows at the bottleneck link. In BSCL, the buffer requirement depends on the harmonic mean of RTTs and the degree of asynchronism. To limit packet-loss rate, the buffer size should be proportional to the number of long TCP flows, when that number exceeds a certain threshold N_{th}. The buffer size can be computed as follows.

$$B = \begin{cases} B_\rho = \dfrac{q(N_b)CT_c - 2MN_b[1-q(N_b)]}{2-q(N_b)} & ,if \quad N_b < N_{th} \\ B_p = K_p N_b - CT_e & ,if \quad N_b > N_{th} \end{cases} \qquad (4\text{-}4)$$

In addition, the authors in [138] make a trade-off between packet-loss rate and RTT. Setting a constraint of maximum queuing delay provides a simple upper bound on the buffer requirement. A problem of BSCL is that packet-loss rate will cause larger queueing delay.

Tiny Buffer Rule [139] is proposed for all-optical networks. All-optical routers could only store a few dozen packets. The number of packets is much less than that required by the rule-of-thumb. The authors argue that if a small amount of link utilization can be sacrificed, buffers can be significantly reduced to $\log_{1/\rho}\left(\dfrac{w_{max}^2}{2(1-\theta)}\right)$, where W_{max} is the maximum size of each flow's congestion window and θ is the effective link utilization. This scheme allows buffer size to be independent of bandwidth, delay and the number of flows, and requires the aggregated arrival process at the bottlenecked link to resemble a Poisson process. Since the access link bandwidth is much smaller than the backbone link bandwidth in real networks, the arrival packets at the backbone router are naturally separated. Even if the access link bandwidth is close to the backbone link bandwidth, the source can change sending mode through TCP pacing mechanism. TCP pacing [143] inserts the time interval d/W_{max} when the source sends packets. Tiny buffer rule not only can ease or even eliminate the optical storage problem, but also can be applied to the current backbone networks. Since the current backbone link utilization is merely 20~30% [158, 159], it is meaningful to sacrifice 10~15% link utilization to get small router buffers. In [144], the authors demonstrate that, when Combined Input-Output Queuing (CIOQ) model is widely used in current routers, router buffers that can accommodate a few dozen packets could satisfy the requirement.

Active Drop-Tail (ADT) [141] is the first adaptive buffer sizing algorithm. At present, most buffer sizing schemes are based on rigorous mathematical models. Because of time-varying and complexity of network traffic, it could not easily find an accurate mathematical model to characterize network behaviors. In [141], the author proposes an adaptive buffer sizing algorithm called ADT, which estimates the current link utilization and adjusts available buffer threshold dynamically according to the relationship between the current and the desired link utilization. The algorithm could minimize queuing delay and still maintain high utilization. The control equation of ADT is expressed as follows:

$$q(k+1) = q(k) + K_\tau (u^* - u(k)) \qquad (4\text{-}5)$$

The parameter u denotes the measured link utilization, u^* is the desired link utilization, and q corresponds to the number of packets that can be accommodated in the buffer. The algorithm could change traffic arrival characteristic by sending available buffer space to the source. The key for this scheme is that, since the traffic arrival is elastic, a feedback loop matches the network load with the available bandwidth in flow layer.

4.4. ANALYSIS OF ROUTER BUFFER SIZING

Two approaches exist to adapt router buffer to high bandwidth-delay networks. The first approach is to modify existing TCP protocol or re-design a fair and efficient congestion control mechanism. Because the existing buffer sizing mechanisms are based on traditional TCP protocols, TCP modification of re-design is a possible approach to enable small buffer to meet the requirements of the high bandwidth-delay networks. The second approach is to set the router buffer space without modifying existing protocols. To maintain back compatibility, it is preferred not to modify the current widely used Internet transport layer and application layer protocols. In the following subsections, the key factors that influence buffer requirements are analyzed and summarized from the above two aspects.

4.4.1. Impact of TCP Congestion Control Mechanism

As buffer size has a close relationship with the TCP congestion-control mechanism, most buffer sizing mechanisms are designed based on the TCP AIMD algorithm. However, rather than designing buffers to accommodate the TCP AIMD algorithm, [155] suggests a simple modification of back-off factor β to the AIMD in the ith periods. The value of β is set as:

$$\beta_i = \frac{RTT_{min,i}}{RTT_{max,i}} \qquad (4\text{-}6)$$

In this way, the queue becomes empty only after a back-off event and the link continues to operate with the expected capacity. This method can also realize effective decoupling between cache partition method and the TCP congestion-control mechanism. The possible problem is that too small back-off factor may slow down the rate of network's convergence to equilibrium. HTCP [108] has partially adopted the Adaptive AIMD mechanism. It has been shown that HTCP has a better perform than other high-speed network protocols according to simulation experiments.

Recently, a series of high-speed TCP congestion-control protocols for high bandwidth-delay networks have been proposed. However, whether these new router buffer mechanisms are reasonable for the high-speed TCP needs further exploration. In [147], the authors study the effect of the router buffer size on the throughput of High-Speed TCP (HSTCP). They first derive an analytical model for HSTCP. Then they show that, for small buffer size equal to 10% of the bandwidth-delay product, HSTCP can achieve more than 90% of the bottleneck capacity. For the buffer size equal to 20% of the bandwidth-delay product, the utilization of HSTCP increases to 98%. On the contrary, setting the buffer size to less than 10% of the bandwidth-delay product can decrease HSTCP's throughput significantly.

4.4.2. Impact of Real-time Traffic and Bursty Traffic

As TCP traffic predominates in the Internet, recent studies have ignored non-TCP traffic. In [149], through the practical experiments on the long haul network in Australian, the author evaluates the end-to-end performance when the router buffer size is changed. The results indicate that, when coexistence with burst real-time traffic, TCP requires larger router buffers to achieve a given fraction of its saturation throughput. However, larger buffers lead to increasing losses for real-time traffic. This suggests that TCP and non-TCP traffic can negatively affect each other, and their performance trade-off need to be considered when sizing router buffers.

In [150], the authors analyze the interaction between buffer size and TCP bursty traffic. Through the analysis of the stability, the authors show that smooth traffic will more easily lead to the network's burst, which results in synchronization loss and low stability of the network. However, the synchronization loss problem of smooth traffic can be solved by using small buffer.

4.4.3. Impact of Various Applications

Although large file transfer based on long-term TCP is a more general application, Internet also offers other applications, such as TCP-based web page download, UDP-based interactive applications and so on. Different applications demand different buffer mechanism.

Web page transfer application is based on short-term TCP flows. The AIMD mechanism in the congestion avoidance phase is no longer a determinant factor on optimal buffer size for this application. As the file size becomes smaller, the impact of queuing delay on completion time of small file transmission is gradually increasing. Recent studies have shown that, for any number of small file transfers, the optimal buffer size is dozens of packets.

Queuing delay and delay jitter are important for UDP-based interactive streaming media applications because it is unaccepted if the round-trip propagation delay is greater than a few hundred milliseconds in the application. As transmission jitter of TCP is too large, most interactive applications are UDP-based. In this case, the UDP-based upper-layer communication protocols control the congestion. The optimal buffer size should be determined by the congestion control algorithm of upper-layer communication protocol.

Overall, different applications focus on different performance indicators, which lead to different buffer demands. Then how to coordinate the buffer needs of various applications is a key factor on determining whether buffer mechanisms are effective in the current Internet environment.

4.4.4. Impact of Network Traffic and Topology

Link load is an important factor of the demand for the buffer. If the link load is light, the queuing delay is small and almost no packet loses. In this case, large buffer size has little effect on overall performance. On the contrary, if the link load is heavy, the queuing delay and packet loss are great. In this case, large buffer size is needed to prevent the collapse of the network caused by excessive packet loss. In [146], the relationship between network link input / output ratio and buffer demand is given theoretically.

Network topology also affects router buffer by affecting the packet forwarding routing. Combination of network load and network topology determines the number of bottleneck links and the queuing delay. In Section 4.5, the impacts of network traffic and topology are shown in the environment of multi-bottleneck and complex topology.

4.4.5. Impact of Flow Synchronization

In the multi-stream aggregation network environment, when the flows are synchronized, a large buffer size is in need to take full advantage of the bandwidth bottleneck, whereas a small buffer size can meet the requirements. Synchronization not only causes a large queueing delay and delay jitter, but also causes decrease of network utilization. In [163], the author gives an analysis of flow synchronization using control theory, and points out that the flow synchronization depends in part on the size of the buffer and the small buffer size can be used to solve the synchronization problem.

4.4.6. Impact of Queue Management

The queue management mechanisms, including queue scheduling strategy and packet dropping strategy, are also important factors that affect the buffer size.

Queue scheduling strategy: FIFO scheduling brings about a number of fairness problems when the buffer size is small. Some flows may occupy the buffer for a long time while other competing flows starvation. In this case, routers can use flow-based fair queuing scheduling strategy [14, 164] to distribute bandwidth justly. In [153], the authors raise the idea that per-flow fair scheduling in router queues can effectively solve the TCP-friendliness, fairness and convergence problems brought by small buffer size.

Packet dropping strategies: Drop-Tail is one of the most common packet dropping strategies. To stabilize the queue length and avoid the loss of synchronization, Active Queue Management (AQM) is proposed. In [165], the authors give the conclusion that RED mechanism can enhance the system stability with the same buffer size. Under a queue-based

AQM with ECN marks, the method in [154] achieves the stable congestion control by setting the buffer size $B(N) = O(N^{\gamma})$, where $\gamma \in [0.5, 1)$.

4.5. SIMULATION RESULTS

(1) Experiment 1: The Performance of Buffer Sizing Methods Under Different Traffic Loads

Figure 4-1 shows the dumbbell-shaped network topology in the experiment. The number of TCP Reno flows is 100 and the bandwidth of bottleneck increases progressively. The purpose of this experiment is to evaluate the performance of five typical buffer sizing methods under different traffic loads. To prevent the occurrence of flow synchronization, the starting time of all TCP flows are randomly selected between 0 and 10s.

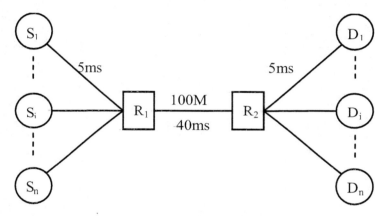

Figure 4-1. Simple dumbbell topology.

As shown in Figure 4-2, the bottleneck link utilization, packet-loss rate and queuing delay are in decrease trend with the increasing of the bottleneck bandwidth. Rule of thumb maintains a high network utilization, but the sustained queue status has also brought a large queuing delay. The small caching mechanisms (Stanford Model and Tiny Buffer Rule) have relatively low queuing delay, but do not make full use of network bandwidth. Under the condition of constant flow, the FPQ mechanism adopts a fixed-size buffer space. Thus, the FPQ's adaptability to different network load is relatively worse.

It is obvious that different buffer sizing approaches adapt to different network load environments. When the bottleneck bandwidth is less than 400M and the network load is heavy, all buffer sizing methods will bring many lost packets. Apparently, how to reduce the packet-loss rate is the primary concern at that time. Then the large buffer sizing methods, Rule of thumb and FPQ, should be adopted. When the bottleneck bandwidth is larger than 400M and the network load is lighter, the network utilization and packet loss are at an acceptable range, while the queuing delay becomes the bottleneck in the network performance. Then the small caching mechanism, Stanford Model and Tiny Buffer Rule, should be adopted to reduce the queuing delay in the bottleneck link.

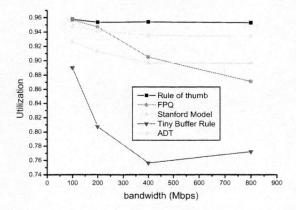

(A) Network utilization rate under different load conditions

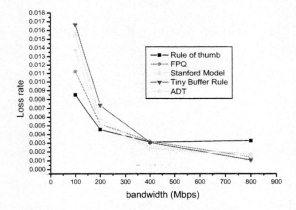

(B) Packet loss rate under different load conditions

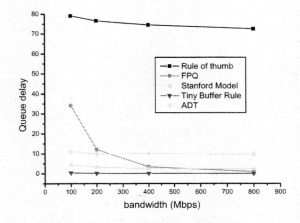

(C) Queuing delay under different load conditions

Figure 4-2. The performance of buffer sizing methods under different traffic loads.

ADT algorithm adjusts the level of the buffer thresholds dynamically based on utilization of bottleneck links. This algorithm can not only maintain more than 90% utilization, but also remain relatively small queuing delay under different load conditions. However, the packet-loss rate of this algorithm is high when the load is heavy. That is because the network will be at the brink of full-queue status of congestion when it is heavy loaded. On the contrary, ADT algorithm will reduce the caching threshold, which may result in more packet loss. This experiment mainly tests the static network environment in which the flow number is fixed. The biggest advantage of ADT algorithm is that it can apply to the network environment in which the flow numbers change dynamically. In the future, ADT algorithm should be validated in the complex network environments.

Based on the above analysis, it can be concluded that network traffic load is an important factor that affects buffer requirements. The appropriate buffer sizing methods should be selected according to different load level of the network status.

(2) Experiment 2: Interactions between High-Speed TCP Protocol and Buffer Size

The experimental network topology is shown in Figure 4-1. The bandwidth of bottleneck link R1-R2 is 100M. The experiment uses TCP Reno and various high-speed TCP protocols, including HSTCP [40], STCP [101], BIC-TCP [41], CUBIC [107], FAST [44] and H-TCP [108]. These connections are between the source-side S_i and destination-side D_i. The 5% UDP background flows with Poisson distribution are included. The buffer size of bottleneck link is set as follows: 0.1/0.2/0.4/0.6/0.8/1 × bandwidth delay product (BDP).

It can be seen from Figure 4-3 that network utilization levels of different TCP protocols increase with the buffer size rising. This is because the more the data packets cached in the network, the higher the network utilization rate is. TCP Reno flows cannot make full use of network bandwidth because of its conservative growth mode of the window. High-speed network protocols, on the contrary, can improve network utilization due to the introduction of new mechanisms to adjust windows. However, the utilization rate of FAST protocol is low when the buffer size is small, which is even lower than TCP Reno protocol. It is mainly because parameter α exists (α=0.6 × BDP in this experiment) in FAST protocol and each FAST flow needs α packets in bottleneck buffer in order to achieve steady state.

Although the high-speed TCP protocols have improved the network throughput, these protocols also bring more packet loss and queuing delay because of the increase in the aggressiveness of the protocols. With the increase of buffer size, the growth of packet-loss rate of high-speed TCP protocols except for FAST TCP is slower than TCP Reno protocol. The performance of HTCP is the best in all high-speed TCP protocols and the curve of its queuing delay is almost consistent with TCP Reno protocol. This is mainly because HTCP adopts the strategy of dynamic adjustment of the window back-off factor based on bottleneck buffer size. It makes TCP congestion control mechanism and the buffer-division method decoupled effectively.

When the buffer is larger than α, the queue length of FAST TCP is stable because FAST TCP based on delayed feedback maintains relatively stable queue utilization. Westwood estimates the available network bandwidth using ACK so that it can dynamically adjust the back-off factor of congestion window and the slow start threshold after losing packets according to available bandwidth and buffer size. As shown in Figure 4-3, Westwood protocol has the minimum queuing delay in various buffer conditions, but it cannot make full use of network bandwidth because the adopted window growth mechanism is the same as TCP Reno.

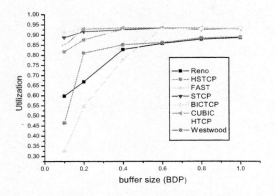

(A) Network utilization rate

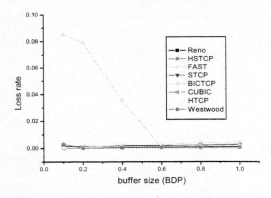

(B) Packet loss rate

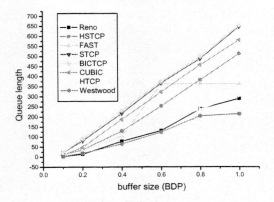

(C) Average queue length

Figure 4-3. The performance of protocols with different buffer sizes.

In short, using a small cache, high-speed TCP protocols can improve the utilization of the network while not introducing large queuing delay. It is clear that high-speed TCP protocols can achieve higher link utilization with relatively small buffer because high-speed TCP protocols adopt window adjustment mechanism that is suitable for high-bandwidth delay networks.

(3) Experiment 3: Interactions between Queue Management Mechanism and Buffer Size

This experiment compares the network layer performance of two types of typical queue management mechanisms, DropTail and RED, under different buffer size. There are 100 TCP Reno flows competing 622Mbps bottleneck bandwidth. Rules of thumb and the Stanford model methods are used as the buffer settings.

Table 4-1. The performance of two queue management algorithms with different buffer sizes

Queue Management Mechanism		Utilization	Loss Rate	Queue Delay	Delay Jitter	JFI
Big buffer (rule of thumb)	DropTail	98.70%	0.39%	72.68ms	20.24ms	0.85
	Gentle RED	97.51%	0.23%	14.65ms	8.86ms	0.96
Small buffer (Stanford Model)	DropTail	90.24%	0.31%	2.07ms	3.19ms	0.93
	Gentle RED	79.68%	0.23%	0.28ms	0.71ms	0.97

As shown in Table 4-1, when large buffer (i.e., a rule of thumb) method is adopted, the level of network utilization and the queue delay of the two queues management mechanism are relatively high. Compared with DropTail, RED's queuing delay and delay jitter are relatively smaller and its fairness index (JFI) is higher. Therefore, it is obvious that RED has improved the network stability and fairness. When small cache (i.e., Stanford model) mechanism is adopted, the delay and delay jitter of the two queue management algorithms have significantly reduced. RED mechanism has further reduced the queuing delay and increased the fairness of the network at the expense of the network utilization. When different buffer sizing methods and queue mechanism are used, the packet-loss rate changed little because the packets loss is mainly caused by the congestion-control mechanisms of the source. If AQM mechanism of ECN marking is used, the packet loss can be effectively prevented.

(4) Experiment 4: The Affection of Router Buffer Size on the Performance of the Application Layer in Complex Multi-Link Environment

This section presents the experiment results in the complicated bottleneck-link network topology environment shown in Figure 4-4. Flows of FTP, HTTP, CBR and ON-OFF are added to simulate the application programs under real network environment. All connections adopt the same round-trip propagation delay. The cache size of the bottleneck link R2-R3 and R4-R5 is changed simultaneously.

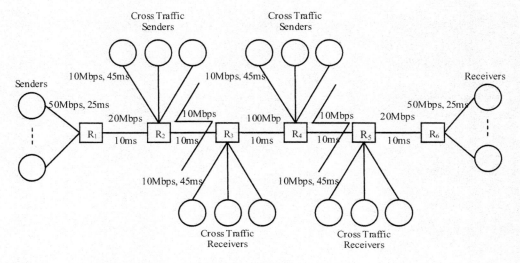

Figure 4-4. Complicated multi-bottleneck links topology.

Figure 4-5 shows the performance indicators of the end-to-end applications: one-way transmission delay of interactive video applications based on CBR flow, effective throughput of the file transfer applications based on long-term TCP flow, and download delays of web page based on short-term TCP.

When the traditional buffer sizing methods of bandwidth-delay product are adopted, the effective throughput of file transfer applications is relatively higher and download time of web page is acceptable. However, one-way propagation delay of interactive applications is as high as 250ms in this multi-bottleneck network environment. It is difficult to accept the large delay in real world in terms of the online video service.

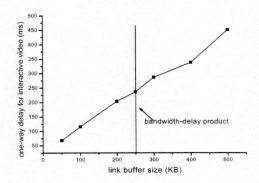

(A) One-way transmission delay of the interactive video applications

Figure 4-5 (continued).

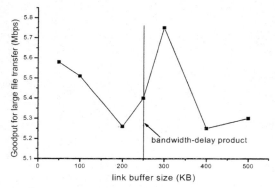

(B) Effective throughput of the file transfer applications

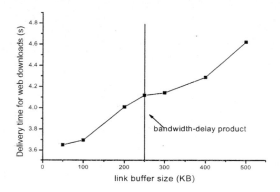

(C) Download delays of web page

Figure 4-5. The performance of applications in the multi-bottleneck topology.

4.6. OPEN ISSUES

Many different buffer sizing methods are proposed in different scenarios and assumptions. However, a series of open issues still exist when these methods are applied to real networks.

1) In these current buffer sizing methods, only the optimization of network layer performance, such as utilization, packet-loss rate and queuing delay, is considered. The performance of transport layer and application layer, such as throughput per flow, file transfer delay via FTP, quality of VoIP and so on, are not taken into account. The implementation of network optimization is based on the viewpoint of administrators. Network users pay more attention to the implementation of application objectives. In [142], the authors point out that network utilization is not the most suitable metric of choosing buffer size, because it cannot effectively reflect the per-flow throughput that users concern. Therefore, how to combine different performance metrics to optimize buffer sizing rules needs to be studied further.

2) Various network parameters used in the improved mechanisms, such as the number of active flows, RTT, the maximum congestion window and so on, are changing constantly in real networks. Since there is a lack of effective communication among routers and end systems in current networks, it is difficult for routers to estimate these parameters accurately. For example, it is essential to change buffer size dynamically according to the number of flows. However, a reliable method that counts the number of TCP flows does not exist. On one hand, the researchers cannot find a method that can distinguish short flow and long flow. One the other hand, the number of active flows is always changing in real networks. Moreover, acquiring TCP's RTT is hard to realize by routers. Routers cannot decide which flow's RTT should be used to compute the optimal buffer size. The optimal buffer size for a connection is not optimal for other connections. Therefore, it is hard to implement the various buffer sizing mechanisms in current real networks.

3) At present, most buffer-setting methods are based on mathematical models with rigorous assumptions. Problems arise when these methods applied to the complex time-varying networks. As buffer requirements mainly depend on the characteristics of traffic arrival, most of buffer mechanisms are based on the model analysis of fixed number of long TCP flows. In fact, more complex traffic characteristics, such as a mixture of a variety of flow length, RTTs and non-TCP traffics and so on, should be considered in real networks. Since the traffic characteristics of the same link are often time-varying, the methods with the fixed buffer size are not suitable inevitably. Therefore, it is necessary to adopt buffer sizing methods that adjust threshold dynamically, such as ADT algorithm.

4.7. CONCLUSION

Some new characteristics of Internet are emerging, such as high bandwidth, high latency, constantly increased number of flows, decreased network utilization and so on. Thus, the weaknesses of traditional rules are shown from the simulation results. A series of improved small buffer mechanisms are proposed. In this chapter, five typical buffer sizing methods are compared with each other via simulations. Then, this chapter analyzes the impact of various high-speed TCP protocols and queue management mechanism on the buffer requirements. It is also pointed out that a small buffer reduces the queuing delay and enhances the overall performance of the network, while maintaining high utilization in the current high bandwidth-delay network environment. Finally, it concludes with some open issues existed in the current study and future work.

PART II. ACTIVE QUEUE MANAGEMENT

A Robust Proportional Controller for AQM Based on Optimized Second-Order System Model

5.1. Introduction

Designing a scalable Active Queue Management (AQM) scheme to co-operate with TCP end-to-end congestion control has received much interest recently [22]. The TCP end-to-end congestion control scheme is effective in preventing congestion collapse, especially when most of the flows are responsive to packet loss in congested routers. Unresponsive flows, however, do not slow down their sending rates when the network becomes congested, and they indeed obtain more bandwidth, which results in a longer time for the network to recover from congestion. Traditional end-to-end congestion control and drop-tail buffer management are insufficient to assure even minimal fairness, delay or loss guarantees, let alone provide quality of service support.

To mitigate such problems, AQM has been proposed at intermediate nodes to improve the end-to-end congestion control [22].Generally, an Internet congestion control mechanism is comprised of two components. The first is a flow control algorithm which runs in end hosts. During the congestion avoidance phase, TCP sources increase the congestion window size by one segment per round-trip time in the absence of congestion, and halve the congestion window size in response to a round-trip time with a congestion event, which is known as Additive Increase and Multiplicative Decrease (AIMD). The second is the link management algorithm executed in intermediate routers. Internet routers trigger the packet dropping (or marking, if Explicit Congestion Notification (ECN) [46] is enabled) in advance when the onset of congestion is perceived, which is the basic idea of AQM. The design objectives of AQM are as follows:

1) Reducing packet loss ratio at routers;
2) Providing high throughput and low end-to-end delay and jitter;
3) Being stable and responsive under dynamic network scenario;
4) Being simple, efficient and scalable to deploy.

In existing AQM schemes, link congestion is estimated through queue length [24], traffic input rate [30, 167], packet loss ratio [82, 29], buffer overflow and emptiness [25], or a combination of these congestion indicators [27, 82]. Queue length (or average queue length) is widely used in RED [24] and most of its variants [166, 72, 74], where packet drop probability is often linearly proportional to the queue length. Many studies have demonstrated that the performance of RED is inherent deficient in parameter settings. Floyd, the designer of RED, and other researchers have made great efforts to provide guidelines in parameter settings, such as gentle-RED [166], ARED [72], SRED [74] etc. Although these schemes work more effectively than RED under a wide range of traffic scenario, the major drawback is that their queue lengths oscillate largely under special network load and traffic conditions, which results in low throughput and high queueing delay. BLUE [25] adjusts the marking (or dropping) probability based upon the buffer overflow and link idle events. The traffic input rate is also used in some AQM schemes such as AVQ [30] to make the input rate match the link output rate. Many other schemes, such as REM [27] and RaQ [82], use both queue length and input rate to estimate congestion level.

In [168], the fluid model of TCP behavior derived in [29] has been linearized by Hollot et al. and a second-order feedback control system was obtained thereafter. Subsequently, a Proportional-Integral (PI) controller [87] is designed to regulate the TCP/AQM interconnection system. The TCP/AQM interconnection system gives a framework for network researchers to design an AQM controller to regulate the system. Based on the system framework, Proportional-Integral-Derivative (PID) controller [169], PIP [170], and LRED [29], are proposed to eliminate the drawbacks in PI controller. These sophisticated controllers indeed enhance the performance in wide network scenarios; however, the connatural demerit of these controllers is that the control parameters are configured in particular network scenarios so that they lack flexibility. The strong correlation between the control parameters and network parameters makes these controllers be prone to be unstable. The *stability* and *convergence* are two important issues which should be considered in the system design. Existing AQM controllers are sensitive to network load and obtain unsatisfactory stability and convergence under dynamic network environment, which motivates us to develop a robust controller with both stable control of queue evolution and fast convergence rate to the desire queue length under a variety of network scenarios.

The design is motivated by the following observation. The TCP throughput formula, which is derived from [16], can be useful in decoupling AQM design from the number of TCP sessions N. Based on the optimized second-order system model which has a small overshoot and fast convergence rate, together with the TCP throughput formula, a robust AQM scheme is proposed, called Adaptive Optimized Proportional Controller (AOPC). AOPC periodically measures the packet loss ratio and uses it to compute a tuning factor of the control parameter. With this tuning factor, the AOPC tunes the control parameter adaptively, tracking the dynamic network load. Besides, AOPC applies the optimized second-order system model to ensure the satisfactory performance and guarantee the system stability. It has a better system closed-loop performance over the approaches tuned by the classical Ziegler-Nichols rule. Through extensive simulations under various network configurations, we show that, compared to existing AQM schemes, such as REM, PI, PID, PIP, and LRED, AOPC scheme offers more stable control of queue length around the desired queue length, thus achieves higher link utilization. AOPC also has better responsiveness and robustness.

The rest of this chapter is organized as follows. In Section 5.2, the control system models are introduced. Section 5.3 presents the AOPC scheme and gives some guidelines for parameter settings. A performance analysis is also presented at the end of this section. AOPC is compared with REM, PI, PID, PIP and LRED through NS simulation in section 5.4. Conclusion about this work is given in section 5.5.

5.2. CONTROL SYSTEM MODEL

In this section, some control system models are introduced, such as the TCP/AQM interconnection system model, the optimized second-order system model, and the general properties of proportional AQM control.

5.2.1. TCP/AQM Interconnection System Model

Transient behavior of networks with AQM routers supporting TCP flows was described by a couple of nonlinear ordinary differential equations [18]. These equations are linearized in [14] and the linear TCP/AQM interconnection system is depicted in Figure 5-1, where q_0 is the desired queue length, $G_1(s)$ is the AQM controller, $G_2(s)$ is the "plant" or TCP window-control and queue dynamics we try to control.

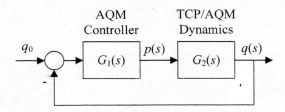

Figure 5-1. Block diagram of TCP/AQM interconnection system.

The objective of the AQM controller is to regulate the queue length to the desired value q_0 by marking (dropping) packets with a probability p as a function of measured queue length deviation between instantaneous and desired value. The transfer function of $G_2(s)$ is:

$$G_2(s) = \frac{K_m}{(T_1 s + 1)(T_2 s + 1)}, \tag{5-1}$$

where,

$$K_m = \frac{(RC)^3}{4N^2}, \quad T_1 = \frac{R^2 C}{2N}, \quad T_2 = R. \tag{5-2}$$

with

$N \equiv$ load factor (number of active TCP sessions)
$R \equiv$ round trip time (RTT)
$C \equiv$ link capacity

Different AQM algorithms (Controllers) are obtained by choosing different forms of $G_1(s)$ and employing different methods to determine the parameters of $G_1(s)$. The widely adopted controller is the general PID (Proportional-Integral-Differential) controller. Due to the modeling inaccuracies, as listed in [170], a parameter tuning structure is 1) to correct this simple plant or controlled object; and 2) insensitive to the drift of system parameters. In previous works, the control parameters of $G_1(s)$ are determined only based on some special network and traffic conditions. A self-tuning proportional controller that can determine the controller parameters dynamically is proposed in this chapter.

5.2.2. Optimized Second-Order System Model

Consider the closed-loop transfer function of the second-order system:

$$G(s) = \frac{K}{\tau^2 s^2 + 2\zeta\tau s + 1},\tag{5-3}$$

where K is the static sensitivity, τ is the time constant, and ζ is the damping factor. The magnitude-frequency characteristic $A(\omega)$ and the phase-frequency characteristic $\varphi(\omega)$ are given by:

$$A(\omega) = \frac{K}{\sqrt{\left(1-\omega^2\tau^2\right)^2 + 4\zeta^2\omega^2\tau^2}},$$

$$\varphi(\omega) = -\arctan\frac{2\zeta\omega\tau}{1-\omega^2\tau^2}.$$

The damping factor ζ is vital to the performance of the second-order system [174]. When ζ is very small (close to zero) at $\omega\tau = 1$, the value of $A(\omega)$ is very large, which is called resonance. With the increasing of ζ, the resonance peak descends. When $\zeta \geq 0.707$, the resonance peak vanishes and $A(\omega)$ is a decreasing function of ω. In engineering, the second-order system is classified into under damping, critical damping, and over damping system corresponding to $\zeta < 1$, $\zeta = 1$ and $\zeta > 1$. The second-order system is optimal when $\zeta = 0.707$. For $0 < \zeta < 1$, the closed-loop poles are a pair of complex conjugates $-\frac{\zeta}{\tau} \pm j\frac{\sqrt{1-\zeta^2}}{\tau}$ in the left-half s-plane, and the step response of the second-order system described by (5-3) is

$$y(t) = K \left[1 - \frac{1}{\sqrt{1-\zeta^2}} e^{-\zeta \frac{t}{\tau}} \cdot \sin \left(\frac{\sqrt{1-\zeta^2}}{\tau} t + \arctan \frac{\sqrt{1-\zeta^2}}{\zeta} \right) \right] \qquad (5\text{-}4)$$

When $t \to \infty$, $y(t) \to 1$, the steady-state error e_{ss} goes to zero. Assume $K \leq 1$ is always satisfied in the proportional AQM control (This assumption is consistently valid, which is shown in section 5.2.3.). Let $y(\infty) = 1$, then the steady-state error e_{ss} and the settling time t_s with admissible error set to be 2%, satisfied with $|y(ts) - y(\infty)| = 0.02y(\infty)$, are obtained as follows:

$$e_{ss} = 1 - K, \qquad (5\text{-}5)$$

$$t_s = \frac{4 - \ln \sqrt{1-\zeta^2}}{\zeta} \tau. \qquad (5\text{-}6)$$

5.2.3. General Properties of Proportional AQM Control

Let θ denote the control parameter for a proportional AQM controller. The closed-loop transfer function of the TCP/AQM control system can be given by:

$$G(s) = \frac{\theta K_m}{T_1 T_2 s^2 + (T_1 + T_2)s + \theta K_m + 1} = \frac{K(\theta)}{\tau^2(\theta)s^2 + 2\zeta(\theta)\tau(\theta)s + 1} \qquad (5\text{-}7)$$

where the static sensitivity K, time constant τ, and damping factor ζ are calculated as functions of θ as follows:

$$K(\theta) = \frac{\theta K_m}{\theta K_m + 1}, \qquad (5\text{-}8)$$

$$\tau(\theta) = \sqrt{\frac{T_1 T_2}{\theta K_m + 1}}, \qquad (5\text{-}9)$$

$$\zeta(\theta) = \frac{T_1 + T_2}{2} \sqrt{\frac{1}{(\theta K_m + 1)T_1 T_2}} \qquad (5\text{-}10)$$

Assume that the TCP/AQM interconnection system is an under damping system. In the following, the monotonicity of steady-state error e_{ss} and settling time ts with the increase of control parameter θ are examined.

Lemma 1 The steady-state error e_{ss} of the TCP/AQM interconnection system is a decreasing function of θ when using a proportional AQM controller.

Proof: The steady-state error calculated from (5-5) is a decreasing function of θ if and only if the parameter K is an increasing function of θ. From (5-8), since K_m is a positive parameter, obviously $K(\theta) < 1$ is always satisfied for all $\theta > 0$ and increases with θ. Therefore, e_{ss} decreases as θ increases.

Lemma 2 The settling time t_s of the TCP/AQM interconnection system is a decreasing function of θ when using a proportional AQM controller.

Proof: From (5-8), (5-9) and (5-10), we have

$$\theta K_m + 1 = \frac{1}{1-K}, \quad \frac{\tau \zeta}{T_1 + T_2} = \frac{1}{2(\theta K_m + 1)} = \frac{1-K}{2}.$$

The derivative of function t_s about θ can be written as follows:

$$\frac{dt_s}{d\theta} = \frac{\partial t_s}{\partial \tau}\frac{d\tau}{d\theta} + \frac{\partial t_s}{\partial \zeta}\frac{d\zeta}{d\theta},$$

where

$$\frac{\partial t_s}{\partial \tau} = \frac{4 - \ln\sqrt{1-\zeta^2}}{\zeta},$$

$$\frac{d\tau}{d\theta} = -\frac{T_1 T_2 K_m}{2(\theta K_m + 1)\sqrt{T_1 T_2 (\theta K_m + 1)}} = -\frac{K_m \tau^2 \zeta}{T_1 + T_2} = -\frac{K_m(1-K)}{2}\tau,$$

$$\frac{\partial t_s}{\partial \zeta} = \left(\frac{\zeta^2 + (1-\zeta^2)\ln\sqrt{1-\zeta^2}}{(1-\zeta^2)\zeta^2} - \frac{4}{\zeta^2}\right)\tau,$$

$$\frac{d\zeta}{d\theta} = -\frac{(T_1 + T_2)K_m}{4(\theta K_m + 1)\sqrt{T_1 T_2(\theta K_m + 1)}} = -\frac{K_m \zeta(1-K)}{2},$$

hence,

$$\frac{dt_s}{d\theta} = \frac{\partial t_s}{\partial \tau}\frac{d\tau}{d\theta} + \frac{\partial t_s}{\partial \zeta}\frac{d\zeta}{d\theta} = -\frac{K_m\left[\zeta^2 + 2(1-\zeta^2)\ln\sqrt{1-\zeta^2}\right](1-K)}{2\zeta(1-\zeta^2)}\tau.$$

From (5-8), it can be seen that $K<1$ is always satisfied for all $\theta \in R^+$. Since the system is an under damping system, that is $0< \zeta < 1$. If $\zeta^2 + 2(1-\zeta^2)\ln\sqrt{1-\zeta^2} > 0$ is valid,

$\dfrac{dt_s}{d\theta} < 0$ will be satisfied. The proof for $\forall \zeta \in (0\,1),\ \zeta^2 + 2(1 - \zeta^2)\ln\sqrt{1 - \zeta^2} > 0$ will be

similar. Thus, $\dfrac{dt_s}{d\theta} < 0$, and the function t_s is a decreasing function of θ.

5.3. THE AOPC SCHEME

5.3.1. Overview of LRED Scheme

The packet loss ratio and queue length are both used to estimate the degree of link congestion in LRED [29]. LRED periodically measures the packet loss ratio, which is then set as the desired stable packet drop probability p_0, in the large time-scale, and updates packet drop probability in the small timescale at each packet arrival. Thus, the packet drop probability is calculated as follows:

$$p = \overline{l(k)} + \beta\sqrt{\overline{l(k)}}(q - q_0),\qquad(5\text{-}11)$$

where β is a pre-configured positive constant, $\overline{l(k)}$ is the measured packet loss ratio at period k, q_0 is the desired queue length. Let $l(k)$ be the packet loss ratio in period k during the latest M measurement periods, then the measured packet loss ratio $\overline{l(k)}$ can be calculated as follows:

$$\overline{l(k)} = mw * \overline{l(k-1)} + (1 - mw) * l(k)\qquad(5\text{-}12)$$

where mw is the measured weight factor.

LRED is a typical proportional controller. The rationale of parameter setting behind LRED is to let the control parameter increase with the measured loss ratio. Thus, when $l(k)$ is a bit large (or small), p will increase (or decrease) with a large (or small) slope so as to guarantee that the packet drop probability in small queue length is much smaller. For comparison of AOPC scheme, a stability condition for LRED is presented as follows.

Stability condition for LRED: Given network parameters $\left(\hat{N}, \hat{C}, \hat{R}\right)$, and assume that β

satisfies $\hat{R}\omega + \arctan(\dfrac{\omega}{k_{11}}) = \dfrac{\pi}{2}, \beta > 0,$ where ω can be calculated as

$$\omega = \sqrt{\dfrac{1}{2}\left(\sqrt{K_{11}^4 + 4K_c^2 H_c^2} - K_{11}^2\right)}, \text{ and } K_{11} = \dfrac{2\hat{N}}{\hat{R}^2\hat{C}}, K_c = \dfrac{\hat{C}^2}{\eta\hat{N}}, H_c = \hat{\beta}\sqrt{p_0} \text{ in LRED.}$$

If

$$\beta < \hat{\beta} = \min(\beta, \frac{\sqrt{2\eta}(2\hat{N})^4}{\hat{R}^3 \hat{C}^3}),$$

(5-13)

then the TCP/LRED system remains stable for every value of $N \geq \hat{N}$ and $R \leq \hat{R}$.

From the stability condition for LRED, it can be seen that the TCP/LRED interconnection system has a strong relation with network variables (N, R) and the parameter tuning rule for LRED is not flexible enough since β is an implicit function of the network variables (N, R). However, the number of TCP sessions N and round trip time R vary dynamically and remain unknowns. Moreover, even N and R are known a priori, the value of β is unable to be obtained through online computation for Internet routers since β is not an explicit function of the network variables (N, R). Therefore, LRED is not scalable for a wide range of traffic conditions and impossible to be deployed in Internet routers. In order to circumvent the obstacle of parameter configuration and simplify the parameter tuning method, an estimation mechanism for network variables should be provided to capture the network dynamics.

5.3.2. AOPC Description

The main goal of the work is to develop a simple AQM controller that can scale to Internet-like environments with significant heterogeneity in link capacities, end-to-end RTTs, route buffer sizes and variable traffic characteristics. "simple" means that an AQM controller does not require per-flow state information and low computation overhead in deployment. AQM schemes need to maintain closed-loop performance in face of varying network conditions. These conditions include variations in the number of TCP sessions N and TCP average round trip time R, and the introduction of short-lived flows into the queue. Due to the fact that 1) the lifetime of a TCP session remains unknown to a network router, 2) nonidentical TCP sessions have various lifetimes, and 3) the number of TCP sessions varies greatly, it is difficult to count the number of TCP sessions directly. Nevertheless, in the TCP/AQM interconnection system model, the system closed-loop performance has a strong relationship to these unknown network state variables.

The motivation behind AOPC is to detach the correlation between control parameters and the network state variables so as to provide an efficient and flexible mechanism for queue management. Proportional AQM control is employed to calculate packet drop probability. AOPC measures packet loss ratio in a large time scale and updates packet drop probability in a small timescale upon each packet arrival. Different from LRED, AOPC tunes its control parameter adaptively according to the packet loss ratio measured in a large time scale to circumvent the drawbacks of LRED. The packet drop probability in AOPC is given by:

$$p = \overline{l(k)} + \gamma(k)(q - q_0),$$

(5-14)

where, $\gamma(\cdot)$ is a variable parameter suitable to current network conditions, $\overline{l(k)}$ is the measured packet loss ratio, and the measurement method is the same as LRED as described in (5-12).

The TCP/AOPC interconnection control system is depicted in Figure 5-2. AOPC has two components:

1) Network Load Estimator, which estimates the average umber of TCP sessions at the end of the latest packet loss ratio measurement period so as to detach the correlation between the control parameter and the number of TCP sessions N;
2) Parameter Optimization Module, which optimizes the TCP/AOPC interconnection system based on the optimized second-order system model.

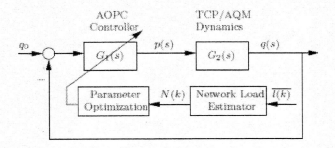

Figure 5-2. Block diagram of TCP/AOPC interconnection system.

In order to acquire current network load information, AOPC estimates the number of TCP sessions N after packet loss ratio measured at the end of each measurement period. The TCP flow number estimation is based on the TCP throughput formula [16], which takes the stable packet drop probability p_0 as an input variable. The key assumption in the estimation is that the measured packet loss ratio $\overline{l(k)}$ can be used to approximate the stable packet drop probability p_0, that is, $\overline{l(k)} \approx p_0$. Thus, the number of TCP sessions can be estimated when having the most recent measured packet loss ratio.

Apart from tuning controller parameters on-line to make system adaptable to network load changes by tracking current network load information, AOPC applies the optimized second-order system model to ensure the efficiency and stability. This controller parameter tuning approach is known to work well for most single-input-single-output (SISO) linear system and results in better system closed-loop performance over those tuned by the classical Ziegler-Nichols rule.

(1) Network Load Estimator

A single TCP flow, which experiences packet drop probability p_0, attains the throughput roughly as follows [16]:

$$x = \frac{1}{R}\sqrt{\frac{2}{3p_0}} \tag{5-15}$$

where R is the round trip time of the TCP flow.

Now consider a link shared by N flows. Let $y = \sum x_i$ ($i = 1, ..., N$) be the total sending rate. Suppose the link has the service rate (link capacity) C and the buffer is large enough to keep the link being fully utilized. Clearly the total sending rate is larger than the service rate, $i.\ e.\ y > C$, so the drop probability p_0 satisfies

$$(1 - p_0)y = C \tag{5-16}$$

Then, from (5-15) and (5-16), the drop probability p_0 is the solution to

$$\sum_{i=1}^{N} \frac{1}{R_i}\sqrt{\frac{2}{3p}}(1-p) = C \tag{5-17}$$

Denoting

$$\frac{1}{R_{eq}} = \frac{1}{N}\sum_{i=1}^{N}\frac{1}{R_i}, \tag{5-18}$$

where R_{eq} is the harmonic mean of the individual round trip times of the flows. In [15], the R_{eq} is interpreted as the equivalent round trip time of the flows, which can be viewed as equivalent to R in TCP/AQM model shown in Figure 5-2. Then the system behaves in the mean as a system with N flows each having an identical equivalent round trip time R_{eq}.

From (5-17) and (5-18), we obtain

$$N = R_{eq}Cf(p_0) \tag{5-19}$$

where,

$$f(p_0) = \frac{\sqrt{3p_0/2}}{1-p_0} \tag{5-20}$$

In (5-20), $f(p_0)$ is a tuning factor for calculating packet drop probability. According to previous assumption that the measured packet loss ratio $\overline{l(k)}$ can be used to approximate the stable packet drop probability p_0, (5-20) can be rewritten as follows:

$$f(p_0) = f\left(\overline{l(k)}\right) = \frac{\sqrt{3\overline{l(k)}/2}}{1-\overline{l(k)}} \tag{5-21}$$

Equation (5-19) illustrates that the number of TCP sessions N largely depends on the harmonic mean R_{eq} of the RTTs yet not on individual RTTs. If the harmonic mean value R_{eq} is a known variable and varies slightly around a stable value, the number of TCP sessions N can be estimated by ignoring the time variant property of R_{eq}. Recent Internet measurements [171] report that roughly 75% ~ 90% of flows have RTTs less than 200ms and the average RTT is distributed around 180ms [172], suggesting an alternate way to improve TCP performance and AQM design.

(2) Parameter Optimization Module

By approximating the stable packet drop probability p_0 as the latest measured packet loss ratio $\overline{l(k)}$, the following formulas can be obtained from (5-2), (5-19) and (5-21):

$$K_m = \frac{R_{eq}C}{4f^2\left(\overline{l(k)}\right)}, T_1 = \frac{R_{eq}}{2f\left(\overline{l(k)}\right)}, T_2 = R_{eq} \tag{5-22}$$

Thus, the TCP and queue dynamics transfer function $G_2(s)$ is greatly simplified. The rule for designing a stabilizing proportional controller to stabilize the TCP/AOPC interconnection system can be given in theorem 1.

Theorem 1 Denoting $\gamma(\cdot)$ to be the control parameter of AOPC. If

$$\gamma(k) = \frac{f\left(\overline{l(k)}\right)[1+4f^2(\overline{l(k)})]}{R_{eq}C}, \tag{5-23}$$

the linear feedback control system in Figure 5-2 using $G1(s)=\gamma(\cdot)$ is asymptotically stable and the system is an optimized system.

Proof: From (5-22), it can be obtained

$$\gamma = \frac{f\left(\overline{l(k)}\right)[1+4f^2\left(\overline{l(k)}\right)]}{R_{eq}C} = \frac{T_1^2 + T_2^2}{2K_mT_1T_2} \tag{5-24}$$

Replacing θ in (5-10) with γ in (5-24), it can be obtained

$$\zeta = \frac{T_1 + T_2}{2} \sqrt{\frac{1}{(\gamma K_m + 1) T_1 T_2}} = 0.707 \tag{5-25}$$

According to the optimized second-order system model discussed in section 5.2, when ζ = 0.707, the system is an optimized second-order system, and it is asymptotically stable. So, TCP/AOPC interconnection system is asymptotically stable and the system is an optimized system.

Compared to the stability condition for LRED, AOPC scheme maintains the closed-loop performance in face of varying network conditions. Meanwhile, AOPC simplifies the tuning method and makes it adaptable to dynamic networks. For AOPC implementation, packet departure can be tracked to obtain the link service rate C. From (5-20), it can be seen that the harmonic mean of individual RTTs, R_{eq}, contributes a very small weight to the control parameter γ. For example, assume the current measured packet loss ratio $\overline{l(k)} = 0.01$, the link capacity is 2500packets/s, when $R_{eq} = 0.2$s, the required AOPC parameter γ is 2.625×10^{-4}; while, when $R_{eq} = 0.15$s, the required AOPC parameter γ is 3.5×10^{-4}. The example shows that even though R_{eq} varies slightly in a range between 150ms and 200ms, the control parameter γ is not obviously affected and can be treated as insensitive to RTT variation in real network condition.

5.3.3. Analysis of Performance Index

This section mainly discusses why AOPC obtains smaller steady-state error and faster convergence rate than LRED. Both AOPC and LRED are proportional controllers. Let θ_a and θ_l denote the control parameter for AOPC and LRED respectively. Then,

$$\theta_a = \gamma = \frac{f(\overline{l(k)})(1 + 4f^2(\overline{l(k)}))}{R_{eq}C}, \text{ and } \theta_l = \beta\sqrt{\overline{l(k)}}.$$

Ordinarily, the packet loss ratio is very small (close to zero), i. e. $\overline{l(k)} \ll 1$. Thus,

$$f(\overline{l(k)}) = \frac{\sqrt{3\overline{l(k)}/2}}{1 - \overline{l(k)}} \approx \sqrt{3\overline{l(k)}/2}.$$

Then it can be obtained

$$\frac{\theta_a}{\theta_l} = \frac{\sqrt{\frac{3}{2}}\left(1 + 6\overline{l(k)}\right)}{\beta R_{eq} C} \qquad (5\text{-}25)$$

Considering the following network conditions: R_{eq} = 0.18s, C = 2500packets/s, and $\overline{l(k)}$ = 0.01. According to [18], β is equal to 0.001. Substituting these values to (5-22), it can be obtained that $\frac{\theta_a}{\theta_l} = 2.885$, that is $\theta_a > \theta_l$. Generally, in most network situations, $\theta_a > \theta_l$ is valid.

Suppose that TCP/LRED remains an under damping system, the following observations could be found:

1) According to Lemma 1, the steady-state error, e_{ss}, is a decreasing function of proportional parameter θ. Therefore AOPC obtains smaller steady-state error than LRED;

2) According to Lemma 2, the settling time, t_s, is a decreasing function of proportional parameter θ, which means that AOPC has a faster convergence rate than LRED.

Although proportional AQM controller always maintains non-zero steady-state error, this demerit can be overlooked in highly dynamic network scenarios as long as the error is sufficiently small. Furthermore, a simple proportional controller can enhance the scalability of AQM algorithms and reduce the computational overhead. The simulations below show that the performance of AOPC is never suffered by its small steady-state error.

5.4. PERFORMANCE EVALUATION

To comprehensively evaluate the performance and the robustness of the proposed AOPC, AOPC scheme is implemented in NS2 [173]. Some representative AQM schemes, namely, REM [27], PI [87], PID [169], PIP [170], and LRED [29], are also simulated for the purpose of comparison. The settings of the parameters for various AQM schemes are based on their authors' recommendations.

The dynamic behaviors of the selected AQM schemes are simulated under a variety of network topologies and traffic models. In particular, the dumbbell network topology is chosen. Unless stated elsewhere, the congested link is configured with 10Mbps, the round trip propagation delays are uniformly distributed over the range [60, 220] ms. The network topology with multiple bottleneck links as shown in Figure 5-3 is also be used in simulations, where each sender-receiver pair has TCP connections as cross traffic. In both scenarios, TCP Reno is used as the transport agent. Unless otherwise specified, the buffer size of each router is set to be 200 packets, and the desired queue length is set to be 50 packets. The total simulation last for 100s.

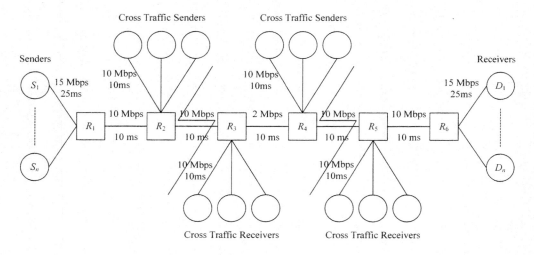

Figure 5-3. Multi-bottleneck topology with two sets of cross traffic.

5.4.1. Single Bottleneck Topology

Homogeneous Traffic: Long-Lived FTP Flows Only

Experiment 1 Stability and responsiveness under sudden traffic load change scenario

In this experiment, the stability and responsiveness of the AQM schemes are investigated under sudden traffic load change scenario. The number of FTP flows is 200 at the beginning and 200 additional FTP flows arrive at the link 50seconds later. The queue evolutions are depicted in Figure 5-4.

It can be seen that, PI is unable to regulate the queue length to the reference value throughout the simulation runtime. Note that REM and PID are not very robust with respect to such sudden traffic load change scenario, which results in long time buffer overflows and heavy queue oscillations during 20-50s and 60-100s. Besides, the queue evolution of REM bears much resemblance to that of PID, due to the fact that REM is in essence a PID-type controller. LRED is too aggressive, resulting in an empty buffer much of the time. AOPC has less overshoots and smaller queue oscillations. On the contrary, the queue lengths of PIP and LRED oscillate over a large range. As shown in Figure 5-4, AOPC is robust against the variation of the number of connections and achieves shorter response time and better stability than other algorithms in the presence of sudden traffic change scenario.

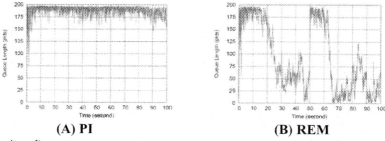

(A) PI   **(B) REM**

Figure 5-4 (continued).

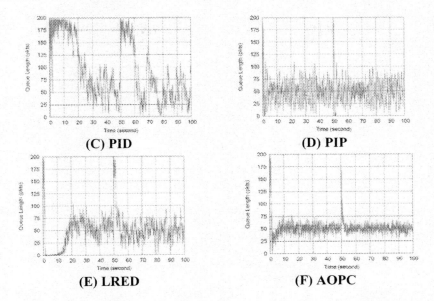

Figure 5-4. Exp. 1: Evolution of the queue length under sudden traffic load change scenario.

Experiment 2 Convergence under Various Number of FTP Flows

The following Convergence Criterion is used to compare the convergence properties of the AQM algorithms.

Convergence Criterion: An AQM algorithm converges to a stable point if and only if it satisfies all the following conditions:

1) the average queue length $AveQLen(t_0, t_0 + \Delta t)$ during $[t_0, t_0 + \Delta t]$ time interval must satisfy $|AveQLen(t_0, t_0 + \Delta t) - q_0| \leq \lambda * q_0$, where Δt, is a slot duration, and λ is a constant which admits negligible queue deviation between real average queue length and reference queue length $q0$;

2) the standard queue deviation $StanQDev(t_0, t_0 + \Delta t)$ of q_0 during $[t_0, t_0 + \Delta t]$ time interval must satisfy $StanQDev(t_0, t_0 + \Delta t) \leq \mu * q_0$, where μ is a constant which admits slight queue oscillation around reference queue length q_0;

3) given any time $t > t_0$, condition 1 and 2 must be always satisfied simultaneously.

Thus, the algorithm converges to a stable point at time $t_0 + \Delta t / 2$.

In the experiment, the total number of FTP flows, N, are varied from 300 to 1000 to imitate different congestion degrees. The value of λ and μ are set to 0.3 respectively, and the slot duration Δt is set to 4s. Using such a customized convergence criterion, the simulation results show that only AOPC is able to converge to a stable point at different congestion degrees while all other algorithms failed. Figure 5-5 plots the convergence times of AOPC, the average queue length, and standard deviation of queue length of all algorithms except PI controller with various congestion degrees. Because PI causes buffer persistent overflows, which leads to large average queue length and small queue deviations. So its performance is not considered here. As shown in Figure 5-5, the convergence rate of AOPC is almost independent to the value N. AOPC always converges to the stable point in less than 4

seconds. Note that the represent lines of PIP and AOPC overlap in the figure of average
queue length. PIP obtains small value of average queue length and LRED may also satisfy
condition 1 in the convergence criterion, however, both of them violate condition 2 due to
their large queue oscillations.

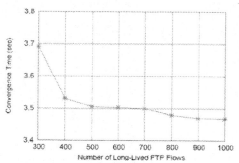

(A) Convergence time of AOPC with λ=0.3, μ=0.3, Δt=4s.

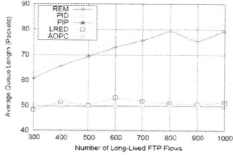

(B) Average queue length.

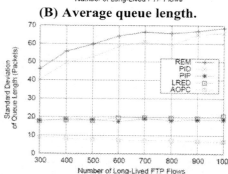

(C) Standard deviation of instantaneous queue length.

Figure 5-5. Exp. 2: Convergence under various number of FTP flows .

Experiment 3 AQM Performances as Functions of Round Trip Time

In this experiment, a series of simulations are conducted to investigate the performance of
the AQM schemes through varying the RTT from 20s to 200s. The performance of queue
deviation, link utilization, and packet loss ratio are studied. Figure 5-6 plots these metrics as
functions of RTT for each AQM schemes except PI controller. As shown in Figure 5-6, as
RTT increases, REM and PID show gradually nice performances in respect of queue
deviation and packet loss ratio. The queue deviation of AOPC keeps small as the RTT
increases, which accounts for its persistent high link utilization. This confirms that small

queue oscillations not only indicate low delay jitter but also a guarantee of high link utilization. An unattractive point is that the AOPC encounters a slightly larger proportional of packet losses than REM and PID. The queue deviations of PIP increase steeply as the RTT increases. On the contrary, LRED maintains a mild increment of queue deviations. However, as a result of the aggressiveness of packet drop behavior, LRED drains the queue for a long time of emptiness and hence falls a large stride in terms of link utilization when RTT is set to larger than 100s.

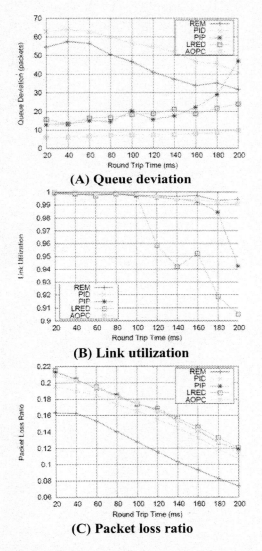

(A) Queue deviation

(B) Link utilization

(C) Packet loss ratio

Figure 5-6. Exp 3: Queue deviation, link utilization, packet loss ratio as a function of round trip time for each AQM algorithm except PI.

Experiment 4 AQM Performances as a Function of Link Capacity

In this experiment, a set of simulations are conducted to investigate the performance of the AQM schemes through varying the bottleneck link capacity from 10Mbps to 90Mbps.

The performance of queue deviation, link utilization, and packet loss ratio are studied in this subsection. Figure 5-7 plots these metrics as functions of link capacity for each AQM schemes except PI controller. As shown in Figure 5-7, AOPC obtains the smallest queue deviation and satisfactory link utilization and packet loss ratio in all configured link capacities. Although REM and PID obtain slightly higher link utilizations when the link capacity is configured with 90Mbps, their larger queue deviations mean more oscillatory in terms of queue evolution. The experiment illustrates that AOPC can scale to high speed links yet with stable control of queue evolution and satisfactory performance.

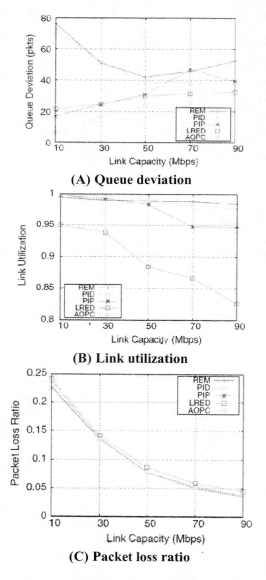

(A) Queue deviation

(B) Link utilization

(C) Packet loss ratio

Figure 5-7. Exp 4: Queue deviation, link utilization, packet loss ratio as a function of link capacity for each AQM algorithm except PI.

Heterogeneous Traffic: Hybrid Flows

Experiment 5 Adding CBR Flows, Web Traffic, and Exponential ON/OFF UDP Flows

The unresponsive CBR flows, short-lived web traffic and ON/OFF UDP flows can influence the control effect of AQM algorithms as the result of queue oscillation or unstable queue evolution. In this experiment, a mixture of FTP, CBR, exponential ON/OFF UDP flows, and web traffic is used to simulate a more realistic network scenario. The number of FTP flows and the number of CBR flows are 100 and 20 respectively. The inter-packet gap of a CBR flow is 0.08s, and the total introduced CBR flows is approximately 1Mbps. 30 exponential ON/OFF UDP flows starting at 10s are introduced and the inter-flow arrival time is exponentially distributed with a mean of 0.1s. The durations of the "ON" and "OFF" states are exponentially distributed with a mean of 1s. Also the introduced ON/OFF flows is approximately 1Mbps. The web traffic is generated by "PagePool/WebTraf" provided by NS2. The page pool attached to each of the congested link contains 5 servers and 5 clients. Each session transfers 1000 pages, such that the sessions never end in the lifetime of the simulation. Other parameters, like the inter-page waiting time, are presented in Table 5-1. Without any other traffic, the random web traffic utilizes about 1Mbps.

Table 5-1. Parameter setting for PagePool/WebTraf in simulations: Inter Session is the inter-session waiting time; Inter Page is the inter-page waiting time; Page Size is the number of objects in one page; Inter Object is the inter-object waiting time; Object_Size is the size of each object

	Inter_Session	Inter_Page	Page_Size	Inter_Object	Object_Size
Average	5s	4s	10	0.01s	10
Distribution	Exponential	Exponential	Exponential	Exponential	Pareto II (shape = 1.2)

Figure 5-8 plots the queue evolution of the AQM schemes. As shown in it, AOPC can robustly stabilize the queue length around 50 packets, while the queue length of PI keeps the peak value for around 60 seconds. REM and PID require much longer time to decrease their queue size from the buffer top. The queue evolutions of PIP and LRED oscillate along with the dynamics of load levels. Despite AOPC is developed on TCP throughput model, it is close to the ideal performance under hybrid traffic conditions. The results show that PIP, LRED and AOPC outperform REM, PI and PID in responsiveness. Moreover, AOPC has a better queue stability than PIP or LRED. The queue length of AOPC also has a smaller oscillation.

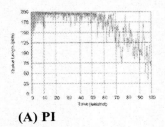

(A) PI

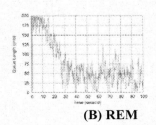

(B) REM

Figure 5-8 (continued).

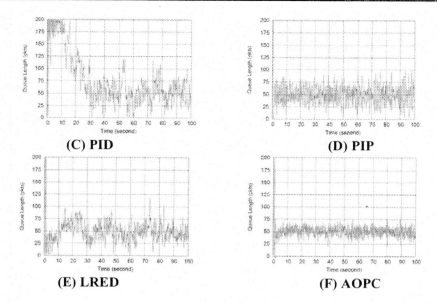

(C) PID   (D) PIP

(E) LRED   (F) AOPC

Figure 5-8. Exp. 5: Queue evolution under hybrid traffic scenario.

5.4.2. Multiple Bottlenecks Topology

Experiment 6 Queue Stability under Multiple Bottlenecks Topology

Using the multiple bottleneck network topology depicted in Figure 5-3, the behavior of different AQM algorithms in the presence of cross traffic are studied. There are 150 FTP flows with senders at the left hand side and receivers at the right hand side. There are 60 FTP flows for each cross traffic senders-receivers pair. It is obvious that links R2-R3, R3-R4 and R4-R5 are the bottleneck links. Queue R1- R2 and R5 - R6 are almost empty, indicating that these two links are not bottleneck links. Since the queue R2 - R3 and R4 -R5 exhibit similar trends, Figure 5-9 plots the queue R3- R4 and R4 -R5.

AOPC significantly outperforms other AQM schemes, which are often sensitive to the network configurations such as TCP loads, presence of unresponsive flows, and cross traffic. In the multiple bottlenecks topological situation, PIP is prone to be unstable with continuous queue oscillation. Meanwhile, LRED suffers an aggressive packet drop behavior and makes the buffer empty for long periods, resulting in poor link utilization and continuous packet losses.

Previous simulations illustrate that stable queue evolutions and small queue oscillations do not only mean small queueing delay and jitters, but also high link utilizations. Note that the system convergence rates of other algorithms are deteriorated with higher loads, thus, the high link utilization are gained at the expense of more sluggish responsiveness, longer queueing delay, and larger delay jitter. On the contrary, AOPC can maintain a fast convergence rate and restrain queue oscillations under various traffic scenarios, achieving high link utilization and being well-suited as an AQM scheme.

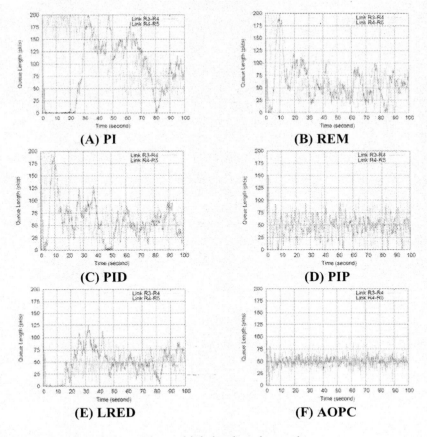

Figure 5-9. Exp 6: Queue evolution under multiple bottlenecks topology.

5.5. CONCLUSION

A novel AQM scheme called AOPC is proposed in this chapter. The AOPC scheme employs proportional AQM control to calculate packet drop probability. It measures packet loss ratio on a large time scale and updates packet drop probability on a small time scale upon each packet arrival. By introducing: 1) a network load estimator, which estimates TCP load based on the TCP throughput formula after packet loss ratio measured; and 2) a parameter optimization module, which optimizes the TCP/AOPC feedback control system based on the optimized second-order system model, AOPC detaches the correlation of control parameter from network load and alleviate the sensitivity to the system parameter variations. By using an optimized second-order system model, AOPC regulates the queue close to the desired length with small oscillations under widely varying traffic conditions.

The performance of AOPC is evaluated in simulations and compared with PI, REM, PID, PIP, and LRED. The performance analysis and simulation results show that AOPC is superior to existing AQM algorithms, including REM, PI, PID, PIP, and LRED. The major advantages of AOPC include:

1) Being stable and responsive in a sudden traffic load change scenario, or in the presence of unresponsive UDP flows and short-lived web traffic;

2) Having a fast convergence rate and small queue oscillations with respect to a large range of traffic scenarios, achieving high link utilization;

3) Having robustness and fast system response under multiple bottleneck link scenarios.

There are also several issues need to be discussed in the future. There are several limitations:

1) The TCP throughput formula used to estimate network load produces uncertain estimation errors, especially in light load networks;

2) The feedback delay is ignored, which might be reasonable in small-delay LAN or MAN, but is definitely harmful to system stability;

3) Different versions of TCP implementation, such as Reno, Vegas, etc, do coexist in the Internet. Actually, the TCP/AQM model only describes the TCP Reno congestion control mechanism. Other unresponsive flows, for example, UDP flows and web traffic, should also be considered in the control system.

Recent technology trends indicate that the future Internet will have a large number of high-bandwidth links. With the transmission rate speeding up, the surge of interest of designing new transmission control protocols is increasingly active [44, 47, 51]. The research of TCP/AQM control system in high speed network is also a hot issue [175, 176]. Therefore, it might be difficult, if not impossible, to employ an accurate model of network traffic and the queue dynamics with fixed parameters. An alternative way to address this issue could be regarding the controlled system as an uncertain system, and employing parameter identification approach to adjust the control laws, i.e., the packet drop behavior, accordingly.

Chapter 6

DESIGN OF A STABILIZING SECOND-ORDER CONGESTION CONTROLLER FOR LARGE-DELAY NETWORKS

6.1. INTRODUCTION

Congestion control in communication networks such as the Internet has become increasingly important today due to the explosive expansion and growth of traffic. From a point view of the control theory, congestion control problems are complex and challenging because they are high-dimensional, nonlinear, and dynamic and, moreover, individual sources have to select their transmission rates in a decentralized way with little information about the rest of the network.

Recent advances in mathematical modeling of congestion control have strongly simulated the research on theoretic analysis of the behavior, such as stability, robustness and fairness, of currently developed Internet congestion control protocols as well as the design of new protocols with higher performance [18, 90, 177, 178, 179]. One of the most important factors in the design of congestion control is its asymptotic stability, which is the capacity of the system to avoid oscillations in the steady-state and to respond properly to external perturbations caused by the arrival/departure of flows, variation in feedback, and other transient effects. Stability proofs for distributed congestion control become progressively more complicated as feedback delays are taken into account. However, most of exist congestion controllers, such as RED [24], REM [27], PI [87], AOPC [180], DC-AQM [103] and so on, neglect the impact on performance caused by large round-trip communication delay. Simulation results in Section 6.2 illustrate that these controllers result in dramatic oscillations in large delay networks, which decreases the utilization of the bottleneck link and introduces the avoidable delay jitter.

It is the goal of this chapter to build a stabilizing congestion control system that maintains both stability and ideal transient performance under arbitrary feedback delays, especially in large round-trip communication delay scenarios. This problem is solved by applying the principle of internal model compensation in control theory to restrict the negative impact on the queue stability caused by feedback delay. The new scheme is called as IMC-PID congestion controller. Instead of using padé approximation to approximate the delay element [103], Taylor series expanding approach is applied to reduce the plant/model mismatch. By choosing appropriate PID parameters, the IMC-PID controller can maintain stability with higher link utilization and smaller queue oscillation than that of other AQM controllers with arbitrary feedback delays.

The rest of the chapter is organized as follows. In Section 6.2, the negative impact of large delay on TCP/AQM system performance is evaluated. Section 6.3 makes an overview of the TCP/AQM control system and internal model control (IMC) principle. In Section 6.4, a robust, stable IMC-PID congestion controller for large-delay networks is developed and some guidelines for parameter settings are given. The performance of IMC-PID is compared with that of REM, PI, and DC-AQM in section V. Finally, the conclusion about this work is present in Section 6.5.

6.2. EFFECT OF LARGE DELAY ON TCP/AQM SYSTEM PERFORMANCE

The dynamics of congestion control may be abstracted as a control loop with feedback delay. A fundamental characteristic of such system is that it becomes unstable for some large feedback delay. A fundamental principle from control theory states that a controller must react as quickly as the dynamics of the controlled signal; otherwise the controller will always lag behind the controlled system and will be ineffective. In the context of current proposals for congestion control, the controller is an AQM scheme. Most previous AQM schemes [24, 27, 87, 180], which configure the parameters in the small delay network scenarios, do not consider the effect of large feedback delay on TCP/AQM system performance. These design approaches cause the system oscillation in large feedback delay networks. Table 6-1 shows the round trip delays to different overseas website from the host at Central South University in China. It can be seen that the maximum average RTT is larger than 1s.

Table 6-1. RTT Statistical Values

URL	Minimum Delay (ms)	Maximum Delay (ms)	Average Delay (ms)
www.ieee.org (61.200.81.134)	411	432	419
www.acm.org (63.118.7.16)	1101	1155	1131
www.yahoo.com (209.73.186.238)	347	355	352
www.mit.edu (18.7.22.83)	298	308	302

In order to investigate the performance of the existing typical AQM schemes, particularly PI, REM and DC-AQM schemes are selected to verify their stability in large delay networks. Two sets of simulations are conducted under the dumbbell network topology scenario shown in Figure 6-1 when RTT=150ms and RTT=400ms respectively. The buffer size is 300 packets, and the reference queue length is set to 150 packets in all AQM schemes. All sources are greedy and sustained FTP applications.

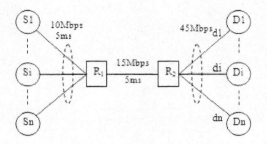

Figure 6-1. Dumbbell network topology.

Figure 6-2 demonstrates unstable dynamic behaviors of these AQM schemes in large-delay networks, though they can converge to steady-state fast in small-delay networks. The large queue oscillations of PI and REM indicate large delay jitter and/or low link utilization. DC-AQM does not converge to the reference queue length which is designed to compensate large delays.

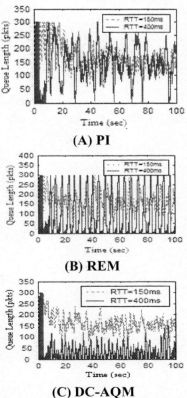

Figure 6-2. Queue evolution under RTT=150ms and RTT=400ms networks.

Table 6-2 summarizes the performance and statistical queue length for each scheme. As shown in Figure 6-2 and Table 6-2, although PI keeps relative high link utilization, the queue is unstable and the queue deviation increase 20 packets. The average queue length of DC-AQM shrinks to 30 packets, which leads to low link utilization. The queue deviation increases 70 packets in REM, which is unfavorable to QoS requirement for real-time applications.

Table 6-2. Link Utilization and Queue Statistics

Schemes	PI		REM		DC-AQM	
RTT (ms)	150	400	150	400	150	400
Link Utilization	99.34%	97.27%	99.31%	91.14%	99.40%	95.50%
Average Queue Length (pkts)	162.42	150.80	154.22	102.67	157.25	32.98
Queue Deviation (pkts)	44.23	63.89	45.16	112.26	28.16	30.81

6.3. TCP/AQM CONTROL SYSTEM AND INTERNAL MODEL CONTROL

In this section, a description of the TCP/AQM interconnection system model and the IMC based PID control are given.

6.3.1. TCP/AQM Control System Model

Nonlinear ordinary differential equations, which describe the transient behavior of networks with AQM routers supporting TCP flows, are developed in [18]. These equations are linearized in [87] and the linear TCP/AQM system model can be depicted as in Figure 6-3, where q_0 is the reference queue size. The action of an AQM controller is to mark (or drop) packets with probability p as a function of the measured difference between the real queue length q and the reference queue length q_0. From Figure 6-3, it is can be seen that the plant transfer function, $P(s)=P_{tcp}(s)P_{que}(s)$, can be expressed in terms of network parameters yielding:

$$P_{tcp}(s) = \frac{\dfrac{R_0 C^2}{2N^2}}{s + \dfrac{2N}{R_0^2 C}}, \qquad P_{que}(s) = \frac{\dfrac{N}{R_0}}{s + \dfrac{1}{R_0}}. \qquad (6\text{-}1)$$

with

$R_0 \equiv$ round-trip time (RTT)
$N \equiv$ the number of active TCP sessions
$C \equiv$ link capacity (packets/sec)

The plant dynamics, denoted by the transfer function $P(s)$, relates how this packet-marking probability dynamically affects the queue length. The following formula can be obtained from (6-1) and Figure 6-3.

$$P(s) = \frac{K_m e^{-sR_0}}{(T_1 s + 1)(T_2 s + 1)} \tag{6-2}$$

where, $K_m = \frac{(R_0 C)^3}{4N^2}$, $T_1 = \frac{R_0^2 C}{2N}$, $T_2 = R_0$.

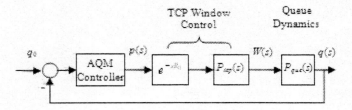

Figure 6-3. TCP/AQM feedback control system model.

6.3.2. Internal Model Control

The IMC (Internal Model Control) was introduced by Garcia and Morari [181]. In designing controller by using the IMC, its complexity depends exclusively on two factors: the complexity of the model and the performance requirements stated by the designer. The control principle of IMC can be illustrated in Figure 6-4, where $G_i(s)$ is the internal model controller, $G_c(s)$ the feedback controller, $G_p(s)$ the real plant, and $\hat{G}_p(s)$ the inner model.

Plant/model mismatch can be caused by model reduction (the representation of a high-order system by a low-order approximate model) or by system parameters which depend on the operating conditions. From Figure 6-4, the relationship between $G_i(s)$ and $G_c(s)$ can be obtained as follows:

$$G_i(s) = \frac{G_c(s)}{1 + G_c(s)\hat{G}_p(s)}, \tag{6-3}$$

$$G_c(s) = \frac{G_i(s)}{1 - G_i(s)\hat{G}_p(s)}. \tag{6-4}$$

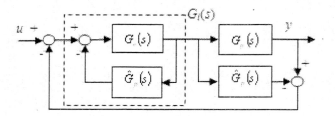

Figure 6-4. IMC and equivalent feedback control structure.

The control of Large-delay system has been a major issue in control theory. Smith predictor [182] is a widely used time-delay compensator; however, it is excessively sensitive to model mismatch. IMC surmounts the Smith predictor's drawback, and enhances the robustness and the ability to against disturbance. The IMC design procedure is very simple and straightforward, which can be divided into the following two steps:

Step 1. Factor the model

$$\hat{G}_p(s) = \hat{G}_{p^+}(s) \cdot \hat{G}_{p^-}(s) \tag{6-5}$$

such that $\hat{G}_{p^+}(s)$ contains all time delays and RHP (right-half plane) zeros; consequently $\hat{G}_{p^-}(s)$ is stable and does not involve predictors.

Step 2. Define the IMC controller by

$$G_i(s) = \hat{G}_{p^-}^{-1}(s) \cdot g(s), \tag{6-6}$$

where $g(s)$ is a low pass filter with

$$g(s) = \frac{1}{(\varepsilon s + 1)^\gamma}, \tag{6-7}$$

where ε is an adjustable filter parameter which determines the speed of response, γ is the order that must be selected such that $G_i(s)$ is proper, namely γ must be equal to or greater than the order of $\hat{G}_{p^-}(s)$. From (6-4), (6-6) and (6-7), it can be obtained

$$G_c(s) = \frac{\hat{G}_p^{-1}(s)}{(\varepsilon s + 1)^\gamma - \hat{G}_{p^+}(s)}. \tag{6-8}$$

6.4. DESIGN OF THE IMC-PID CONGESTION CONTROLLER

6.4.1. IMC-PID Parameter Tuning Guideline

The goal of this subsection is to show that the IMC design procedure leads naturally to PID-type controllers for the simple TCP/AQM congestion control model.

Theorem 1. Given a model $\hat{G}_p(s) = \hat{G}_{p^+}(s) \cdot \hat{G}_{p^-}(s)$ such that $\hat{G}_{p^+}(s)$ contains all time delays and RHP zeros; consequently $\hat{G}_{p^-}(s)$ is stable and does not involve predictors.

Let $f(s) = \hat{G}_{p^-}^{-1}(s) \bigg/ \dfrac{(\varepsilon s + 1)^{\gamma} - \hat{G}_{p^+}(s)}{s}$, If $\hat{G}_{p^+}(0) = 1$, then the ideal PID controller

$G_c(s) = K_c\left(1 + \dfrac{1}{T_i s} + T_d s\right)$ can be used to regulate the plant, and the PID control

parameters are configured as follows:

$$K_c = f'(0), \ T_i = \frac{f'(0)}{f(0)}, \ T_d = \frac{f''(0)}{2f'(0)} \tag{6-9}$$

where $f'(0)$ and $f''(0)$ are respectively the first- and second-order derivatives of $f(s)$ at $s=0$.

Proof: Recalling that the transfer function of the feedback controller $G_c(s)$ in (6-8), $\hat{G}_{p^+}(0) = 1$ makes zero denominator polynomial of $G_c(s)$, which matches the condition of system control without steady-error. Therefore, $G_c(s)$ contains integral element, and (6-8) can be denoted as $G_c(s) \equiv \dfrac{1}{s} f(s)$, where

$$f(s) = \frac{\hat{G}_{p^-}^{-1}(s)}{\dfrac{(\varepsilon s + 1)^{\gamma} - \hat{G}_{p^+}(s)}{s}}.$$

Expanding $f(s)$ according to Taylor series, it can be obtained

$$G_c(s) = \frac{1}{s}\left(f(0) + f'(0)s + f''(0)s^2 + \cdots\right) = K_c\left(1 + \frac{1}{T_i s} + T_d s + \cdots\right),$$

where, $K_c = f'(0)$, $T_i = \dfrac{f'(0)}{f(0)}$, $T_d = \dfrac{f''(0)}{2f'(0)}$, and K_c, T_i, T_d correspond to PID control parameters.

As given in Theorem 1, TCP/AQM system is a linear feedback system with delay. The stability of such system can be regulated by the IMC-PID controller. Different from the former IMC-PID parameter tuning approach [103], which employs padé approximation for the delay element to yield a low-order approximate model, the Toylor series is applied in tuning IMC-PID parameters to reduce the plant/model mismatch caused by model reduction.

The control parameters are determined by the complicated function $f(s)$, and the calculation of its first- and second-order derivatives at $s=0$ is given as follows.

Let $D(s)$ denote the denominator polynomial of $f(s)$, that is

$$D(s) = \frac{(\varepsilon s + 1)^\gamma - \hat{G}_{p^+}(s)}{s} \tag{6-10}$$

By Applying Taylor series to expand $D(s)$, it can be obtained

$$D(0) = \gamma\varepsilon - \hat{G}'_{p^+}(0), \tag{6-11}$$

$$D'(0) = \frac{\gamma(\gamma-1)\varepsilon^2 - \hat{G}''_{p^+}(0)}{2!}, \tag{6-12}$$

$$D''(0) = \frac{\gamma(\gamma-1)(\gamma-2)\varepsilon^3 - \hat{G}'''_{p^+}(0)}{3!}, \tag{6-13}$$

According to (6-10)-(6-13), the function $f(s)$, its first- and second-order derivatives at $s=0$ can be calculated as follows:

$$f(0) = \frac{1}{K_m D(0)}, \tag{6-14}$$

$$f'(0) = -\frac{\hat{G}'_{p^-}(0)D(0) + K_m D'(0)}{(K_m D(0))^2}, \tag{6-15}$$

$$f''(0) = f'(0)\left(\frac{\hat{G}''_{p^-}(0)D(0) + 2\hat{G}'_{p^-}(0)D'(0) + K_m D''(0)}{\hat{G}'_{p^-}(0)D(0) + K_m D'(0)} + \frac{2f'(0)}{f(0)}\right), \tag{6-16}$$

where, $K_m = \hat{G}_{p^-}(0)$ is the proportional amplification coefficient of the model.

6.4.2. Application to TCP/AQM Control System

This subsection mainly describes the design of IMC-PID congestion controller according to Theorem 1 and the IMC design procedure. Assume the internal model for the IMC-PID congestion controller is

$$\hat{G}_p(s) = P(s) = \frac{K_m e^{-sR_0}}{(T_1 s + 1)(T_2 s + 1)}, \tag{6-17}$$

According to the IMC design procedure, $\hat{G}_p(s)$ can be factored as

$$\hat{G}_{p^-}(s) = e^{-sR_0}, \qquad \hat{G}_{p^-}(s) = \frac{K_m}{(T_1 s + 1)(T_2 s + 1)}. \tag{6-18}$$

Therefore,

$$\hat{G}_{p^-}(0) = K_m, \tag{6-19}$$

$$\hat{G}'_{p^-}(0) = -K_m(T_1 + T_2), \tag{6-20}$$

$$\hat{G}''_{p^-}(0) = 2K_m(T_1^2 + T_2^2 + T_1 T_2), \tag{6-21}$$

$$\hat{G}_{p^+}(0) = 1, \quad \hat{G}'_{p^+}(0) = -R_0, \quad \hat{G}''_{p^+}(0) = R_0^2, \quad \hat{G}'''_{p^+}(0) = -R_0^3. \tag{6-22}$$

The variable γ is set to 2 in the low pass filter $g(s)$ to guarantee the properness of the IMC controller $G_i(s)$. Substitute $\gamma=2$ into (6-11)-(6-13), the following can be obtained:

$$D(0) = 2\varepsilon + R_0, \quad D'(0) = \frac{2\varepsilon^2 - R_0^2}{2}, \quad D''(0) = \frac{R_0^3}{6}.$$

By substituting these expressions into (6-14)-(6-16), the values of $f(0), f'(0)$ and $f''(0)$ can be obtained. Thus the controller parameters can be derived according to (6-9).

6.4.3. Implementation of IMC-PID Congestion Controller

Now, the IMC-PID congestion controller is obtained, which has the ability to restrict the negative impact on the system oscillations caused by large feedback delay. For a digital implementation, the time-continuous system need be converted into time-discrete system by using sample technique. Let T denote the sample interval and the initial value of the drop probability is zero. In the kth sample interval, the arrival packet will be dropped with probability

$$p(kT) = p((k-1)T) + K_c \left\{ \left(1 + \frac{T}{T_i} + \frac{T_d}{T} \right) e(kT) - \left(1 + \frac{2T_d}{T} \right) e((k-1)T) + \frac{T_d}{T} e((k-2)T) \right\} \quad (6\text{-}23)$$

where $e(kT)=q(kT)-q_0$.

In order to implement the controller, the value of ε and T should be determined. T is set approximately equal to the average RTT, in particular $T=0.4$sec. Great numbers of simulations using MATLAB with different network parameters are conducted to investigate the impact of parameter ε on system performance, all of which demonstrate that the system has a small overshoot and small settling time when $\varepsilon = 0.3R_0 \sim 0.5\ R_0$ (see Figure 6-5).

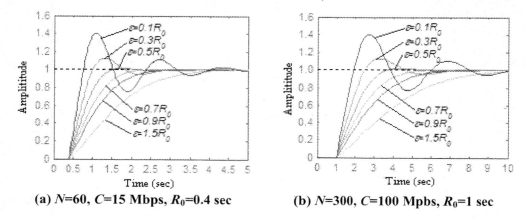

(a) $N=60$, $C=15$ Mbps, $R_0=0.4$ sec   (b) $N=300$, $C=100$ Mpbs, $R_0=1$ sec

Figure 6-5. Step response under different network parameters with various ε value.

Consider a network scenario in which mean packet size = 500 bytes, $C = 3750$ packet/sec (or equivalently, 15Mbps), $N = 60$, and $R_0 = 0.40$ sec, choosing $\varepsilon=0.5R0$, then the IMC-PID congestion controller can be calculated as:

$$G_c(s) = 2.9067 \times 10^{-5} \left(1 + \frac{1}{5.45s} + 0.4157s \right) \quad (6\text{-}24)$$

According to (6-23), the equation for updating the drop probability can be calculated as follows:

$$p(kT) = p((k-1)T) + 6.14111 \times 10^{-5} e(kT) - 8.94889 \times 10^{-5} e((k-1)T)$$
$$+ 3.21111 \times 10^{-5} e((k-2)T) \quad (6\text{-}25)$$

6.5. PERFORMANCE EVALUATION

In this section, the performance of IMC-PID congestion controller is investigated through NS simulations. The dynamic behaviors of the previous AQM schemes are simulated under a variety of network topologies. In particular, the dumbbell network topology is considered, which is depicted in Figure 6-1. Then the network topology with multiple bottleneck links as shown in Figure 6-6 is also considered, where the maximum buffer of each router is also 300 packets, and each sender-receiver pair has TCP connections as cross traffic. In both scenarios, TCP Reno is used as the transport agent.

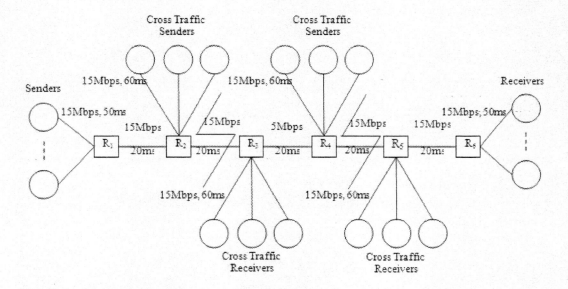

Figure 6-6. Network topology with multiple bottleneck links and cross traffic.

6.5.1. Simple Dumbbell Topology Network

(1) Queue Stability

For completeness, the simulation in section 2 is continued to investigate the stability of IMC-PID with RTT=150ms and RTT=400ms respectively. The queue evolutions are plotted in Figure 6-7 and the performance are tabulated in Table 6-3. Simulation results demonstrate that IMC-PID can restrict the negative impact on the queue stability caused by the large delay. Moreover, it gains fast convergence rate when RTT=150ms. Compared to the results of other AQM schemes, IMC-PID obtains higher link utilization, relative better controls of queue length, and smaller queue deviations.

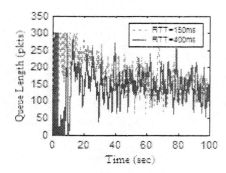

Figure 6-7. Queue evolution of IMC-PID with RTT=150ms and RTT=400ms.

Table 6-3. Link Utilization and Queue Statistics of IMC-PID

	Link Utilization	Average Queue Length (pkts)	QueueDeviations (pkts)
RTT=150ms	99.33%	175.88	46.52
RTT=400ms	97.30%	149.72	42.16

(2) Packet Drop Behavior

The large queue oscillations aroused in PI and REM and undesired queue evolution of DC-AQM probably result from the misbehaving controller output, i.e. packet drop probability. Figure 6-8 plots the packet drop probability of each AQM controller.

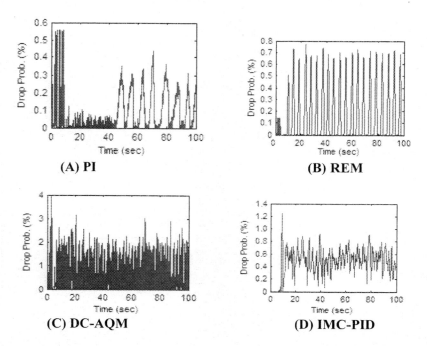

Figure 6-8. Packet drop probability of each AQM controller.

Obviously, IMC-PID controller maintains more stable packet drop behavior, and other controllers yield dynamic outputs which result in the queue oscillations. The undesired queue evolution of DC-AQM results from the large packet drop probability.

(3) Relationship between RTT, Reference Queue Length and Link Utilization

In order to study the effect on link utilization caused by various RTT and reference queue length, RTT is varied from 50ms to 1000ms with 20 segments, and q_0 is varied from 25 packets to 150 packets with 5 partitions, which would form a grid on XY plane. Figure 6-9 gives the bottleneck link utilization after every experiment. As shown in Figure 6-9, IMC-PID obtains roughly the same link utilization when RTTs are equal and its performance is hardly affected by the reference queue length. However, this is not true for other controllers. The link utilizations of other schemes, especially REM, decrease dramatically with large delay and small reference queue length.

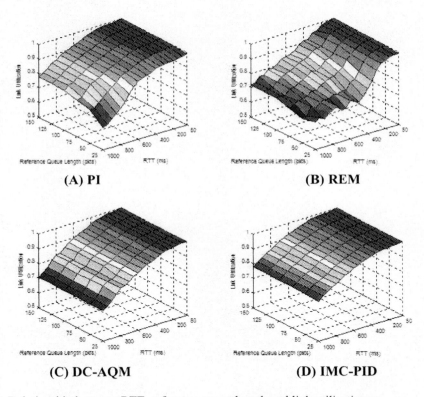

(A) PI (B) REM

(C) DC-AQM (D) IMC-PID

Figure 6-9. Relationship between RTT, reference queue length and link utilization.

6.5.2. Multiple Bottleneck Topology with Cross Traffic

Using the multiple bottleneck network topology depicted in Figure 6-6, the behavior of different AQM algorithms in the presence of cross traffic is studied. There are 120 FTP flows with senders at the left hand side and receivers at the right hand side. There are 90 FTP flows for each traffic cross sender-receiver pair. The queue lengths for the AQM schemes of the congested routers are collected. The instantaneous queues of R2 for different AQMs are depicted in Figure 6-10, and those of R3 are plotted in Figure 6-11. Simulation results show that R2's queue and R4's queue exhibit similar trends, so the data of R4's queue is not plotted. R1's queue and R5's queue are almost empty, indicating that these two links are not bottleneck links.

As shown in Figure 6-10 and Figure 6-11, all the AQM schemes have noticeable oscillations in this case with multiple bottlenecks and cross traffic; yet IMC-PID controls the queue length significantly better than others. The queue length of DC-AQM schemes is still frequently below the expected value (150 packets). REM oscillates largely in all congested routers, and often causes buffer overflows and emptiness. PI exhibits entirely different queue evolutions between R2 and R3. IMC-PID regulates queue length around the expected value (150 packets) and obtains better control effect than other schemes.

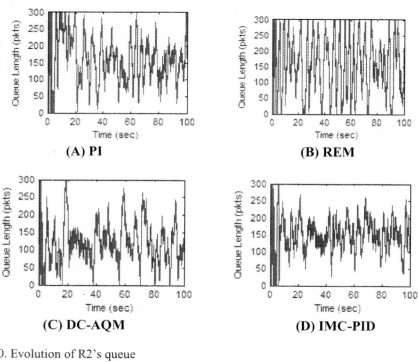

(A) PI   (B) REM

(C) DC-AQM   (D) IMC-PID

Figure 6-10. Evolution of R2's queue

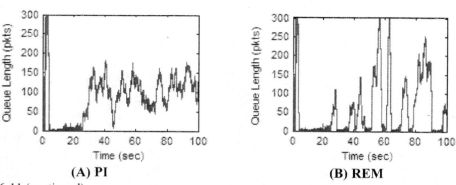

(A) PI   (B) REM

Figure 6-11 (continued).

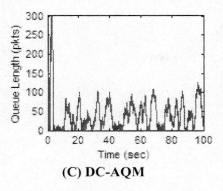

(C) DC-AQM

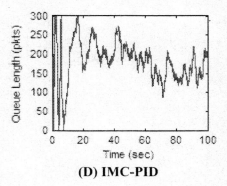

(D) IMC-PID

Figure 6-11. Evolution of R3's queue.

6.6. CONCLUSION

In this chapter, a congestion controller is proposed, called IMC-PID, to address the problem of stability of congestion control in large-delay networks. Simulations demonstrate that the existed AQM controllers yield unstable queue evolutions and result in low link utilizations and/or high delay jitters in networks with large communication delays. By using internal model control theory, an IMC-PID controller is designed to restrict the negative impact on queue stability caused by large delay. Extensive simulations are conducted and the performance of IMC-PID is comprehensively compared with that of PI, REM and DC-AQM. Simulation results show that the performance of IMC-PID outperforms that of others and maintains high link utilization as well as small queue deviation.

Chapter 7

PFED: A PREDICTION-BASED FAIR ACTIVE QUEUE MANAGEMENT ALGORITHM

7.1. INTRODUCTION

A number of active queue management (AQM) algorithms have been proposed since Random Early Detection (RED) [24] was introduced in 1993. RED is the most widely accepted AQM algorithm. However, many studies show that the performance of RED heavily depends on whether or not its parameters are properly tuned. RED is known to be unfair to individual flows, unable to achieve high link utilization and low packet loss rate simultaneously, and exhibit short-term fluctuation in the queue length. Thus, many alternative AQM algorithms have been proposed to amend these disadvantages. Unfortunately, few of these algorithms can amend these disadvantages simultaneously.

In this chapter, a number of well-known AQM algorithms are analyzed and their advantages and disadvantages are discussed. Then a novel AQM algorithm — Prediction based Fair Early Drop (PFED) is proposed.

The main objectives of PFED are:

1) To stabilize the queue length at a desirable level through more accurate traffic prediction and more reasonable calculation of packet drop probability;
2) To impose effective punishment upon misbehaving flow;
3) To maintain queue arrival rate bounded by queue service rate.

PFED is implemented in NS2 [173] and is compared with a number of well-known AQM algorithms such as RED and CHOKe [26]. The algorithms are examined in terms of stability (i.e., the variance rate of queue length) and fairness, in addition to their complexity. Simulation results show that PFED outperforms RED and CHOKe in stabling instantaneous queue length and in fairness. It is also shown that PFED enables the link capacity to be fully utilized by stabilizing the queue length at a desirable level, while not incurring excessive packet loss ratio.

The rest of this chapter is organized as follows. Section 7.2 discusses related work (analysis of a few well-known AQM algorithms). Section 7.3 describes PFED algorithm.

Section 7.4 compares PFED with other AQM algorithms in NS2. Finally, Section 7.5 concludes the work.

7.2. RELATED WORKS

Active queue management has been extensively studied since early 1990s, and RED is the most widely accepted one. RED detects incipient congestion at network routers in order to promptly notify sources to reduce their rates, punish misbehaving flows without being biased against burst traffic, and avoid global synchronization. RED maintains a long term average of the queue length (buffer occupancy) of the routers to detect incipient congestion, and randomly drops packets in proportion to this buffer occupancy value.

However, RED's performance is extremely sensitive to its parameters. It is difficult to tune the parameters to achieve good performance in different networks.

Furthermore, queue length is only an indirect reflection of traffic load, many studies showed that queue length should not be the only parameter to be observed and controlled.

When mixed traffic types share a link, RED allows unfair bandwidth sharing since RED imposes the same loss rate on all flows regardless of their bandwidths. To amend this weakness, FRED (Flow RED) [183], proposed in 1997, uses per-active-flow accounting to impose on each flow a loss rate depending on the flow buffer occupancy. Unfortunately, the per-active-flow accounting in FRED suffers from the problem of scalability.

CHOKe [26] is another improved AQM algorithm based on RED, targeting to improve the fairness of RED. The basic idea behind CHOKe is that the contents of the FIFO buffer form a "sufficient statistic" about the incoming traffic and can be used in a simple fashion to penalize misbehaving flows. When a packet arrives at a congested router, CHOKe draws a packet at random from the FIFO buffer and compares it with the arriving packet. If they both belong to the same flow, then they are both dropped, else the randomly chosen packet is left intact and the arriving packet is admitted into the buffer with a probability that depends on the level of congestion (this probability is calculated exactly as in RED). The reason for doing this is that the FIFO buffer is more likely to have packets belonging to a misbehaving flow and hence these packets are more likely to be chosen for comparison. Further, packets belonging to a misbehaving flow arrive more numerously and are more likely to trigger comparison. The intersection of these two high probability events is precisely the event that packets belonging to misbehaving flows are dropped. As a consequence, packets of misbehaving flows will be dropped more often than packets of well-behaved flows.

The main contribution of CHOKe is its fairness over RED. Although CHOKe cannot realize absolute fairness (or max-min fairness), it does punish the misbehaving flows effectively. Moreover, CHOKe does not use per-flow-state, thus maintains the simplicity and scalability of RED. However, CHOKe also inherits the disadvantages of RED, such as instability of instantaneous queue length, and parameter sensitiveness etc.

CSFQ (Core Stateless Fair Queue) [76] is another improved AQM algorithm. The goal of CSFQ is to realize max-min fairness through packet dropping. In CSFQ, a technique named DPS (Dynamic Packet State) [184] is used to relieve core nodes from per-flow-state management, thus improve the scalability of the algorithm.

In CSFQ, network routers are divided into edges and cores. The edge routers maintain per-flow state, estimate the incoming rate of each flow, and insert a label into each packet based on the estimation. The core routers maintain no per-flow state, but use FIFO packet scheduling augmented by a probabilistic dropping algorithm, which uses the packet labels and an estimate of the aggregate traffic at the router.

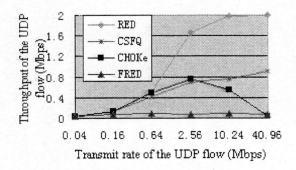

Figure 7-1. Fairness comparison of AQM algorithms.

Theoretically, CSFQ can achieve more fairness than other AQM algorithms. But in experimental studies, the fairness of CSFQ is not as good as expected, especially when there are TCP flows.

Figure 7-1 is the simulation results of several AQM algorithms, aiming to compare their fairness. In this simulation, many TCP flows and a UDP flow compete bandwidth at a bottleneck link (the bandwidth of this bottleneck link is 2Mbps), and the UDP flow's transmit rate increase from 0.04Mbps to 40.96 Mbps. As shown in Figure 7-1, the UDP flow gets different bandwidth (throughput) under different algorithms with the increasing of the transmit rate of the UDP flow.

In RED, the UDP flow occupies more and more bandwidth with the increasing of transmit rate. Finally, it occupies total bandwidth of the bottleneck link. FRED, on the other hand, can achieve good fairness due to its utilization of per-active-flow accounting. The fairness of CSFQ and CHOKe is between that of FRED and RED. With the increasing of the transmit rate of the UDP flow, the UDP flow achieves more and more bandwidth at the bottleneck link, but when the transmit rate of the UDP flow reaches a certain value, the throughput of the UDP flow in CHOKe begins to decrease, while the throughput of the UDP flow in CSFQ still increases steadily, which means that the fairness of CSFQ is even worse than that of CHOKe.

This experimental results show that the fairness of CHOKe is not as good as that of FRED. But CHOKe can impose effective punishment on misbehaving flow. Why the fairness of CSFQ is not as good as expected when there are TCP flows? In CSFQ, the fairness is heavily dependent on the measurement of each flow's rate at the edge routers because the rate is used to calculate the drop probability. However, the transmit rate of TCP flows changes so frequently that it cannot be measured accurately by exponential averaging used in CSFQ, which leads to the decline of fairness.

7.3. PFED ALGORITHM

To achieve these goals of PFED, which are described in Section 7.1, the following techniques are used in the PFED algorithm:

1) Detecting incipient congestion by using queue length measurement and traffic prediction (measurement), which uses a simple and effective MMSE (Minimum Mean Square Error)[185] predictor to predict arrival rate in the next interval;
2) Punishing the misbehaving flow by using the method borrowed from CHOKe;
3) Calculating packet drop probability by using load information.

In particular, all of these techniques are very easy to implement, no per-flow state management and no complex computation are involved. The number of parameters needed to be configured is less than that of RED. As a consequence, the PFED algorithm is easy to implement in the current network infrastructures.

7.3.1. Congestion Detection and Arrival Rate Prediction

As described in former sections, using queue length as the only congestion indicator is not sufficient. Queue length is only an indirect reflection of traffic load, thus is just an indirect reflection of network congestion.

In PFED, load information, which is combined with queue length information as the indicator of congestion, is used.

The load information used in PFED is the load factor defined as the ratio of periodically measured arrival rate and service rate (service rate is the link bandwidth). The load factor LF is:

$$LF = \frac{r}{C} \qquad (7-1)$$

where r is the arrival rate, and C is the link bandwidth. A high load factor value indicates congestion and a low value indicates link underutilization.

In PFED, the arrival rate is measured periodically (every τ time), then MMSE predictor is used to predict the future arrival rate in the next interval. Thus the load factor in the next interval can be calculated. The load factor, combined with the measured queue length as the congestion indicator, is used to detect incipient congestion. In detail, when the load factor is larger than 1 (LF >1) and the current queue length is larger than half of the queue buffer size (i.e., QL >QS /2, QL is the current queue length, QS is the queue buffer size), the congestion is estimated to occur in the next interval.

In the detection of congestion, the most important task is to predict the arrival rate in the next interval. To select a good predictor, two criterions have to be considered. One is the accuracy of the predictor and the other is the simplicity of the predictor, because the predictor will be run online.

MMSE is selected as the predictor of PFED algorithm because MMSE is simple enough to be run online and the accuracy of MMSE is also desirable. In the following subsection a detailed description of MMSE is given.

7.3.2. MMSE Predictor

A number of recent empirical studies of traffic measurements from a variety of working packet networks have convincingly demonstrated that network traffic is self-similar or Long-Range Dependent (LRD) in nature [189, 190, 191]. Considering the LRD nature of network traffic, the best traffic predictors are FBM [186] and FARIMA [187]. Unfortunately, FBM and FARIMA include lots of complex calculation, so they are improper for online predictions.

Recently, studies of real traffic traces indicate that the Hurst parameter rarely exceeds 0.85 (Hurst parameter is an indicator of LRD) [188, 189, 190]. Under this circumstance, the MMSE predictor shows performance as good as FBM or FARIMA. Furthermore, studies in [191] showed that the predictability of aggregate flow is better than that of single flow. In PFED, we only use MMSE is used only to predict aggregate flow rate, not single flow rate, so the prediction accuracy of MMSE is good enough to be used in PFED.

The following is the description of MMSE.

Let $\{X_t\}$ denote a linear stochastic process and suppose that the next value of $\{X_{t+1}\}$ can be expressed as a linear combination of the current and previous observations. That is:

$$X_{t+1} = WX'+\varepsilon_t \tag{7-2}$$

where

$$W = (w_m, w_{m-1}, ..., w_1) \tag{7-3}$$

$$X = (X_t, X_{t-1}, ..., X_{t-m+1}) \tag{7-4}$$

m is the order of regression.

Let $\hat{W}$ denote the estimated weight vector, and $\hat{X}_{t+1}$ denote the predicted value of X_{t+1}. While minimizing the mean square error, i.e., minimizing $E[e_t^2] = E[(X_{t+1} - \hat{X}_{t+1})^2]$, the following can be get

$$\hat{W} = [\rho_m \quad \cdots \quad \rho_1] \times \begin{bmatrix} \rho_0 & \rho_1 & \cdots & \rho_{m-1} \\ \rho_1 & \rho_0 & \cdots & \rho_{m-2} \\ \cdots & \cdots & \cdots & \cdots \\ \rho_{m-1} & \rho_{m-2} & \cdots & \rho_0 \end{bmatrix}^{-1} \tag{7-5}$$

where $\rho_k = \dfrac{1}{m} \displaystyle\sum_{t=k+1}^{m} X_t X_{t-k}$.

The benefit of using MMSE is the simplicity of implementation. There are only some matrix manipulations that can readily be implemented in hardware and software at a very high speed. Moreover, there are approximation approaches called NMMSE (Normalized MMSE) [192, 193] for computing the weight vector $\hat{W}$, which eliminate matrix inversion and autocorrelation computations by adaptive and recursive solutions. That is

$$\hat{W}_{t+1} = \hat{W}_t + \mu \frac{X}{\|X\|^2} e_t \qquad\qquad (7\text{-}6)$$

where μ is the adaptation constant and determines the convergence speed. NMMSE is convergent in the mean square error sense if μ satisfies the condition $0 < \mu < 2$.

7.3.3. Punishing Misbehaving Flow

In order to impose effective punishment on misbehaving flow, the method used in CHOKe is introduced to PFED. When a packet arrives at a congested router, PFED draws a packet at random from the FIFO buffer and compares it with the arriving packet. If they both belong to the same flow, they are both dropped, else the randomly chosen packet is left intact and the arriving packet is dropped with a probability that depends on the level of congestion. The drop probability P_{drop} is calculated as shown in the next subsection.

7.3.4. Calculating Drop Probability

In PFED, load factor and queue length are combined to calculate the packet drop probability P_{drop}.

$$P_{drop} = (\frac{r-C}{r})\frac{Q_L}{Q_S} = (1-\frac{C}{r})\frac{Q_L}{Q_S} = (1-\frac{1}{LF})\frac{Q_L}{Q_S} \qquad\qquad (7\text{-}7)$$

where LF is the load factor, r is the arrival rate, C is the link bandwidth, Q_L is the current queue length, and Q_S is the queue buffer size.

Using load factor to calculate drop probability can keep the queue arrival rate at or below the queue service rate. This is also helpful for improving the stability of queue length.

7.3.5. Pseudo Code of PFED Algorithm

For completeness, the pseudo code of PFED algorithm is given in Figure 7-2.

```
    on receiving packet p
    if (interval> τ ) {
      calculate the arrival rate in last interval;
      use MMSE to predict the arrival rate in the next
interval;
      calculate LF using Equation (7-1);
    }
    if ((LF >1) && (Q_L > Q_S /2)) {
      draw a packet at random from the queue;
      if (both packets from the same flow) {
        drop both packets;
      } else {
        calculate P_drop using Equation (7-2);
        if (random(0,1)< P_drop)
          drop packet p;
        else
          enque (p);
      }
    } else {
      enque (p);
    }
```

Figure 7-2. Pseudo code of PFED.

7.4. SIMULATION RESULTS AND ANALYSIS

To verify the performance of PFED, PFED is implemented along with RED and CHOKe in NS2. A simulation study is conducted to compare the performance of PFED with other AQM algorithms. The behavior of these algorithms is examined in a variety of network topologies and traffic sources.

The parameter used in PFED is: τ=0.02s (measurement and prediction interval). The parameters of RED are set as w_p=0.002, min_{th}=20, max_{th}=70. The parameters of CHOKe are set the same as RED. Queue buffer capacity (QS) is set to 100 packets in all experiments.

7.4.1. Single Bottleneck Topology

Firstly, the stability and other properties of PFED are compared with these of RED and CHOKe in single bottleneck topology. The topology of the simulation is shown in Figure 7-3, the bandwidth of the bottleneck link is 2Mbps, and the delay is 1ms.

In this experiment, k TCP connections are established over the single bottleneck link, where k varies from 50 to 100.

Figure 7-4(a) gives the standard deviation of instantaneous queue length under different algorithms where the number of connections varies from 50 to 100. Figure 7-4(b) gives the packet loss ratio under different algorithms. Figure 7-4(c) gives the link utilization under different algorithms.

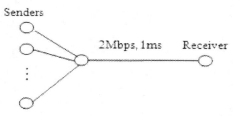

Figure 7-3. The single bottleneck topology.

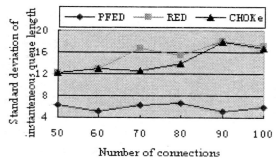

(A) Standard deviation of instantaneous queue length

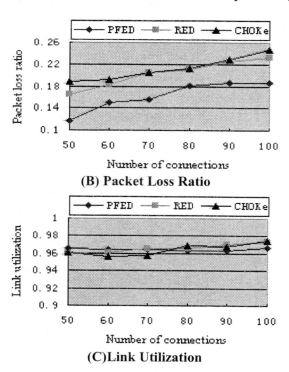

(B) Packet Loss Ratio

(C)Link Utilization

Figure 7-4. Comparisons of different algorithms in single bottleneck topology.

As shown in Figure 7-4, the instantaneous queue length of PFED is much more stable than that of RED and CHOKe, the packet loss ratio of PFED is less than that of RED and CHOKe, and the link utilization of these three algorithms are close.

7.4.2. Multiple Bottlenecks Topology

The same experiment is repeated in a network with multiple bottlenecks, which is shown in Figure 7-5. The bandwidth of all bottleneck links is 2Mbps, and the delay is 1ms. There are 5 queues (Q1, Q2, Q3, Q4, Q5) among which Q2 and Q4 are shared with cross traffic of 30 TCP connections. There are k TCP connections with the senders at the left hand side and the receivers at the right hand side, where k varies from 50 to 100.

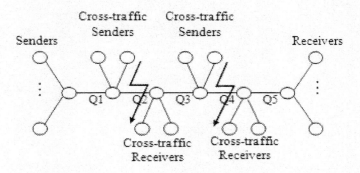

Figure 7-5. Multiple bottlenecks topology.

Simulation results show that the queue length at Q5 is always 0 or 1, which suggests that the link is not a bottleneck link. The other four queues exhibit similar trends as far as the performance comparison is concerned. Figure 7-6 gives the standard deviation of instantaneous queue length of Q4, the packet loss ratio of Q4, and the link utilization of Q4 to show the performance of different algorithms.

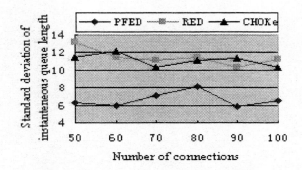

(A) Standard deviation of instantaneous queue length

Figure 7-6 (continued).

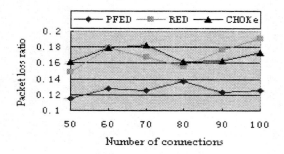

(B) Packet Loss Ratio

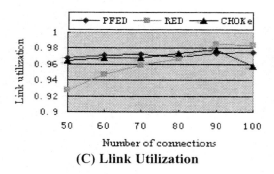

(C) Llink Utilization

Figure 7-6. Comparisons of different algorithms in multiple bottlenecks topology.

As shown in Figure 7-6, PFED outperforms RED and CHOKe with respect to stability of instantaneous queue length and packet loss ratio, but the link utilization of these three algorithms are close.

7.4.3. Fairness Comparison

To show the effectiveness of punishment for misbehaving flow with different algorithms, this experiment is done in the topology shown in Figure 7-3. There are 49 TCP flows and 1 UDP flow, and the transmit rate of the UDP flow increases from 0.04Mbps to 40.96Mbps.

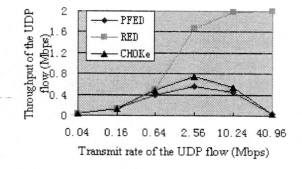

Figure 7-7. Fairness comparison of different AQM algorithms.

As shown in Figure 7-7, the UDP flow gets different bandwidth (throughput) under different algorithms with the increasing of the transmit rate of the UDP flow. The throughput of the UDP flow in PFED is much less than that in RED, and a little less than that in CHOKe, which means that the fairness of PFED is better than that of RED and CHOKe.

In fact, the method of punishing misbehaving flow in PFED is the same as that in CHOKe, but more accurate congestion detection in PFED contributes to its better fairness.

7.5. CONCLUSION

A novel AQM algorithm, called PFED, is proposed in the chapter. The main objectives of PFED are to stabilize the queue length at a desirable level with consideration of future traffic and with more reasonable calculation of packet drop probability; and to impose effective punishment upon misbehaving flow with a full stateless method. The complexity of PFED is no more than that of RED and CHOKe, so PFED can be easily implemented in current networks. The validity of PFED is demonstrated by simulation on NS2. A variety of network topologies and traffic sources are used in the simulation to test the performance of PFED. Simulation results show that the stability and fairness of PFED are much better than those of RED and CHOKe. Through the simulation, it is also shown that by stabilizing the queue length at a desirable level, PFED enables the link capacity to be fully utilized without incurring excessive packet loss ratio.

Chapter 8

DOWNLINK TEMPORAL FAIRNESS IN 802.11 WLAN BASED ON VIRTUAL QUEUE MANAGEMENT

8.1. INTRODUCTION

In 802.11 wireless local area network (WLAN), wireless channel condition mainly depends on the location of wireless node because of signal fading and interference. Many existing rate adaptation mechanisms can dynamically switch data rates to match the channel conditions, with the goal of selecting the rate that will give the optimum throughput for the given channel conditions. Examples of such mechanisms include ARF [193] and RBAR [194]. These mechanisms lead to rate diversity in WLAN, where wireless nodes use different data rates to communicate with the Access Point (AP) in uplink and downlink directions.

The Access Point plays an important role for relaying the traffic between the wired network and the wireless network. Since the bandwidth in wireless networks is much smaller than the bandwidth in wired networks, the bandwidth disparity between wired networks and wireless networks makes the AP become the potential congestion bottleneck in the downlink direction. Even worse case occurs if classical TCP services like web browsing or file retrieval are considered, since the traffic volume ratio is dramatically biased in favor of the downlink direction.

Several active queue management (AQM) algorithms in WLAN have been proposed. In [195], the authors explored applying RED algorithm to control congestion and achieve some quality of service (QoS), such as low delay, low packet loss rate and high throughput. However, the main purpose of RED algorithm is not to improve the fairness among flows. To resolve the fairness problem, VQ-RED in [196] treats all the flows fairly through managing their single flow lengths. It sets the same drop threshold for all single flows on AP. In this way it guarantees the throughput fairness among the flows. In [197], the author proposed multi-class RED algorithm on AP. Multi-class RED algorithm sets different drop thresholds for different class flows to guarantee proportional throughput fairness.

These throughput fair AQM algorithms all assumed that the wireless network can transmit or receive packets by using the only single data rate. But in multi-rate WLAN, wireless channel is shared by all competing flows. When some wireless nodes use a lower data rate than the others, the performance of all wireless nodes is considerably degraded [198]. This is because when a wireless node with a low data rate captures the channel, it takes more time than a node with a higher data rate, and hence the utilization of the channel is degraded. So in the multi-rate WLAN, if previously proposed throughput fair AQM algorithms are applied, the overall throughput in WLAN will be brought down.

TTPDE [199] is a queue management algorithm in multi-rate WLAN. When the queue on AP is full, TTPDE algorithm chooses the packet which has the longest transmission time to be dropped. When AP wants to transmit a packet, TTPDE algorithm chooses the packet of the shortest transmission time. TTPDE algorithm utilizes high data rate efficiently in multi-rate WLAN. But this algorithm sacrifices fairness and may suffer wireless nodes with low date rate in long time.

To provide QoS in a multi-rate WLAN, the throughput of each wireless node should be independent of the transmission cost of other nodes, which is defined as the channel usage time. Thus, in order to achieve a better utilization of channel usage time, temporal fairness among single flows should be guaranteed to increase network efficiency.

In this chapter, a temporal fair AQM algorithm on AP, named TFRED (Temporal Fair RED), is proposed to address the congestion, efficiency, and fairness problems in WLAN. TFRED algorithm not only alleviates congestion, but also guarantees the temporal fairness among the flows. In this way, TFRED algorithm greatly improves network efficiency.

8.2. THE TEMPORAL FAIR RED ALGORITHM

Let IEEE 802.11b be the MAC protocol in WLAN for the purposes of discussion. Depending on the wireless link condition of a wireless node, it can support data rates of 11 Mbps, 5.5 Mbps, 2 Mbps or 1 Mbps.

8.2.1. Description of TFRED Algorithm

When the congestion happens, TFRED drops the high rate transmitted packet with low probability and drops the low rate transmitted packet with high probability. TFRED keeps the queue length of each single flow at its target queue length, which is determined by the data rate of the single flow.

Actually there is no real queue for each flow. AP only records the number of packet waiting to be transmitted to wireless nodes (virtual queue length of each active flow). Each virtual queue is for a particular active flow. In this chapter, each flow is identified by receiving wireless node. A flow may contain TCP traffic, UDP traffic or both. To avoid lockout and global synchronization, the packet is dropped randomly in virtual queue of each active flow.

Figure 8-1 shows the pseudo-code of TFRED algorithm. When a new packet arrives, TFRED algorithm will deal with it as follows:

1) Classifies the arriving packet and dispatches it to a proper virtual queue.
2) Estimates target queue length *targetlength* of each flow based on its wireless data rate.

3) Uses a low pass filter with an exponential weighted moving average to calculate the average queue length *avg* of aggregate flow, which is maintained and compared with two thresholds: minimum threshold min_{th} and maximum threshold max_{th}. The packet dropping probability p_{drop} is determined in different ways according to the average queue size *avg* of aggregate flow:

If $avg < min_{th}$, no packet is dropped.

If $min_{th} \leq avg < max_{th}$, with probability p_{drop} do: find the flow with max(*currentlength-targetlength*) and randomly remove a packet from the flow queue.

If $max_{th} \leq avg$, find flow with max(*currentlength-targetlength*) and randomly remove a packet from the flow queue.

---

on receiving packet *P*
$i = classify(P)$
$l_i = estimate\_per\_flow\_targetlength(i)$
$avg = (1-wq) \times avg + wq \times \sum currentlength_i$
if $(avg \geq max_{th})$ $drop = 1$
if $(avg < min_{th})$ $drop = 0$
if $(min_{th} \leq avg < max_{th})$
   $p_{drop} = (avg - min_{th}) \times max_p / (max_{th} - min_{th})$
   if $(random[0,1] \leq p_{drop})$ $drop = 1$
   else $drop = 0$
if $(drop == 1)$
   find the flow *j* with max(*currentlength_i − l_i*)
random remove packet from flow *j*
$enque(P)$

Figure 8-1. Pseudo-code of TFRED algorithm.

8.2.2. Estimate Flow's Target Queue Length

To guarantee the temporal fairness, TFRED algorithm should estimate target queue length based on wireless data rate.

Assume that AP in 802.11b WLAN transmits a single data frame. If the propagation time is neglected, the overall channel usage time $t_{channel}$ is composed of the transmission time and a contention overhead t_{ov}:

$$t_{channel} = \frac{s_d}{r} + t_{ov} \qquad (8\text{-}1)$$

where s_d is the data frame length in bits, r is the data rate. Assume that no collision with another data packet occurs and the backoff time is chosen from a uniform distribution, the contention overhead time can be calculated based on the IEEE 802.11b system parameter (As shown in Table 8-1.):

$$t_{ov} = \frac{CW_{min} \times Slot\ time}{2} + DIFS + 3 \times SIFS + \frac{RTS + CTS + ACK + PHY_{header}}{Basic\ Rate} \qquad (8\text{-}2)$$

Table 8-1. IEEE 802.11 System Parameters

Parameter	Parameter Value
PHY header	192 bits
RTS frame	160 bits + PHY header
CTS frame	112 bits + PHY header
ACK frame	112 bits + PHY header
Basic rate	1 Mbps
Slot time	20 μs
SIFS	10 μs
DIFS	50 μs
CW$_{min}$	31

For a FCFS service discipline, the output data rate of each flow is proportional to its buffer occupancy, which is determined by its queue length. So the probability p_i of AP transmitting a packet in flow i can be calculated as follows:

$$p_i = l_i \Big/ \sum_{i=1}^{n} l_i \qquad (8\text{-}3)$$

where l_i is the current queue length of flow i, n is the number of flows. Assume that the data frame length is the same in WLAN. So the channel usage time T_i of flow i is:

$$T_i = (\frac{S_d}{r} + t_{ov}) \times p_i \times T \qquad (8\text{-}4)$$

where T is the total channel usage time of all flows. From (8-3) and (8-4), it is obvious that in order to let all flows have the equal channel usage time, queue length l_i should be inversely proportional to $s_d/(r_i+t_{ov})$. So the target queue length of flow i is:

$$l_i = L \times \frac{1}{\frac{S_d}{r_i} + t_{ov}} \Big/ \sum_{i=1}^{n} \frac{1}{\frac{S_d}{r_i} + t_{ov}} \qquad (8\text{-}5)$$

where L is the queue target length of aggregate flow in AP. To avoid buffer overflow, L is set to $(max_{th}+min_{th})/2$.

8.3. COMPARISON AND ANALYSIS

In multi-rate WLAN, throughput fair AQM algorithm guarantees equal throughput for each wireless node, which penalizes fast flows and privileges slow flows; temporal fair AQM algorithm guarantees equal channel usage time for each wireless node, which provides per-flow throughput protection. Lemma 1 shows that temporal fair AQM algorithm can achieve more network efficiency than throughput fair AQM algorithm.

Lemma 1: If rate diversity exists in 802.11 networks, temporal fair AQM algorithm can achieve more total throughput than throughput fair AQM algorithm.

Proof: Assume that AP transmits n flows to n wireless nodes respectively and all flow use the same data frame length s_d. Let t_{ov} be the contention overhead for each packet to transmit, r_i be wireless data rate of flow i. If the propagation time is neglected, the throughput t_i of AP transmitting a packet in flow i becomes:

$$t_i = s_d \bigg/ (\frac{s_d}{r_i} + t_{ov}) \tag{8-6}$$

Under the temporal fairness, each flow achieves an equal share of channel usage time. So the total throughput T_{tf} in temporal fair WLAN will be:

$$T_{tf} = \frac{1}{n} \sum_{i=1}^{n} t_i \geq \sqrt[n]{\prod_{i=1}^{n} t_i} \tag{8-7}$$

Under the throughput fairness, the fraction of the time required to transfer packets in single flow to the total time required for all flows is $\dfrac{1}{t_i} \bigg/ \sum_{i=1}^{n} \dfrac{1}{t_i}$. So the total throughput T_{rf} in throughput fair WLAN will be:

$$T_{rf} = \sum_{j=1}^{n} (t_j \times \frac{1}{t_j} \bigg/ \sum_{i=1}^{n} \frac{1}{t_i}) = \frac{n}{\sum_{i=1}^{n} \frac{1}{t_i}} \leq \sqrt[n]{\prod_{i=1}^{n} t_i} \tag{8-8}$$

From (8-7) and (8-8), it is obvious $T_{tf} \geq T_{rf}$. When $r_1 = r_2 = \ldots = r_n$, $T_{tf} = T_{rf}$. So to guarantee temporal fairness is also to guarantee throughput fairness in single data rate WLAN. But if rate diversity exists, temporal fair AQM algorithm can achieve more network efficiency.

8.4. PERFORMANCE EVALUATION

The performance of the TFRED algorithm is evaluated, together with that of the other three algorithms: RED, VQ-RED and TTPDE. All simulations were run on the NS-2 simulator [173]. Each wireless node, including the AP, has a protocol stack. In this protocol stack, the routing protocol uses the NO Ad-Hoc Routing Agent (NOAH) [200] and the interface queue is located between the link layer (LL) and the Medium Access Control (MAC) protocol. The MAC protocol conforms to the IEEE 802.11b specification, and the Ricean model [201] of propagation is used. In Ricean model, parameter k is defined as the ratio between the deterministic signal power and the variance of multi-path fading. In this chapter, a large value of k, for example $k=256$, is chosen because the channel condition of fixed wireless nodes should be stable. The automatic data rate selection algorithm of the MAC protocol uses the receiver-based auto rate (RBAR) [194].

8.4.1. Simulation 1: Throughput Comparison

In Simulation 1, the throughputs of RED, VQ-RED, TTPDE and TFRED are tested in the simulation topology given in Figure 8-2. Node A–E are located at 10 m, 60 m, 80 m, 102 m and 10m from the AP, and initially are connected to the AP with data rates of 11 Mbps, 5.5 Mbps, 2 Mbps, 1 Mbps and 11 Mbps respectively. While the simulation is running, Node E is moving away from the AP at 1 m/s. In the meantime, the data rate of node E changes successively from 11 Mbps to 5.5 Mbps, 2 Mbps and 1 Mbps. In this environment, 5 CBR connections are generated, which are modeled as 5 Mbps flows (the packet size is 1000 bytes). The five CBR connections are flow 1-5(from Node 1-5 to Node A-E). All wired bandwidths are set to 25M. AP's buffer size is 100 packets. The parameters for RED, VQ-RED and TFRED algorithms are set as follows: $w_q=0.002$, $min_{th}=40$, $max_{th}=60$, $max_p=0.1$.

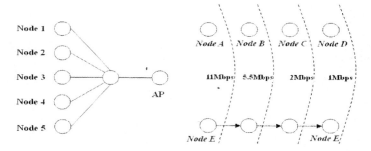

Figure 8-2. Simulation Scenario 1.

Figure 8-3 shows the throughputs of each flow when RED is used as AQM in AP. As shown in Figure 8-3, the throughputs of all 5 flows show some oscillations and they also decrease a little. Figure 8-4 shows that when VQ-RED algorithm is used, the throughputs of all 5 flows are almost the same. This is because VQ-RED can guarantee throughput fairness. Node E degrades the throughput of the other nodes. Figure 8-5 shows that TTPDE algorithm guarantees fast flows' throughput, but fails to protect slow flows. As shown in Figure 8-6, the throughput of each flow is differentiated and dependent on data rate when TFRED is used as AQM in AP. As the data rate of flow 5 is decreased, the throughputs of the other flows are protected. The decreased data rate of flow 5 means a decrease in the number of packets served by flow 5. As the number of packets served by flow 5 drops, the time consumed by contention becomes a free resource and is reallocated to all the other flows. Therefore, the throughput of the other flows increases as the node E moves away from the AP. Figure 8-7 shows that compared with RED and VQ-RED algorithm, TFRED achieves a 40% increase in total throughput.

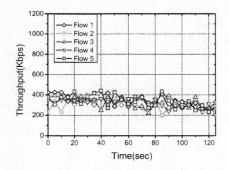

Figure 8-3. Throughput per flow when using RED in AP.

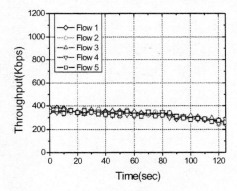

Figure 8-4. Throughput per flow when using VQ-RED in AP.

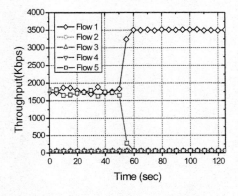

Figure 8-5. Throughput per flow when using TTPDE in AP.

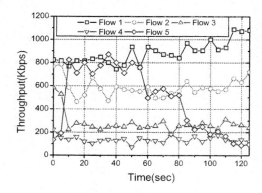

Figure 8-6. Throughput per flow when using TFRED in AP.

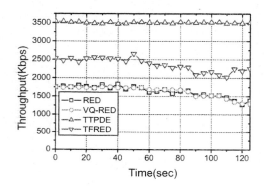

Figure 8-7. Total throughput when using RED, VQ-RED, TTPDE and TFRED in AP.

8.4.2. Simulation 2: Fairness Comparison

In Simulation 2, the temporal fairness and throughput fairness indices of RED, VQ-RED, TTPDE and TFRED is tested in the simulation topology given in Figure 8-8. Nodes A–E are all located at 10 m from the AP. Other settings used are the same as settings in simulation 1.

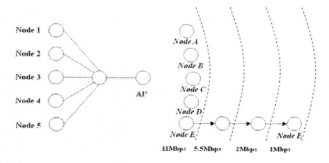

Figure 8-8. Simulation Scenario 2.

Two fairness indexes [97] are used to represent the relative fairness achieved for each flow. Assume that AP transmits n flows to n wireless nodes respectively. The sets of channel usage time and throughput of n flows is $(T_1, T_2, ..., T_n)$ and $(T_1', T_2', ..., T_n')$. The temporal fairness index is calculated as follows:

$$temporal\ fairness\ index = \left(\sum_{i=1}^{n} T_i \right)^2 \bigg/ \left(n \sum_{i=1}^{n} (T_i)^2 \right) \tag{8-9}$$

The throughput fairness index is calculated as follows:

$$throughput\ fairness\ index = \left(\sum_{i=1}^{n} T_i' \right)^2 \bigg/ \left(n \sum_{i=1}^{n} (T_i')^2 \right) \tag{8-10}$$

Figure 8-9 shows the temporal fairness index of the four algorithms. As shown in Figure 8-9, the temporal fairness index remains close to 1 when TFRED is used, despite the mobility of the node. This means that all flows receive almost the same channel usage time. In Figure 8-10, when data rates of all flows are equal, the throughput fairness indexes of the four algorithms remains close to 1. When the data rate of node E changes from 11 Mbps to 5.5 Mbps, throughput fairness index of the TTPDE algorithm decreases to 0.8 and node E's throughput is zero (in "starve" state). When the data rate of node E changes, throughput fairness index of the TFRED algorithm only decreases a little. But this is the tradeoff between total throughput and throughput fairness.

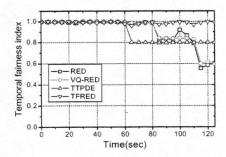

Figure 8-9. Temporal fairness index.

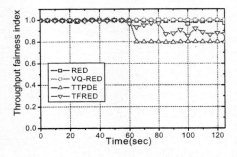

Figure 8-10. Throughput fairness index.

8.5. CONCLUSION

This chapter has proved that temporal fair AQM algorithm can achieve more total throughput than throughput fair AQM algorithm in multi-rate 802.11 WLAN, and proposed a temporal fair AQM algorithm (TFRED) with the following properties:

1) TFRED outperforms the throughput fair AQM algorithms in terms of total throughput, since it guarantees an equal share of the wireless channel usage time to each flow;
2) TFRED can provide congestion control on AP, by controlling the queue length;
3) TFRED can be easily implemented without changing the existing network protocols.

Chapter 9

AN ADAPTIVE LOSS DIFFERENTIATION ALGORITHM BASED ON QUEUE MANAGEMENT

9.1. INTRODUCTION

High Bit Error Rate, fading and blackout become non-negligible factors in wireless network, which is different from wired networks. If a TCP connection traverses over a wireless link, for example a WLAN network, packets may be corrupted and get lost due to wireless errors. However, in traditional TCP, a sender considers all losses as congestion signals and reacts to random wireless loss by decreasing the sending rate unnecessarily [202]. To avoid such performance degradation, TCP should let the sender be clear about the cause of losses and make correct control on adjusting the congestion windows.

There are two types of losses. One is congestion loss due to buffer overflow and the other is wireless loss due to wireless error. In general, a procedure of Loss Differentiation Algorithms should be [203]: firstly, capturing the state variables implying some kind of losses through analysis, secondly, measuring the newly value of these variables, and lastly, applying some rules on metrics to diagnose losses. Currently, most Loss Differentiation Algorithms are based on end_to_end measurement, which can be classified into the following three groups.

(1)Algorithms Based on Single Metric

Many TCPs are extended to endow with this kind of algorithm because it is easy to be implemented. The commonly used metrics are: round trip time, such as NCPLD [204]; one way trip time, such as TCP-Spike [205]; interval of packets arrival, such as TCP-Biaz [206].

(2) Algorithms Based on Multiple Metrics

The aim of this kind of algorithm is to exploit the correlation of these metrics. In [207], the authors proposed a discriminator with four metrics, that are IDD (Inter Delay Difference), STT (Short Term Throughput), POR(Packet Out-of-order Rate), PLR(Packet Loss Rate). It could be a detailed discriminator, but the duration of value is difficult to determine.

(3)Algorithms Based on Inference

Since the network is dynamic, the more reasonable approach should be based on change of the metrics. If the change of metrics is modeled by learning from history, the model could be used as a predictor to infer from current measure. In Bayes_TCP [128], a HMM model of condition probability is built on RTT sample from events including congestion losses and wireless losses, and used to infer the current losses. Similarly, the authors proposed a fuzzy logic approach to detect the TCP errors and diagnose losses in [208]. In this kind of algorithms, extra cost must be taken on training the predictors.

However, packet dropping doesn't happen at the end point, so it is difficult to maintain accuracy of the end_to_end measurement in heterogeneous networks. Since the low layer will detect losses earlier, a BQM discriminator [209] is proposed based on loss pattern on routers, and it is easy to be deployed on the network. In this chapter, because BQM is unfit to dynamic network states, an Adaptive BQM (Biased Queue Management) is proposed to solve this problem. The aim is to keep the accuracy of loss differentiation as network state varying by adjusting parameters used to track loss pattern adaptively. The simulation results show that the performance of A_BQM is better than that of BQM under different states and it benefits TCP improving in wired-wireless hybrid networks.

9.2. ADAPTIVE BQM

9.2.1. BQM and its Problem

BQM (Biased Queue Management) is similar to diff_serv [210] but quite different in detailed technique. The main idea of BQM is that packets are marked *in* or *out* by the TCP sender. While buffer overflowing occurs in routers, packets marked *out* are dropped first with probability 1. Situations of congestion_induced loss and wireless_induced loss are given in Figure 9-1 [209].

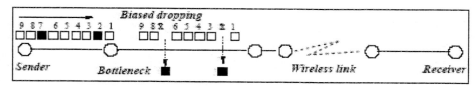

(A) Situation of congestion_induced loss

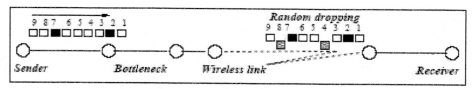

(B) Situation of wireless_induced loss

Figure 9-1. Illustration of BQM.

As shown in Figure 9-1, it is messages marked with "in, out" that are inject into a TCP connection, which every packet is marked with "*out*" after N packets. Under situation of congestion_induced loss, routers will drop packets marked with "*out*" because of its low priority. Under situation of wireless_induced loss, routers will drop packets randomly. So the exhibited fingerprint of loss pattern could be used to distinguish congestion losses from wireless losses.

In BQM, a pattern function is used to track the loss pattern on routers:

$$F(x,r,k) = 1 - \left\lfloor k \cdot \frac{x}{r} \right\rfloor \tag{9-1}$$

where x is the number of lost packets marked *out* and r is the number of losses within the ordered set at TCP receiver, k is a variable factor corresponding to mark intervals at TCP sender. If $F(x,r,k) > 0$, which implies few *out* packets is dropped, the losses are diagnosed as wireless losses and ACK is marked with ELN (Explicit Loss Notify) [211] to avoid decreasing the sending rate incorrectly. Using BQM in wired_wireless hybrid networks could eliminate the effect on wireless link and improve TCP performance to some degree.

The accuracy of BQM scheme may reach 1 only if the interval marking out, named *bias*, is less than *1/PC* (*PC*: congestion loss rate). So *bias* is crucial for BQM. For a special scenario in [209], a best value around 8 is suggested by simulations. Since a fixed *bias* is used in BQM, numbers and distribution of *out* packets is identical with various losses pattern.

Indeed, as wireless loss rate is becoming higher, out packets would be dropped together with other packets if there are no enough *out* packets in router buffer. As a result, there are some mistakes on partial wireless losses. Therefore, it seems reasonable to change bias with wireless loss rate, as well as bandwidth of bottleneck link. With the increasing of congestion losses, the number of out packets should be increased too. In conclusion, *bias* should be adjusted to be suitable for various loss patterns on routers.

9.2.2. Introduction of A_BQM

There are two key points in A_BQM, which can track losses pattern adaptively.

The first is what should be used to adjust the parameters *bias*? The ACK events are selected to trigger the change. *Bias* will be increased as three consecutive ACKs arrival which indicates a normal network, while decreased as three consecutive "DUPACKs corresponding to out packets arrival which indicates severe losses.

In simulations, AIMD is found to be the best for adjusting *bias* because it can adapt to the change of network states smoothly and efficiently. In addition, the adjustment should be within a range to assure the validity of A_BQM. The range is defined as [*min, max*], where *min* should be a reasonable decimal and *max* should be corresponding to the buffer size of TCP sender. In the following simulations, the value of *min* and *max* is set to 4 and buffersize/2 respectively.

The second is a simple probability statistics substituting the pattern function. Upon a disorder for a packet P, the receiver will judge that the loss is caused by congestion if the packet P is marked *out*. Otherwise the receiver will judge the loss as wireless losses and add the ELN flag to its ACK. As to multiple losses occurring in the same window of packets in flight, searching for lost packets will begin from the packet with lowest sequence number and stop as soon as a lost packet with *out* mark is found in the window. Then the consecutive loss will be diagnosed to be caused by congestion, otherwise it will be diagnosed to be caused by wireless errors.

A_BQM scheme is described in detail as following.

(1) TCP Sender

Firstly, TCP sender sets the value of interval *bias* according to ACK events. Then all packets are marked by the new *bias*. Its pseudo code is given in Figure 9-2.

At the arrival of ACK packet, TCP sender will check the ELN flag in ACK head. If its value is "1", TCP sender should retransmit the corresponding packet without halving the "*cwnd*" when it is a DUPACK. Otherwise, TCP is as normal as before. At the same time, TCP sender will refresh its ack[], which is used to count for 3 consecutive event. As shown in Fig 9-2(b), the mark interval "*bias*" will be adjusted according to these ACK events.

```
Recv(Packet *pkt)
{Update(in,out);  //adjust the value of Biasmax
 if (ELN=1) tcp_eln ; /
else dealing with it as Newreno;
if (elements of in[ ] are all with value "1")
cwnd=cwnd/2;
}


Output(int seqno)
// packets to be sent are marked with 0 (corresponding to out) with interval bias
{ if (a normal packet to be sent)
{ tcph->bias( )=bias;
   mark=(mark+1)%bias; }
else bias=biasmax;   //// retransmitted packet shouldn't be dropped firstly
}
```

(A) Pseudo code of transmission process

```
Update (in, out)
{if (Dupack) {if (pkt->bias()==out) out[i++]=1;
else ack[i++]=1;
if (being counted for 3 times)  reset in,out;
if (elements of out[i] are all with value "1")&&(bias>min)  biasmax=biasmax/2;
if (elements of ack[i] are all with value "1")&&(bias<max)  biasmax=biasmax+1;
return biasmax;
}
```

(B) Pseudo code of biasmax adjusting

Fig 9-2. pseudo code of TCP sender in A_BQM.

(2) Router

In router, if the buffer is overflowing, the packet will be dropped according to its marked flag.

```
Ack(Packet *pkt)
{ state=2;
if (seq > next) {
  for ( i=next; (i <= maxseen-1); i++) {
    if (seen[i & wndmask] == 0) {
      if (!(i%biasmax)) {state=1; break; }
  if (state>1) mark ELN in ACK with 1
  }
```

Figure 9-3. pseudo code of TCP receiver in A_BQM.

(3) TCP Receiver

The pseudo code is given in Figure 9-3, where *seq* is the sequence number arrived recently, *next* is the next expected sequence number, *maxseen* is the max sequence number seen so far within current window [*0...wndmask*].

At the arrival of packets in flight, TCP receiver will search these disorder packets in buffer. If there are packets with "out" flag, these losses will be identified as congestion induced. Otherwise, these losses will be identified as wireless induced. Subsequently, an ELN flag will be set and be feedback to TCP sender.

9.2.3. Analysis of A_BQM

It is premier for BQM to exploit the exhibited fingerprint of packet dropping through the pattern function, which is shown in (9-1).

While this pattern matching is substituted by the searching for *out* packet upon consecutive losses in A_BQM. Is the simple approach successful?

Assume that S is the total number of packets in ordered set $\{P_{nxt}, ..., P_{hi}\}$, in which the number of out packets is y. The marked sequence will be (the value of bias is b):

$$P^1_{nxt}, ..., P^{b-1}_{nxt+b-1}, P^0_{nxt+b}, P^1_{nxt+b+1}, ..., P^{b-1}_{nxt+2b-1}, P^0_{nxt+2b}, ...$$

That is :

$$P^{in}_{nxt}, ..., P^{in}_{nxt+b-1}, P^{out}_{nxt+b}, P^{in}_{nxt+b+1}, ..., P^{in}_{nxt+2b-1}, P^{out}_{nxt+2b}, ...$$

Suppose that r packets among S are lost as a cause of wireless error. The pattern of r losses should appear to be a result as a random sampling. Let X be a random variable representing the number of packets marked out within the S packets, then

$$p(X = x) = \frac{\binom{y}{x}\binom{r-x}{s-y}}{\binom{s}{r}} \tag{9-2}$$

In A_BQM scheme, $p(X = x) = \varepsilon$ is considered correct if $x \geq 1$. Proof for this hypothesis is as follows.

Let $x = 1$, its hypergeometric distribution should be:

$$P(X = 1) = \frac{\binom{y}{1}\binom{r-1}{s-y}}{\binom{s}{r}} = \frac{y*(r-1)!*r!*(s-r)!}{(s-y)!*(r-1-(s-y))!*s!} \tag{9-3}$$

where y is the number of "out" packets in S. If *bias* can be set to be an accurate interval, that is to say $r = y$, (9-3) can be rewritten as:

$$P(X = 1) = \frac{y*(y-1)!*y!*(s-y)!}{(s-y)!*(2y-1-s))!*s!} = \frac{y*(y-1)!*y!}{(2y-1-s))!*s!} \tag{9-4}$$

For an ideal process, all the *out* packets in A_BQM are dropped exactly, then $y = s*p$ (p is the loss rate). According to (9-4), it can be obtained:

$$P(X = 1) = \frac{s*p*(s*p-1)!*(s*p)!}{(s*(2p-1)-1)!*s!}$$

$$\approx (s*p)*\frac{(s*p)!}{(2*s*p))!}*\frac{(s*p)!}{s!}$$

$$= \frac{1}{2}*\frac{1}{(2*s*p-1)*...*(s*p+1)}*\frac{1}{s*(s-1)*...*(s*p+1)} \tag{9-5}$$

From (9-5), it can be concluded that $P(X=1)=0.5*P(X = 1) = 0.5*\varepsilon1*\varepsilon2$, where $\varepsilon1$ and $\varepsilon2$ are very small variables, which are corresponding to the last two parts of (9-5) respectively. For example, for a TCP connection with $s=10$ and $p=0.1$, $P(X=1)=0.14*10^{-6}$.

In short, the assumption: if $x \geq 1$, $p(X = x) = \varepsilon$ comes into existence for an ideal A_BQM scheme.

9.3. PERFORMANCE ANALYSIS

A_BQM algorithm is implemented in NS2 [173] and is compared with BQM. Figure 9-4 shows the topology used in the simulations. Two TCP flows labeled TCP1, TCP2 share the bottleneck link between R1 and R2. UDP0 is a crossing flow occupying 20% bandwidth of the bottleneck link. The last hop of TCP1 is wireless link, so TCP1 is mainly concerned in the section. The propagation delay of wired link is 2ms and that of wireless link is 10ms.

To evaluate discriminators, the following metrics are used:

$P[W|W']$: the probability of identifying wireless loss correctly, where W is the number of lost packets caused by wireless signal and W' is the number of packets that are correctly identified as wireless loss.

$P[C|C']$: the probability of identifying congestion loss correctly, where C is the number of lost packets caused by congestion and C' is the number of packets that are correctly identified as congestion loss.

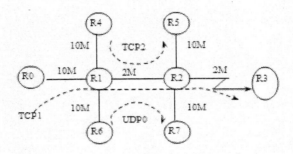

Figure 9-4. network topology.

9.3.1. Impact of Wireless Loss

Wireless loss model located between R2 and R3 is corresponding to the degree of wireless losses. In this section, loss rate is varying from 0.02 to 0.1. The accuracy of BQM and A_BQM are shown in Figure 9-5. As shown in Figure 9-5, $P[W|W']$ of BQM decreases distinctly with the increasing of wireless loss rate, while loss rate has much less impact on $P[C|C']$. In contrary, $P[C|C']$ and $P[W|W']$ of A_BQM both maintain highness in the same condition.

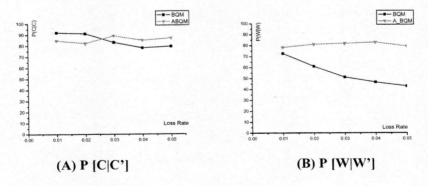

(A) P [C|C']   (B) P [W|W']

Figure 9-5. Impact of wireless loss on Accuracy.

9.3.2. Impact of Congestion Loss

Bandwidth of bottleneck within R1 and R2 is corresponding to congestion losses and changes from 1.5M to 0.4M. The experiment results plotted in Figure 9-6 show that accuracy of BQM decreases distinctly with the increasing of congestion loss, while the impact of congestion loss on $P[W|W']$ is less relatively. Instead, the impact on $P[C|C']$ and $P[W|W']$ of A_BQM is small and the two metrics of A_BQM keep high with varied bottleneck bandwidth.

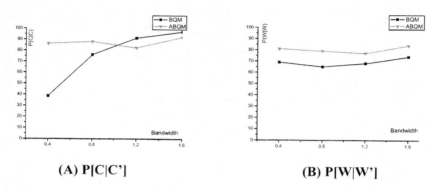

(A) P[C|C']   (B) P[W|W']

Figure 9-6. Impact of congestion loss on Accuracy.

9.3.3. Impact of Real Loss Model

The error in wireless transmission is caused by different phenomena, including path loss, fast fading, and noise from other devices. Thus the BER is not uniform. A more reasonable model that describes the bit error of wireless channel is the Gilbert-Elliot model, in which the process can be either one of the two states, namely the "good" state (its BER is 0.01) or the "bad" state (its BER is 0.07). The transition between the two states is modeled as a continuous-time Markov chain with probability P_{GB} and P_{BG}. With this real loss model, the accuracy of the two discriminators is depicted in Table 9-1. It is obvious that BQM with any fixed *bias* has much mistake because it is susceptibility to loss rate, whereas the improvement of A-BQM can be quite significant.

All these results lead to the conclusion that A_BQM is more adaptive to varied states of network and more robust under dynamic circumstance.

Table 9-1. Accuracy with Gilbert-Elliot Model

BQM			A_BQM	
Bias	P(C|C)	P(W|W)	P(C|C)	P(W|W)
8	76%	12.5%	91%	86.1%
20	38.8%	35%		
50	33.3%	68.8%		

9.4. CONCLUSION

In this chapter, an adaptive Loss Differentiation Algorithm based on queue management is proposed. This new approach makes the diagnosis by analyzing the loss pattern on routers. Since parameters in A_BQM are adjusted by ACK events, the characters of queue management could be captured more accurately. Therefore A_BQM scheme is of great flexibility and superiority.

It is remarkable that the unfairness problem between wired and wireless flow is prominent if TCP sender reduces its windows frequently as error bit occurring. Thus the flows traverse wireless link would be staved in the end. Therefore an adaptive Loss Differentiation Algorithm is significant for TCP improvement in wired_wireless hybrid networks.

Chapter 10

A PREDICTION-BASED AQM ALGORITHM FOR DIFFSERV NETWORKS

10.1. INTRODUCTION

Multimedia information is transported besides the data on the Internet with the development of multimedia technology. But it has different demand for quality of service, compared with the data. Therefore, traditional service of best effort can't provide the guarantee of QoS for the multimedia communication [212]. In order to meet the requirement of QoS for the applications about multimedia, IETF has proposed two different models: integrated services (IntServ) and differentiated services (DiffServ).

Resource ReSerVation Protocol (RSVP) [213], which provides the consultation policy of QoS, is used in IntServ where per node need keep the state information of per flow so that there is a problem of scalability. Later, RSVP for aggregation proposed in [214] mitigates the problem effectively, but doesn't solve it thoroughly.

DiffServ classifies the network nodes into boundary nodes and interior nodes. IP flows are classified and aggregated into different forwarding classes, marked with different levels of priority on the boundary node and dropped with different dropping mechanisms on the interior node according to the priority in the packet header [215]. Only by deploying the traffic conditioner on the boundary node, DiffServ can implement some simple services, such as premium service and assured service. There isn't problem of scalability in DiffServ because the interior node doesn't keep the state information of per flow. So DiffServ has become the preferred model for addressing QoS in the IP network.

Assured service provides statistical assurance for the committed information rate which is specified in the service level agreement and should be provided to the customer. Its basic idea is: the packet marking mechanism monitors and marks packets according to the committed information rate on the boundary node. If the measured flow conforms to the committed information rate, the packets belonging to this flow are marked with high priority (e.g., marked as IN) and receive assured service. Otherwise, the packet belonging to the non-conformant part of a flow are marked with low priority (e.g., marked as OUT) and received best effort service. The queue management mechanism, deployed on the core node, gives preferential treatment to high priority packets [216, 217].

RIO (Red with In or Out) [216] is an active queue management method in DiffServ, which is the extension of RED [22]. It is configured with two sets of parameters, one for IN packets (*min_in*, *max_in*, P_{max_in}) and another for OUT packets (*min_out*, *max_out*, P_{max_out}). The probability of dropping an IN packet depends on the average queue length for IN packets, and the probability of dropping an OUT packet depends on the average total queue length for all arriving packets (both IN and OUT). The choice of parameters meets the following specification: *min_out<min_in* and $P_{max\_out} > P_{max\_in}$. Generally *max_out≤min_in*, RIO drops IN packets after dropping all OUT packets when it detects persistent congestion and the objective is to protect IN packets better. There is also a problem that the queue length is unstable because RIO is the extension of RED. However, the stable queue length can keep high bandwidth utilization and predictable queuing delay. ARIO-D [218] is the improvement on RIO in under-subscribed network and provides the stabilized average queue length. In [218], the authors point out that the improvement of the stabilization of queue is at the cost of the increase of packet loss ratio in ARIO-D. ARIO-D will not take effect on stabilizing the queue length when the UDP flows exist in the network because the stabilization analysis of RIO is based on the TCP flows.

A prediction-based active queue management algorithm, named PIO, is proposed in this chapter by using the predicting traffic method, which is also used in the PFED algorithm [78]. It stabilizes the queue length at a desirable level whether the network is under-subscribed or over-subscribed on the basis of statistical assurance for the subscribed bandwidth. The PIO algorithm predicts the average arrival rate of IN packets and all packets. It decides whether or not to drop the arriving packet according to the queue length for IN packets or the total queue length for all packets, combined with the predicted arrival rate for IN packets or all packets in the next interval. The simulation results indicate that compared with the RIO, PIO not only improves the stabilization of the queue, but also reduces packet loss ratio and keeps high throughput.

10.2. PREDICTION OF ARRIVAL RATE

The most important step in PIO is how to predict the average arrival rate for IN packets and all packets in the next interval. The choice of predictor is a tradeoff between the prediction accuracy and computational overhead. Recently, a number of empirical studies have convincingly demonstrated that network traffic is long-range dependent (LRD) in nature [189] [191] and studies of real traffic traces indicate that the Hurst parameter rarely exceeds 0.85 (Hurst parameter is an indicator of LRD) [219]. Under this circumstance, the MMSE (Minimum Mean Square Error) predictor performs as accurately as FBM [186] or FARIMA [220] and has less computational overhead than them. Furthermore, studies in [191] show that the predictability of aggregate flows is better than that of single flow. In PIO, MMSE is used to predict the arrival rate for IN packets and all packets in aggregate flows, so the prediction accuracy of MMSE is good enough to be used in PIO. The following is the description of MMSE.

Let $\{X_t\}$ denote a linear stochastic process and suppose that the next value of $\{X_{t+1}\}$ can be expressed as a linear combination of the current and previous observations. That is:

$$X_{t+1} = WX' + \varepsilon_t \tag{10-1}$$

where $W = (w_m, w_{m-1}, ..., w_1)$, $X = (X_t, X_{t-1}, ..., X_{t-m+1})$, m is the order of regression.

Let $\hat{W}$ denote the estimated weight vector, and $\hat{X}_{t+1}$ denote the predicted value of X_{t+1}. While minimizing the mean square error, i.e., minimizing $E[e_t^2] = E[(X_{t+1} - \hat{X}_{t+1})^2]$, it can be obtained:

$$\hat{W} = [\rho_m \; \cdots \; \rho_1] \times \begin{bmatrix} \rho_0 & \rho_1 & \cdots & \rho_{m-1} \\ \rho_1 & \rho_0 & \cdots & \rho_{m-2} \\ \cdots & \cdots & \cdots & \cdots \\ \rho_{m-1} & \rho_{m-2} & \cdots & \rho_0 \end{bmatrix}^{-1} \tag{10-2}$$

where $\rho_k = \dfrac{1}{m} \sum_{t=k+1}^{m} X_t X_{t-k}$ [192].

The benefit of using MMSE is the simplicity of implementation. There are only some matrix manipulations that can readily be implemented in hardware and software at a very high speed. The detail of network traffic prediction is presented in [78].

10.3. PIO Algorithm

The PIO algorithm uses the predicted arrival rate in the next interval to calculate the probability of dropping the packet. If the current queue length for IN packets is below or equal to the threshold TH_{in}, the arriving IN packet is queued into the buffer to make the queue length near to TH_{in}. Otherwise, the PIO algorithm decides whether or not to drop the arriving IN packet according to the predicted arrival rate for IN packets, and controls the queue length near to the threshold TH_{in} by controlling the source sending rate. If the current total queue length for all packets is below or equal to the threshold TH, the arriving OUT packet is queued into the buffer to make the queue length near to TH. Otherwise, the PIO algorithm decides whether or not to drop the arriving OUT packet according to the predicted arrival rate for all packets. The pseudo code of PIO is given in Figure 10-1.

10.3.1. Calculating Drop Probability for IN Packet

In PIO, the predicted load factor for IN packets LF_{p-in} in the next interval is defined as the ratio of the predicted arrival rate for IN packets r_{p-in} in the next interval and service rate C (service rate is the link bandwidth). LF_{p-in} is

```
Upon receiving packet p:
if (interval>τ) {
calculate arrival rate in last interval;
use MMSE to predict arrival rate in next interval;
calculate LF_p-in with equation (10-3);
calculate LF_p-total with equation (10-5);
}
if (p is IN packet){
if(Q_L_in>Thin && LF_p-in>1){
if(LF_p-in<2){
calculate P_drop-in with equation (10-4);
drop the packet with probability P_drop-in;
}
else
    drop(p);
}
else
    enque (p);
}
else{
if(Q_L≤TH)
    enque(p);
else if(LF_p-in <u){
    if(LF_p-total<1)
        enque(p);
    else if(LF_p-total <2){
        calculate P_drop-out with equation (10-6);
        drop the packet with probability P_drop-out;
}
else
        drop(p);
}
else
        drop(p);
}
```

Figure 10-1. Pseudo code of PIO algorithm.

$$LF_{p-in} = \frac{r_{p-in}}{C} \qquad (10\text{-}3)$$

In PIO, the arrival rate for IN packets r_{in} is measured periodically (every τ time). PIO algorithm uses MMSE predictor described in Section 10.2 to predict the future arrival rate for IN packets r_{p-in} in the next interval, and calculates the load factor LF_{p-in} in the next interval according to (10-3).

If the current queue length for IN packets is below or equal to the threshold TH_{in}, the arriving IN packet is queued into the buffer. Otherwise, if the predicted load factor for IN packets LF_{p-in} in the next interval is smaller than 1 ($LF_{p-in} <1$), the arriving IN packet is also queued into the buffer; the arriving IN packet is dropped if the predicted load factor for IN packets LF_{p-in} in the next interval is larger than 2 ($LF_{p-in}>2$); the arriving IN packet is dropped with the probability $P_{drop-in}$ if the predicted load factor for IN packets LF_{p-in} in the next interval is between 1 and 2 ($2\geq LF_{p-in} \geq 1$). The probability $P_{drop-in}$ is

$$P_{drop-in} = \frac{LF_{p-in}}{2} \times \frac{Q_{L\_in}}{Q_S} = \frac{r_{p-in}}{2C} \times \frac{Q_{L\_in}}{Q_S} \qquad (10\text{-}4)$$

where Q_{L_in} is the current queue length for IN packets, Q_S is the queue buffer size.

If the predicted load factor for IN packets LF_{p-in} in the next interval is larger than 2 ($LF_{p-in} >2$), PIO enforces the TCP sources to decrease the sending rate by dropping all arriving IN packets in this interval directly with the objective of reducing the queue length to TH_{in}.

When the predicted load factor for IN packets LF_{p-in} in the next interval is between 1 and 2 ($2\geq LF_{p-in} \geq 1$), the larger the predicted arrival rate r_{p-in} in the next interval is, the larger the probability of dropping the arriving IN packet is. In this case, the objective is to make the queue length not far away from TH_{in} and the buffer not to overflow. The longer the current queue length Q_{L_in} for IN packets is, the larger the probability of dropping the arriving IN packet is, the objective is also to make the current queue length near to the threshold TH_{in}. Therefore, PIO calculates the drop probability by combining the predicted arrival rate r_{p-in} in the next interval with the current queue length Q_{L_in} for IN packets to keep the queue length stable.

10.3.2. Calculating Drop Probability for OUT Packet

In PIO, the predicted load factor for all packets $LF_{p-total}$ in the next interval is defined as the ratio of the predicted arrival rate for all packets $r_{p-total}$ in the next interval and service rate C (service rate is the link bandwidth). $LF_{p-total}$ is

$$LF_{p-total} = \frac{r_{p-total}}{C} \qquad (10\text{-}5)$$

MMSE predictor described in Section 10.2 is also used to predict the future arrival rate for all packets $r_{p-total}$ in the next interval. When the current queue length for all packets is above the threshold TH, the arriving OUT packet is dropped if the predicted load factor for IN packets LF_{p-in} in the next interval is larger than or equal to u ($LF_{p-in}\geq u$, u is constant). Otherwise, the PIO algorithm decides whether or not to drop the arriving OUT packet according to the predicted load factor for all packets $LF_{p-total}$ in the next interval.

The arriving OUT packet is queued into the buffer if the predicted load factor for all packets $LF_{p-total}$ in the next interval is smaller than 1 ($LF_{p-total} <1$); the arriving OUT packet is dropped if the predicted load factor for all packets $LF_{p-total}$ in the next interval is larger than 2 ($LF_{p-total} >2$); the arriving OUT packet is dropped with the probability $P_{drop-out}$ if the predicted load factor for all packets $LF_{p\text{-}total}$ in the next interval is between 1 and 2 ($2 \geq LF_{p\text{-}in} \geq 1$). The probability $P_{drop\text{-}out}$ is

$$P_{drop\text{-}out} = \frac{LF_{p\text{-}total}}{2} \times \frac{Q_L}{Q_S} = \frac{r_{p\text{-}total}}{2C} \times \frac{Q_L}{Q_S} \tag{10-6}$$

where Q_L is the current queue length, Q_S is the queue buffer size.

If the predicted load factor for IN packets $LF_{p\text{-}in}$ in the next interval is larger than or equal to u ($LF_{p\text{-}in} \geq u$), which indicates that an amount of IN packets will arrive in the next interval, OUT packets will be dropped directly to avoid tail drop of IN packets, which can assure the subscribed bandwidth. Dropping OUT packets will also make those flows that excess the committed information rate decrease the sending rate and make the queue length stable around TH.

If the predicted load factor for IN packets $LF_{p\text{-}in}$ in the next interval is smaller than u ($LF_{p\text{-}in} < u$), which indicates that the amount of OUT packets will arrive in the next interval, all OUT packets are still dropped, which may bring about the problem of global synchronization, unstable queue length and low throughput. Therefore, the PIO algorithm drops OUT packets with the probability calculated by combining the predicted arrival rate $r_{p\text{-}total}$ in the next interval with the current queue length Q_L for all packets to keep the queue length near to TH.

Large value of u indicates that OUT packets are also dropped with probability even though the arrival rate for IN packets is large, which brings about the drop of IN packets and can not assure the subscribed bandwidth and keep the queue length stabilized. So the value of u is set to 0.2 in PIO algorithm.

10.4. SIMULATION AND RESULTS

10.4.1. Simulation Scenario and Parameters

To verify its performances, PIO is implemented in NS2 [173] and compared with RIO. Due to the space limitation, only a small set of the simulations is given, which is the most representative.

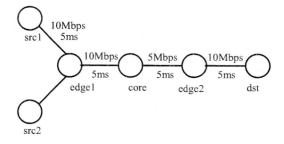

Figure 10-2. Simulation network topology.

The topology of the simulation is shown in Figure 10-2. *src1* and *src2* represent the senders, and *dst* represents the receiver. *edge1* and *edge2* are the ingress edge router and the egress edge router respectively, and *core* is the core router. The link between *core* and *edge2* is the bottleneck. The bandwidth and delay of every link is given in Figure 10-2. The marking algorithm TSW2CM is deployed on the edge router and the RIO and PIO algorithm are deployed on the core router respectively. The simulation time is 85 seconds.

The parameters of RIO and PIO are set in the following. The two sets of parameters for the RIO are (10, 20, 0.1) for OUT packets and (20, 40, 0.02) for IN packets. In PIO, measurement and prediction interval τ is set to 0.02, the threshold *TH* for OUT packets is set to 20 and the threshold TH_{in} is set to 40. Queue buffer size Q_S is set to 50 packets in all experiments.

10.4.2. Simulation Results and Analysis

PIO is compared against RIO with respect to the stabilization of queue, packet loss rate and attainable throughput. In this chapter, the performance of RIO and PIO are studied under the different subscription ratio when the number of connections is fixed and under the different number of connections when the subscription is fixed.

1) When 40 TCP connections are established and a UDP flow whose rate is 1M coexists in the network, PIO is compared against RIO with respect to instantaneous queue length under the different subscription ratio. Here, the simulation results are given in the under-scribed network (the subscription ratio is 10% and 60%), exactly-provisioned network (the subscription ratio is 100%) and over-subscribed network (the subscription ratio is 140%).

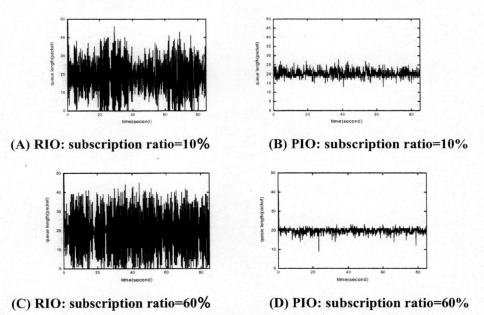

(A) RIO: subscription ratio=10%   (B) PIO: subscription ratio=10%

(C) RIO: subscription ratio=60%   (D) PIO: subscription ratio=60%

Figure 10-3. The instantaneous queue length in under-subscribed network.

Figure 10-3 shows the instantaneous queue length of RIO and PIO in under-subscribed network. Compared with RIO, PIO indeed keeps the queue length around *TH* and better stabilizes the queue. Figure 10-3(b) and Figure 10-3(d) show that the stabilization of the queue under 10% subscription ratios is worse than under 60% subscription ratio in PIO. This is because an amount of OUT packets exist in the network under 10% subscription ratio.

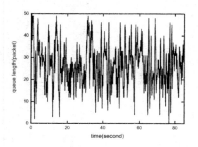
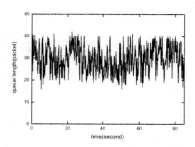

(A) RIO: subscription ratio=100%   **(B) PIO: subscription ratio=100%**

Figure 10-4. The instantaneous queue length in exactly-provisioned network.

Figure 10-4 shows the instantaneous queue length of RIO and PIO in exactly-provisioned network. The stabilization of the queue of RIO and PIO both become quite bad. This is because the network change from under-subscribed case to over-subscribed case and RIO and PIO have two sets of different parameters for IN packets and OUT packets. Figure 10-4(a) shows that the instantaneous queue length of RIO frequently oscillates between empty and full. Figure 10-4(b) shows that the instantaneous queue length of PIO oscillates between *TH* and TH_{in}.

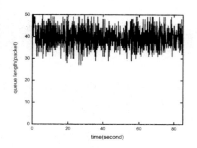
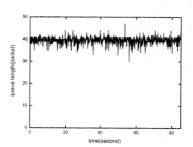

(A) RIO: subscription ratio=140%   **(B) PIO: subscription ratio=140%**

Figure 10-5. The instantaneous queue length in over-subscribed network.

Figure 10-5 shows the instantaneous queue length of RIO and PIO in over-subscribed network. Compared with RIO, PIO indeed keeps the queue length around TH_{in} and better stabilizes the queue.

2)   When 40 TCP connections are established and a UDP flow whose rate is 1M coexists in the network, PIO is compared against RIO with respect to the standard deviation

of the instantaneous queue length, packet loss ratio and attainable throughput under the different subscription ratio.

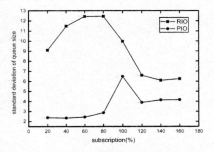

(A)The standard deviation of the instantaneous queue length

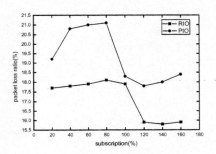

(B) Packet loss ratio

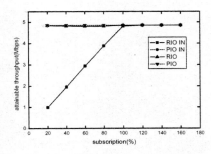

(C) Attainable throughput

Figure 10-6. Network performances with fixed connections.

Figure 10-6(a) shows the standard deviation of the instantaneous queue length of RIO and PIO. RIO performs quite poor with respect to the stabilization of queue in under-subscribed network. This is because RIO drops OUT packets with a large probability when the average queue length is smaller than max_{out} in under-subscribed network. The stabilization of queue becomes better in over-subscribed network, because there are almost IN packets in the buffer in over-subscribed network. PIO performs better than RIO with respect to the stabilization of queue whatever the subscription ratio is, especially in over-subscribed network. With 60% subscription ratio, the standard deviation of the instantaneous queue length of PIO is only 2.6, but the standard deviation of the instantaneous queue length of RIO reaches 12.5. It is evidenced in Figure 10-6(b) that PIO performs better than RIO with respect to packet loss ratio whatever the subscription ratio is. Figure 10-6(c) gives the attainable total throughput and IN throughput of RIO and PIO. It is obvious that the attainable throughput of both algorithms is very close and they also can provide guaranteed throughput for IN packets.

3) When the subscription ratio is 60% or 140%, PIO is compared against RIO with respect to the standard deviation of the instantaneous queue length, packet loss ratio and attainable throughput under the different number of connections.

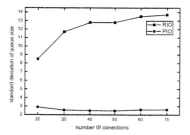

(A)The standard deviation of the instantaneous queue length

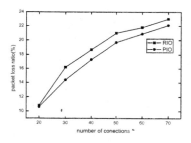

(B) Packet loss ratio

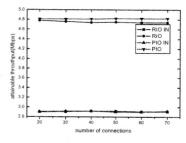

(C) Attainable throughput

Figure 10-7. Network performances with 60% subscription ratio.

Figure 10-7 shows the standard deviation of the instantaneous queue length, packet loss ratio and attainable throughput where the number of connections varies from 20 to 70 when the subscription ratio is 60%. Figure 10-7(a) shows the standard deviation of the instantaneous queue length. The stabilization of PIO queue becomes better and that of RIO becomes worse with the increase of the number of the connections. PIO always performs better than RIO with respect to the stabilization of queue. It is obvious in Figure 10-7(b) that the packet loss ratio of RIO and PIO becomes larger with the increase of the number of the connections and PIO always performs better than RIO with respect to packet loss ratio. Figure 10-7(c) shows the attainable total throughput and IN throughput of RIO and PIO. The attainable IN throughput performances are exactly the same and the attainable total throughput of PIO is slightly higher than that of RIO. Both RIO and PIO can provide guaranteed throughput for IN packets.

Figure 10-8 shows the standard deviation of the instantaneous queue length, packet loss ratio and attainable throughput where the number of connections varies from 20 to 70 when the subscription ratio is 140%. Figure 10-8(a) shows the standard deviation of the instantaneous queue length. When the number of the connection is little, RIO and PIO don't perform well with respect to the stabilization of queue, but the stabilization of queue of RIO and PIO becomes better with the increase of the number of the connections. PIO always performs better than RIO with respect to the stabilization of queue. It is obvious in Figure 10-8(b) that the packet loss ratio of RIO and PIO becomes larger with the increase of the number of the connections and PIO always performs better than RIO with respect to packet loss ratio. As shown in Figure 10-8(c), the attainable total throughput of RIO and PIO are very close, and IN throughput have the similar attribute with the total throughput.

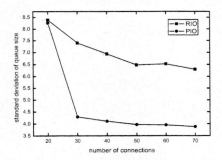

(A)The standard deviation of the instantaneous queue length

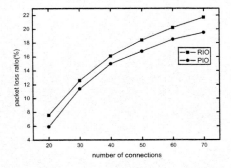

(B) Packet loss ratio

Figure 10-8 (continued).

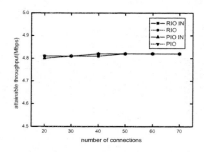

(C) Attainable throughput

Figure 10-8. Network performances with 140% subscription ratio.

10.5. CONCLUSION

RIO, which is an active queue management (AQM) in DiffServ, provides statistical assurance for the bandwidth, but can't keep the queue length stabilized and doesn't have low packet loss ratio. A prediction-based active queue management algorithm, named PIO, is proposed in this chapter, which improves the stabilization of queue and reduces the packet loss ratio efficiently by introducing the traffic predictability into queue management. Through the simulation, this chapter analyzes the PIO performance with respect to the stabilization of the queue, packet loss ratio and attainable throughput under different subscription ratio and different number of connections. The simulation results indicate that compared with RIO, PIO can improve the stabilization of queue reduces packet loss ratio efficiently and keep high throughput whether the network is under-subscribed or over-subscribed.

PART III. TCP in High Speed Network

ARROW-TCP: ACCELERATING TRANSMISSION TOWARD EFFICIENCY AND FAIRNESS FOR HIGH-SPEED NETWORKS

11.1. INTRODUCTION

The AIMD congestion control strategy that is employed by TCP is known to be encountered with scalability issues as the bandwidth-delay product grows exponentially in the recent decade. With rapid advances in the deployment of very high speed links in the Internet and growing requirements of huge volume of data to be transported over the high bandwidth-delay product networks, the need for a survivable replacement of TCP has grown more and more imperative.

Motivated by the inability of traditional TCP to accommodate the requirement of fast transmission, researchers proposed several novel transport protocols for accelerating transmission over high bandwidth-delay product networks. Based on their operation modes, they can be classified into end-to-end congestion control protocols (E2ECCPs), such as HSTCP [40], STCP [101], CUBIC [107], HTCP [108], FAST [44], Westwood [109], and many others, and distributed congestion control protocols (DCCPs), such as VCP [48], XCP [47], MaxNet [230], EMKC [50], RCP [93], JetMax [51], CLTCP [226], and so on. In the end-to-end mode, the network is regarded as a black box and the end takes the responsibility of congestion detection by perceiving packet loss event, monitoring the change of RTT, or estimating the available bandwidth. In a distributed mode, intermediate routers explicitly feed the network load information back to the sources. With the aid of the feedback, the source adjusts its sending rate or congestion window size in a more reasonable way.

From the point view of a control system, the performance of a congestion control protocol can be characterized by *stability*, *convergence*, and *transient behavior*. Recent advances in mathematical modeling of congestion control have stimulated the research on theoretic analysis of the stability of currently developed Internet congestion control protocols as well as the design of new protocols [221–223], [18], [225]. Unfortunately, whether these protocols are stable or not depends not only on the control parameters of the protocols but also on the network parameters, such as link capacity, feedback delays, and the number of active competing flows. Therefore, protocols are prone to be unstable if these parameters are not located in the region that satisfies stability criterions. With regards to the issue of convergence, it is usually depicted by two aspects: convergence to *efficiency* and convergence to *fairness* [224]. A protocol with fast convergence rate signifies that it can not only exploit available bandwidth efficiently but also share bottleneck resources as fair as possible with other competing flows. Another important requirement of congestion control protocols is transient behavior. Transient behavior deals with the procedure that a protocol transits from an arbitrary state to the steady state. Monotonic transitions between two states are more acceptable than oscillatory transitions since an oscillatory transition often leads to capacity overshooting and yields transient packet losses.

From the recent research works on performance evaluations of TCP variants, it seems that DCCPs exploit bandwidth more efficiently than E2ECCPs. However, existing DCCPs can exhibit different deficiencies in terms of stability and convergence. Suppose that the available bandwidth of a flow in a steady state is P. The AIMD algorithm converges linearly to efficiency and fairness within $O(P)$ time. VCP and EMKC only improve the convergence to efficiency from $O(P)$ to $O(\ln P)$. By using a logarithm function in the source algorithm to regulate the sending rate fast to the desired value, CLTCP improves the convergence to efficiency and the convergence to fairness to $O(\ln \ln P)$. XCP and RCP allocate the fair share of each flow directly and their convergence to efficiency and fairness is $O(1)$, i.e., constant convergence rate. As investigated in some research works [227-230], XCP and RCP can be unstable in multi-router networks and can not always achieve max-min fairness. In particular, the large initial overshoot of sending rate when new RCP flows join the network will induce the injection of a large number of packets into the network, which will occupy the router buffer immediately and result in many packet losses. JetMax achieves capacity-independent exponential convergence rate. However, in certain multi-router network scenarios, inconsistent bottleneck assignment will force the newly-starting JetMax flows to wait for a long time to increase their sending rate and also result in rate oscillations of other competing flows.

Motivated by the limitations of existing congestion control protocols, a new distributed congestion control protocol, called ARROW-TCP, is proposed based on explicit rate pre-assignment mechanism. Theoretical analysis and performance evaluations have demonstrated that ARROW-TCP achieves both strong stability and fast convergence to efficiency and fairness without introducing much excess traffic into networks in multi-router bottleneck scenarios. Moreover, the convergence rate is independent of link capacity. Since ARROW-TCP can monotonously converge to efficiency and fairness without too much burstiness, it does not rely on the router buffer size. Besides, ARROW-TCP obtains zero packet loss, zero queuing delay, and full link utilization in the steady state. In other words, it coincides with the router buffer management rationale: match rate, clear buffer as proposed in [27].

The rest of the chapter is organized as follows. Section 11.2 describes the notation used throughout the chapter. The high level illustration of ARROW-TCP protocol and the design guideline are shown in Section 11.3. Performance analysis about stability and convergence of ARROW-TCP are given in Section 11.4. Subsequently, the implementation details are discussed in Section 11.5 and the ARROW-TCP's performance through NS2 simulations is investigated in Section 11.6. Finally, the chapter is concluded in Section 11.7.

11.2. NOTATION

A communication network with a set $\mathcal{L} = \{1, \ldots, L\}$ of L links shared by a set $S = \{1, \ldots, S\}$ of S sources is considered in this chapter. For each link $l \in \mathcal{L}$, the index set of sources using link l is denoted by $S_l \subseteq S$. Equivalently, for each flow $r \in S$, its route involves a set of links, which is a subset of L, denoted by L_r. In order not to introduce too many redundant notations, $l \in \mathcal{L}$ is used to indicate the router which is associated with the egress link l. Also, $r \in S$ is used to denote the flow originated from source r. Further, the *bottlenecked flow* of link l is defined as this flow is really throttled by link l; otherwise, the flow is labeled *unbottlenecked flow* of link l. Let S_l^c be the set of *bottlenecked flows* of link l, and S_l^u be the set of *unbottlenecked flows* of link l.

For each source r, the following can be obtained:

- The congestion window wr (t) (in number of packets);
- The packet size sr (in bits);
- The RTT τr, which is the sum of the forward delay $\overrightarrow{\tau_{lr}}$ to its bottleneck link 1 ($r \in S_l^c$) and the backward delay $\overleftarrow{\tau_{lr}}$ from link 1, i.e., $\tau_r = \overrightarrow{\tau_{lr}} + \overleftarrow{\tau_{lr}}$;

The throughput xr (in bits/s).

- For each link l, the following can be obtained:
- The associated link capacity $C_l > 0$ (in bits/s);
- The target link utilization $\gamma_l \leq 1$;
- The number of its *bottlenecked flows* N_l;
- The aggregate rate y_l (in bits/s) of all sources which use link l;
- The aggregate rate of its *unbottlenecked flows* u_l;
- The fair rate g_l which is the desired amount of resource shared by link l's *bottlenecked flows*;
- The price p_l, used to indicate its *bottlenecked flows* the link congestion level.

11.3. DESIGN RATIONALE

In this section, a high level illustration of ARROW-TCP is given for the comprehension of the overall architecture.

ARROW-TCP is a window-based protocol whose goal is to maintain stability and achieve max-min resource allocation in multi-bottleneck networks. However, the window is not the amount of data segment to be sent in a RTT timescale but it is the amount of data segment to be sent in a constant control interval. In ARROW-TCP, the sources and routers operate in the same control interval to update their congestion window and calculate their fair rate, respectively. Like XCP, ARROW-TCP provides a joint design of source and router algorithms.

11.3.1. Source Algorithm

For the convenience of design and upgrading asynchronously, the control mechanism in the source is separated into three components, i.e., *window control, burstiness control*, and *bottleneck membership management*. The window control component is responsible for the updating of congestion window in a time interval and the burstiness control component smoothes out transmission of packets in fluid-like manner. The bottleneck switch and confirmation are governed by the bottleneck membership management. This section mainly concentrates on the design of window control and burstiness control components and the bottleneck membership management component is left to Section 11.5 which deals with the implementation of ARROW-TCP.

(1) Window Control

Source r uses the feedback from its bottleneck link l to update its congestion window. The evolution of the congestion window through time is described by the following differential control law:

$$\dot{w}_r(t) = \alpha_r \left[w_r^*(t - \tau_{lr}^{\leftarrow}) - w_r(t - \tau_r) \right] \tag{11-1}$$

where α_r is a control gain and w_r^* is the desired optimal sending window that relies on the fair rate g_l from source r's bottleneck link l. ARROW-TCP is named from the equation, where ARROW stands for "*AcceleRating tRansmission towards Optimal Window size.*" From Eq. (11-1), the change rate of current window size is related to the past window size one RTT ahead and the fair rate from bottleneck link l which is delayed with $\tau_{lr}^{\leftarrow}$. When the resource is underutilized, as in early stages of window growth, it functions as an efficiency controller by encouraging the users to increase their congestion windows. Otherwise, it functions as a fairness controller by forcing the users to reduce their congestion window to the optimal window size. Finally, fair resource allocation is achieved in the steady state. Suppose the packet size in source r is s_r, and let Δ denote the window updating period, the optimal window size is calculated from the fair rate g_l as follow:

$$w_r^*(t) = \frac{g_l(t) * \Delta}{s_r} \tag{11-2}$$

For a digital implementation of the window control law, the time-continuous system need be converted into time-discrete system by using sampling technique. by using the aforementioned period Δ as the sample interval, the discrete window control law can be obtained as follow:

$$w_r(k+1) = w_r(k) + \beta_r \left[w_r^*(k - d_{lr}^{\leftarrow}) - w_r(k - d_r) \right] \qquad (11\text{-}3)$$

where, $\beta_r = \Delta \cdot \alpha_r$ is a control gain, $d_{lr}^{\leftarrow} = \tau_{lr}^{\leftarrow} / \Delta$ represents the number of intervals from the bottleneck link l to the source r, and $d_r = \tau_r / \Delta$ is the number of intervals in a round trip time. Thus, sources update their congestion windows periodically with an interval of Δ.

(2) Burstiness Control

Many researchers have observed that the burstiness nature of traditional TCP in sub-RTT timescale can lead to large traffic oscillation with the negative impact on network efficiency. Pacing mechanism has been proposed to counteract these effects by spacing the data packet evenly over an entire round trip time, so that the data are not sent in a burst. Pacing has been quantitatively evaluated in many research works that demonstrate that paced TCP offers better fairness, higher throughput and lower packet loss rates than unpaced TCP [143], [231].

In ARROW-TCP, sources do not send all data packets into the network immediately after updating congestion window but space all data packets evenly over the window control interval Δ. Therefore, the inter-packet interval δ_r is calculated as:

$$\delta_r(k) = \frac{\Delta}{w_r(k)} \qquad (11\text{-}4)$$

Different from the variation property of RTT, Δ is a preconfigured constant, so that pacing in ARROW-TCP is quite simple.

11.3.2. Router Algorithm

The major task of ARROW-TCP router is to compute the fair rate for its bottlenecked flows. The main idea of computing fair rate is to divide the residual bandwidth $\gamma_l C_l - u_l(k)$ equally among all bottlenecked flows. Like source, the router also periodically computes the fair rate $g_l(k)$ in the same time interval:

$$g_l(k) = \frac{\gamma_l C_l - u_l(k)}{N_l(k)} \qquad (11\text{-}5)$$

In order to compute the fair rate, the router should know the number of its bottlenecked flows, $N_l(k)$, and the combined rate of the *unbottlenecked flows*, $u_l(k)$. These two issues are left to Section 11.5.

In addition to the fair rate allocation, routers should assist sources for bottleneck membership management. The bottleneck of a source may shift from link l_i to l_j ($l_i, l_j \in \mathcal{L}_r$, $i \neq j$) due to the arrival/departure of other flows. To fulfill this purpose, routers use link price to manage bottleneck switch. This section only discussed the concept of link price and the bottleneck switch is left to Section 11.5. The link price p_l is calculated based on the combined rate:

$$p_l(k) = \frac{y_l(k) - \gamma_l C_l}{y_l(k)} \tag{11-6}$$

From Eq. (11-6), it can be seen that link price p_l is an increasing function of combined rate y_l and ranges from $-\infty$ to 1. In other words, network load increases with link price. $p_l(k) <$ 0 indicates that the link l is under-utilized and users can properly increase their sending rate. Contrarily, $p_l(k) > 0$ implies that the combined rate is larger than the service rate and queue will be built up. Users should reduce their sending rates. Resources are fully utilized when $p_l(k) = 0$ and users can keep their sending rate in equilibrium.

11.4. PERFORMANCE ANALYSIS

This section starts by deriving stability criterion of ARROW TCP. Subsequently, it performs the analysis of transient behavior of ARROW-TCP. Then it conducts convergence analysis and concludes that ARROW-TCP can obtain exponential convergence rate and converge to efficiency and converge to fairness in a constant time.

11.4.1. Stability Analysis

The stationary window size of each flow has the following lemma.

Lemma 1: Given that flow r is bottlenecked by a link l of capacity C_l together with $N_l - 1$ other flows, its stationary sending window is $\hat{w}_r = w_r^* = (\gamma_l C_l - \hat{u}_l) \cdot \Delta / (N_l \cdot s_r)$, where $\hat{u}_l$ is the combined steady-state rate of all *unbottlenecked flows* at link l.

Proof: In the steady state, the fair rate of link l is $\hat{g}_l = (\gamma_l C_l - \hat{u}_l) / N_l$ and the desired window size of source r is w_r^*. From Eq. (11-3), it is can be obtained that $w_r(k+1) = w_r(k) = w_r(k - d_r) - w_r^*$ in steady state for source r. Therefore, the stationary window size of source r is w_r^*. Furthermore, the stationary window size of source r is $\hat{w}_r = w_r^* = \hat{g}_l \cdot \Delta / s_r = (\gamma_l C_l - \hat{u}_l) \cdot \Delta / (N_l \cdot s_r)$.

The stability of ARROW-TCP is determined by the control gain β_r. The following shows that asymptotic stability of source r, β_r is only related to d_r.

Taking the z-transform of source r's window update Eq. (11-3) yields:

$$\left(z^{d_r+1} - z^{d_r} + \beta_r\right) W_r(z) = \beta_r z^{\vec{d_{lr}}} W_r^*(z) \tag{11-7}$$

where, $W_r(z)$ and $W_r^*(z)$ are the z-transforms of $w_r(k)$ and $w_r^*(k)$, respectively. Eq. (11-7) results in the transfer function

$$H_r(z) = \frac{N_r(z)}{D_r(z)} = \frac{W_r(z)}{W_r^*(z)} = \frac{\beta_r z^{\overrightarrow{d_{lr}}}}{z^{d_r+1} - z^{d_r} + \beta_r} \tag{11-8}$$

The stability of the window control is determined by analyzing the roots of the denominator $D_r(z)$, which gives the characteristic equation

$$D_r(z) = z^{d_r+1} - z^{d_r} + \beta_r = 0 \tag{11-9}$$

A necessary and sufficient condition for source r to be asymptotically stable is that the roots of the characteristic Eq. (11-9) lie inside the unit circle in z space. i.e., for any root $z_i \in \{z \mid z^{d_r+1} - z^{d_r} + \beta_r = 0\}$, $|z_i| < 1$. The location of these roots relative to the unit circle can be determined by using a bilinear transformation $v = (z+1)/(z-1)$ and then applying the Routh-Hurwitz stability criterion [174] to the transformed equation. The bilinear transformation of the complex variable z into the new complex variable v transforms the interior and the exterior of the unit circle in the z-plane onto the open left half and open right half of the v-plane, respectively. After the bilinear transformation, the stability of a time-discrete system with characteristic Eq. (11-9) can be determined by examining the locations of the roots of

$$\hat{D}_r(v) = D_r(z)\Big|_{z=\frac{v+1}{v-1}} = (v+1)^{d_r+1} - (v+1)^{d_r}(v-1) + \beta_r'(v-1)^{d_r+1} = 0 \tag{11-10}$$

in the v-plane. Therefore, the asymptotic stability of source r can be determined by examining whether all the roots of Eq. (11-10) lie in the open left half of the v-plane by applying Routh-Hurwitz stability criterion. The stable region of β_r obtained by Routh-Hurwitz stability criterion is given in Theorem 1.

Theorem 1: Under any consistent bottleneck assignment that does not change over time, source r is asymptotically stable and converges to its stationary window size w_r^* if and only if

$$\beta_r \leq \overline{\beta}_r \approx 2.0052/(1.1369d_r + 0.9970).$$

Proof: The local stability of flow r is determined by the control gain β_r. Moreover, the stability region of β_r can be obtained by applying Routh-Hurwitz stability criteria on Eq. (11-10). Collecting terms in powers of $(v+1)^{d_r}$ and $(v-1)^{d_r+1}$ of Eq. (11-10), the following equation can be obtained:

$$\hat{D}_r(v) = \beta_r(v-1)^{d_r+1} + 2(v+1)^{d_r} = 0 \tag{11-11}$$

Using the binomial expansion, and further collecting terms in power of v yield

$$\hat{D}_r(v) = \sum_{k=0}^{d_r+1} \frac{d_r!}{k!(d_r+1-k)!} \left[2k + (-1)^k (d_r+1)\beta_r \right] v^{d_r+1-k} = 0 \tag{11-12}$$

The roots of this polynomial equation must lie in the open left-half v-plane for stability. Aweya et al. [232] examine the location of the roots by enumerating the upper bound of β_r for different d_r using Routh-Hurwitz stability criterion. Take $d_r = 3$ for example, the Routh array becomes

v^4	β_r	$6+6\beta_r$	$2+\beta_r$
v^3	$2-4\beta_r$	$6-4\beta_r$	
v^2	$\dfrac{(2-4\beta_r)(6+6\beta_r)-\beta_r(6-4\beta_r)}{2-4\beta_r}$	$2+\beta_r$	
v^1	$\dfrac{((2-4\beta_r)(6+6\beta_r)-\beta_r(6-4\beta_r))(6-4\beta_r)-(2-4\beta_r)^2(2+\beta_r)}{(2-4\beta_r)(6+6\beta_r)-\beta_r(6-4\beta_r)}$		
v^0	$2+\beta_r$		

The Routh-Hurwitz stability criterion requires that no changes should be in sign in the first column in the Routh array for a stability system. Since β_r is a positive parameter, the system will be stable if $0 < \beta_r < 0.4450$. The upper bound of β_r with $d_r = 3$ is determined by row 4 (corresponding to row v^1) in the Routh array. By examining the upper bound of β_r for different d_r, Aweya et al. [232] arrive at the following observations:

For $d_r = 1$, the upper bound of β_r is prescribed by the entry in row $(d_r + 1)$, i.e., row v^1, in the first column of Routh array.

A close approximation to the upper on β_r for different d_r is given by the first entry in row 2 of the respective Routh array, i.e.,

$$\bar{\beta}_r(d_r) \approx \beta_r^{row2}(d_r) = \frac{2}{d_r+1} \tag{11-13}$$

This is more clearly seen by referring to Table 11-1 where both the upper bound on β_r and the approximation obtained from row 2 is tabulated for various values of d_r.

In [232], Aweya et al. only tabulate the upper bounds of β_r by varying d_r from 0 to 7. Motivated by the observation that the difference between $\bar{\beta}_r(d_r)$ and $\beta_r^{row2}(d_r)$ is approximately 0.05 when $d_r \leq 7$, they further make a closer approximation of $\bar{\beta}_r(d_r)$ as follow

$$\bar{\beta}_r(d_r) = \frac{2}{d_r + 1} - 0.05$$

$$(11\text{-}14)$$

Table 11-1. The upper bound on β_r vs d_r

d_r	$\beta_r^{row2}(d_r)$	$\bar{\beta}_r(d_r)$	d_r	$\beta_r^{row2}(d_r)$	$\bar{\beta}_r(d_r)$
0	2.0000	2.0000	9	0.2000	0.1652
1	1.0000	1.0000	10	0.1818	0.1495
2	0.6667	0.6180	11	0.1667	0.1365
3	0.5000	0.4450	12	0.1538	0.1256
4	0.4000	0.3473	13	0.1429	0.1163
5	0.3333	0.2846	14	0.1333	0.1083
6	0.2857	0.2411	15	0.1250	0.1013
7	0.2500	0.2086	16	0.1176	0.0952
8	0.2222	0.1845			

However, approximation equation (11-14) will yield negative upper bound of β_r for $d_r \geq$ 40. The upper bound of β_r is further examined by varying d_r up to 16. As shown in Table 11-1, the difference between $\bar{\beta}_r(d_r)$ and $\beta_r^{row2}(d_r)$ decreases as d_r increases. So another proper approximation for the upper bound of β_r should be considered. Noting that $\beta_r^{row2}(d_r)$ can approximate $\bar{\beta}_r(d_r)$ with smaller and smaller difference as d_r increases, the following approximation is used:

$$\bar{\beta}_r(d_r) = \frac{\sigma_1}{\sigma_2 d_r + \sigma_3}$$

$$(11\text{-}15)$$

where, σ_1, σ_2, and σ_3 are the unknown parameters to be determined. By using the approach of curve fitting with LSM (Least Square Method), the following approximation can be obtained for $\bar{\beta}_r(d_r)$:

$$\bar{\beta}_r(d_r) \approx \frac{2.0052}{1.1369 d_r + 0.9970}$$

$$(11\text{-}16)$$

According to the above stability analysis, we can obtain Theorem 1.

Finally, under any consistent bottleneck assignment, ARROW-TCP is globally stable if each source r ($r \in S$) converges to its own stationary window size w_r^*.

Theorem 2: Under any consistent bottleneck assignment that does not change over time, ARROW-TCP is globally stable if each source r ($r \in S$) is locally asymptotically stable.

Proof: From Lemma 2 in [51], it can be obtained that at least one router has no *bottlenecked flows* under any consistent bottleneck assignment when link price is computed as Eq. (11-6). Since bottlenecks do not shift over time, without loss of generality, assume that the set $L_c = \{1, 2,\dots,L_c\}$ of L_c links have *bottlenecked flows*, where $L_c \subset L$ and $L_c < L$. Since each flow has only one bottleneck link, the set S can be partitioned into L_c separated subsets $(S_1 \cup S_2 \cup \dots \cup S_{Lc} = S$ where $S_i \cap S_j = \varnothing$ for any $S_i, S_j \subset S)$ and subset S_i contains a set of link i's bottlenecked flows. For any link l ($l \in L_c$) shared by a set S_l^c of *bottlenecked flows*, if each source in S_l^c is locally asymptotically stable, then link l is fully utilized. Since l is an arbitrarily selected link from L_c, it can be concluded that ARROW-TCP is globally stable if each source r ($r \in S$) is locally asymptotically stable.

Theorem 2 reveals that if each source r follows Theorem 1, then ARROW-TCP is globally stable.

11.4.2. Transient Behavior

To investigate the transient behavior of ARROW-TCP, a single-source single-link network with equivalent capacity of 10 000/Δ packets/s is examined. So the index of the source can be dropped in subsequent analysis. In particular, assume the round trip time $\tau = 10\Delta$. Let $\beta = \lambda /(1.1369d + 0.9970)$, $\lambda = 1.4$, 1.0, 0.6, and 0.4 are chosen respectively to examine the window evolution trajectory, which is presented in Figure 11-1.

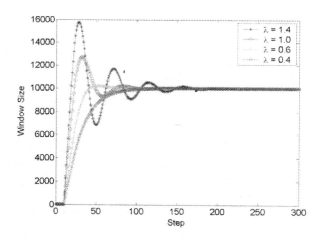

Figure 11-1. Window size dynamics vs. different configuration of β, where $\beta = \lambda /(1.1369d + 0.9970)$, by setting $\lambda = 1.4$, 1.0, 0.6, and 0.4, respectively.

Figure 11-1 illustrates that the transient behavior of the window dynamic is affected significantly by different configuration of β. When β is large, the window size reaches stationary value much faster but shows more oscillating transients. For a smaller β, the window size reaches stationary value slowly and has smaller oscillating transients. For example, when $\lambda = 1.4$, the source initially overshoots the link capacity by 60% and then converges to the stationary value with decaying oscillations. As λ decreases, the initial overshoot descends and the settling time to steady state reduces, indicating less extra load introduced into the network. In ideal congestion control, sources should avoid overshooting the link capacity in case the router buffer is rapidly occupied by surges of packets and so that large transient packet losses occur. As a result, it is important to find the right value of β that a reasonable tradeoff between fast convergence rate and stable control of window dynamics can be achieved. Extensive numerical simulations are conducted with wide range of RTT varying from 1~2000Δ. The simulation results demonstrate that the window size monotonically converges to the stationary value when $\lambda \leq 0.5$. Therefore, the best tradeoff seems occur at $\lambda = 0.5$ since a bit larger λ can result in an initial overshoot of link capacity and a smaller λ can slow convergence rate to the steady state. This guideline of parameter configuration right coincides with the design objective — "free packet loss, zero queuing delay."

11.4.3. Capacity-Independent Exponential Convergence to Efficiency and Fairness

Under any consistent bottleneck assignment that does not change over time, ARROW-TCP converges to efficiency and fairness exponentially fast, and the convergence rate is independent of link capacity, i.e., ARROW-TCP achieves constant convergence rate for each source. Without loss of generality, the analysis can focus on a single link that is shared by N sources since every two links with bottlenecked flows are independent of each other. In the analysis, assume the N sources are homogeneous and they are with the same feedback delay d.

(1) Convergence to Efficiency

Firstly, the following definition about efficiency is given.

Definition 1 ((1 − ε)-efficiency): For a given small positive constant ε ($0 \leq \varepsilon < 1$), the system converges to $(1 - \varepsilon)$-efficiency in $k_e(\varepsilon)$ steps if the system starts with $y(0) = 0$ and $k_e(\varepsilon)$ is the smallest integer satisfying

$$\forall k \geq k_e(\varepsilon): \frac{\gamma C - y(k)}{\gamma C} \leq \varepsilon \tag{11-17}$$

Theorem 3: Under any consistent bottleneck assignment that does not change over time, ARROW-TCP converges to $(1-\varepsilon)$-efficiency exponentially and the convergence rate is independent of link capacity.

Proof: Consider an arbitrary link shared with N homogeneous bottlenecked flows with the same feedback delay d. Since all flows share the same bottleneck link and behave in a synchronized mode, the index for each flow can be dropped. Denote $x(k) = w(k)*s/\Delta$ as the sending rate of each flow. Window update equation (11-3) can be converted into rate update equation as follow:

$$x(k+1) = x(k) + \beta\left[x^* - x(k-d)\right] \tag{11-18}$$

Taking the summation of (11-18) for all N flows, it can be gotten that the combined rate $y(k) = \sum_{i=1}^{N} x_i(k)$ forms a delayed linear system:

$$y(k+1) = y(k) + \beta[\gamma C - y(k-d)] \tag{11-19}$$

Further, denoting $u(k) = (\gamma C - y(k))/\gamma C$, and so the initial value $u(0) = u(1) = \ldots = u(d) = 1$. According to Definition 1, the objective is equivalent to proving that $u(k)$ can converges to zero exponentially. Eq. (11-19) can be further written as:

$$u(k+d+1) - u(k+d) + \beta u(k) = 0 \tag{11-20}$$

Taking the z-transform of (11-20), it can be obtained

$$\left[z^{d+1}U(z) + z^{d+1}u(0) + \cdots + zu(d)\right] - \left[z^d U(z) + z^d u(0) + \cdots + zu(d-1)\right] + \beta U(z) = 0. \tag{11-21}$$

Substituting $u(0) = u(1) = \cdots = u(d) = 1$ into above equation, it can be obtained:

$$U(z) = \frac{z^{d+1}}{z^{d+1} - z^d + \beta}$$

In previous subsection, the stability has been analyzed. The system is stable if and only if all roots of equation $z^{d+1} - z^d + \beta = 0$ lie inside the unit circle, i.e., $\forall i \in \{1, 2, \ldots, d+1\}$, $|z_i| < 1$. Therefore, $U(z)$ can be expressed as

$$U(z) = \frac{z^{d+1}}{(z-z_1)(z-z_2)\cdots(z-z_{d+1})} = \frac{m_1 z}{z-z_1} + \frac{m_2 z}{z-z_2} + \ldots + \frac{m_{d+1} z}{z-z_{d+1}} \tag{11-22}$$

where, m_i are coefficients to be determined and $\sum_{i=1}^{d+1} m_i = 1$. Using

$$\lim_{z \to z_i}(z - z_i)U(z) = \frac{z_i^{d+1}}{(z_i - z_1)\cdots(z_i - z_{i-1})(z_i - z_{i+1})\cdots(z_i - z_{d+1})} = m_i z_i$$

the undetermined coefficients m_i can be calculated as

$$m_i = \frac{z_i^d}{\prod\limits_{j=1, j \neq i}^{d+1} (z_i - z_j)}.$$

Taking the invert z-transform of Eq. (11-22), the following equation can be obtain:

$$u(k) = m_1 z_1^k + m_2 z_2^k + \ldots + m_{d+1} z_{d+1}^k \qquad (11\text{-}23)$$

Since $|z_i| < 1$, each component $m_i z_i^k$ in Eq. (11-23) approaches to zero exponentially. Moreover, the convergence rate of $u(k)$, i.e., $k_u(\varepsilon)$, is dependent in the roots z_i and independent of link capacity. Furthermore, it can be concluded that $k_u(\varepsilon)$ is determined by the delay d and the control gain β.

Theorem 3 indicates that each ARROW-TCP source converges to $(1 - \varepsilon)$-efficiency within a constant time and the convergence time is related to the RTT value. More specifically, the convergence time is determined by d, the number of control intervals in a round trip time.

(2) Convergence to Fairness

Firstly, the definition of fairness is given.

Definition 2 ((1 − ε) -fairness): For a given small positive constant ε $(0 \leq \varepsilon < 1)$, $(1 - \varepsilon)$ - fairness is reached in $k_f(\varepsilon)$ steps if the system starts in the maximally unfair state and $k_f(\varepsilon)$ is the smallest integer satisfying

$$\forall k \geq k_f(\varepsilon) : \frac{\left| x_r(k) - x_r^* \right|}{x_r^*} \leq \varepsilon, \forall r \in S \qquad (11\text{-}24)$$

Theorem 4: Under any consistent bottleneck assignment that does not change over time, ARROW-TCP converges to $(1-\varepsilon)$-fairness exponentially and the convergence rate is independent of link capacity.

Proof: Consider the case where a new flow joins the network after other $N - 1$ flows consuming all link capacity. The proof for Theorem 4 shows much similarity to that of Theorem 3. For each source r, let $e_r(k) = (|x_r(k) - x_r^*|)/x_r^*$, the same equation as Eq. (11-20) can be obtained. According to the derivation in Theorem 3, the conclusion of Theorem 4 can be gotten. Here, the detailed proof is omitted.

From the above analysis, ARROW-TCP converges to $(1 - \varepsilon)$-efficiency and $(1 - \varepsilon)$-fairness in the same time. The convergence time is determined by d, i.e., the ratio of RTT/Δ. To make a quantitative analysis of the convergence time, a set of numerical computations are conducted for convergence time to $(1 - \varepsilon)$-efficiency and $(1 - \varepsilon)$-fairness with $\varepsilon = 0.02$ and $\beta = \lambda/(1.1369d + 0.9970)$ ($\lambda = 0.4, 0.45,$ and 0.5, respectively) by varying the ratio of RTT/Δ from 1 to 20. The convergence time is measured in the number of RTT. The result is shown in Figure 11-2. From Figure 11-2, it can be seen that the convergence time is decreased with λ and the ratio of RTT/Δ. With the increase of the ratio of RTT/Δ, the system converging to (1

$- \varepsilon$)-efficiency and $(1 - \varepsilon)$-fairness requires less number of RTT, which will benefit long-distance flows.

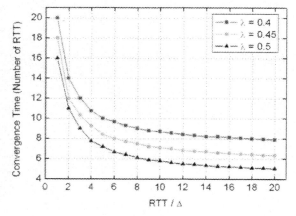

Figure 11-2. Convergence time of ARROW-TCP.

11.5. IMPLEMENTATION

This section discusses the implementation in detail, which includes the design of packet header format, calculating the number of bottlenecked flows, eliminating transient packet loss, and bottleneck link management.

11.5.1. Packet Header Format

The header format of an ARROW-TCP packet is illustrated in Figure 11-3. The *Window Size* field carries current window size of a source. A router calculates the number of bottlenecked flows by summing up the reciprocal value of the window size if the incoming packet belongs to its bottlenecked flows (see Eq. (11-26)). Otherwise, the combined rate of *unbottlenecked flows* is computed by averaging the aggregate window size of the *unbottlenecked flows* on the time interval Δ. Thereby, the fair rate can be achieved according to Eq. (11-5), which is assigned in the *Fair Rate* field in the packet header and carried back to source by ACK packet, then, the source updates its window size according to Eq. (11-3). The usage of other fields in the header is illustrated in subsequent sections.

R_T	R_C	R_S	Unused
Link Price: p_l			
Fair Rate: g_l			
Proposed Size: s_r^+		Flags	
Window Size: w_r			
←————————— 32 bits —————————→			

Figure 11-3. Format of ARROW-TCP packet header.

11.5.2. Calculating the Number of bottlenecked Flows

The first important issue to be addressed is how to calculate the number of bottlenecked flows for each link, which directly affects the allocation of network resources. Without loss of generality, assume link l is shared with a set S_l^c of bottlenecked flows. Figure 11-4 is used to illustrate the notation of calculating the number of bottlenecked flows.

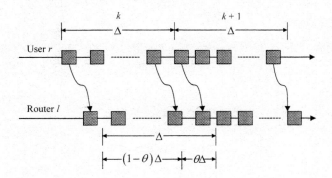

Figure 11-4. Illustration of calculation of the number of bottlenecked flows.

For a given flow r, the start packet and end packet in an interval Δ of router l generally belongs to the kth and $(k + 1)^{st}$ control interval of source r, respectively. Recall that sources and routers operate in the same control interval Δ. The router control interval can be partitioned into two segments, that is $(1 - \theta)\Delta$ and $\theta\Delta$, which are illustrated in Figure 11-4, where $\theta < 1$ is a positive fraction, and packets in the first segment of $(1 - \theta)\Delta$ are from the kth control interval and packets in the remain $\theta\Delta$ time are from the $(k+1)^{st}$ control interval. Since packets are sent in a fluidlike manner with inter-packet interval calculated by Eq. (11-4), the number of packets from source r in $(1 - \theta)\Delta$ and $\theta\Delta$ time in router l are $(1 - \theta)w_r(k)$ and $\theta w_r(k+1)$, respectively. Therefore, we have

$$\sum_{i=1}^{(1-\theta)w_r(k)} \frac{1}{w_r(k)} + \sum_{j=1}^{\theta w_r(k+1)} \frac{1}{w_r(k+1)} = 1 \tag{11-25}$$

Generalizing the case to all N_l bottlenecked flows bottlenecked by link l, it can be gotten

$$\sum_{r \in S_l^c} \left(\sum_{i=1}^{(1-\theta)w_r(k)} \frac{1}{w_r(k)} + \sum_{j=1}^{\theta w_r(k+1)} \frac{1}{w_r(k+1)} \right) = N_l \tag{11-26}$$

Eq. (11-26) indicates that the number of bottlenecked flows in link l can be figured out by taking the summation of the reciprocal value of the window size of all incoming packets belonging to its bottlenecked flows in a control interval Δ.

11.5.3. Eliminating Transient Packet Loss

Considering such a case that the RTT of flow r is much larger than that of flow s, and that flow s joins in the network after flow r saturates the bottleneck link. In that case, if flow s increases its window size immediately after starting, the link capacity will be certainly overshot, which thereafter leads to burst of packet losses in transient time because flow r can not release the resource quickly enough due to the large communication delay. In this chapter this issue is addressed by employing the similar approach in JetMax, called "Propose-Approve" approach.

Assuming that flow r starts to increase its window size from w_r to w_r^+, it keeps the sending window size of w_r and notifies to routers with the proposed window size of w_r^+. The proposal will be approved if the combined proposed rate does not overshoot the capacity of flow r's bottleneck link and will be rejected otherwise.

This "Propose-Approve" approach can be easily realized in practical system. The total proposed traffic of flow r to be sent in the next control interval is $s_r w_r^+(k)$. However, flow r practically sends $w_r(k)$ packets in current control interval. Therefore, flow r can convey its proposed window size to the router by including a virtual packet size s_r^+ in the *Proposed Size* field in each header such that

$$s_r^+ = s_r \frac{w_r^+(k)}{w_r(k)} \tag{11-27}$$

The router can approximate the combined proposed rate $y_l^+(k)$ by adding up the virtual packet sizes and normalizing them by the control interval Δ, that is

$$y_l^+(k) = \frac{\sum_{r \in S_l} \sum_{i=1}^{w_r(k)} s_r^+}{\Delta} \tag{11-28}$$

The bottleneck link approves or declines the proposed rate at the end of its control interval Δ based on whether $y_l^+(k)$ is greater than $\gamma_l C_l$ or not. The approval/decline decision is carried by a bit in the Flags field in packet header.

11.5.4. Bottleneck Membership Management

The bottleneck membership management in ARROW-TCP is on the basis of that in JetMax with an extension of bottleneck confirmation mechanism. In the packet header, three 8-bit router-ID fields are allocated: R_T, R_C, and R_S. All IDs are in terms of hop count from the source. The R_T field records the router ID of the true bottleneck link for each flow; the R_C field carries the hop number of the packet and increases by each router; and the R_S field contains the router ID that is modified by the routers which perceive their congestion level to be higher than that experienced by the flow at the preceding routers. The detailed description of the bottleneck membership management is depicted as follows.

Upon each packet arrival, router l increases R_C by one and then checks which case of the following is satisfied:

1) The local link price $p_l(k)$ of router l is greater than the one carried in the *Link Price* field;
2) The local fair rate $g_l(k)$ of router l is less than that carried in the *Fair Rate* field when both the local link price $p_l(k)$ and the one carried in the packet are zero.

If either case is true, the router overwrites the *Link Price* field and *Fair Rate* field in the packet header and sets the R_S field to the value of R_C field obtained from the header. At the source, if the suggested router ID R_S carried in the ACK packet is different from the true bottleneck ID R_T, the source notices that a bottleneck switch is suggested and indicates a switch to R_S.

Besides that, a bottleneck confirmation mechanism is provided. Source will respond to the bottleneck switch suggestion only if both cases in the following are satisfied:

1) The previous bottleneck switch suggestion has elapsed at least 5Δ time when source receives a new bottleneck switch suggestion;
2) Current sending rate is not less than the fair rate carried in the arrival ACK packet.

Case (1) can largely reduce the number of inconsistent bottleneck switch suggestions, and transient false suggestions are eliminated in case (2). An experiment is used to validate the effectiveness of the bottleneck confirmation mechanism. The simulation topology is shown in Figure 11-5(a) and each link is with 20 ms delay. Flows 1-4 initially start at $t = 0$ second, and flow 5 joins at $t = 50$ second. The simulation results are shown in Figure 11-5(b) and Figure 11-5(c). In this experiment, it can be observed that the value of R_S field in JetMax flow 5 frequently changes between link 1, 2, 3, and 4 for approximately 20 seconds, which results in the starvation of flow 5 for a long time. Without bottleneck confirmation mechanism, JetMax flow 5 first finds the true bottleneck, i.e., link 4, and thereafter flow 4 also bottlenecked by link 4 will release its bandwidth to flow 5. However, after that the link price in link 4 will be less than that in other links and flow 5 will switch its bottleneck to other links subsequently. This inconsistent bottleneck switch will occur irregularly among link 1 through link 4 and finally will fix in link 4 after approximately 20 seconds. ARROW-TCP, however, effectively eliminates the inconsistent bottleneck switch and converges to fair allocation as soon as possible because of the introduction of bottleneck confirmation mechanism.

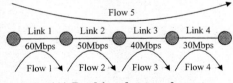

(A) Parking-lot topology

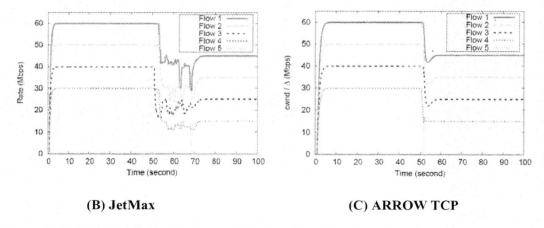

(B) JetMax   **(C) ARROW TCP**

Figure 11-5. Validation of the effectiveness of bottleneck confirmation mechanism.

11.6. SIMULATION

The performance of ARROW-TCP is validated in NS2 simulator [173], meanwhile XCP and RCP are selected for the purpose of comparison. For XCP and RCP, the parameters suggested in their original papers are used, i.e., $\alpha = 0.4$, $\beta = 0.226$ in XCP, $\alpha = 0.4$, $\beta = 1.0$ in RCP. For ARROWTCP, the parameter , for tuning the control parameter β is set to be 0.4. Unless stated elsewhere, packet size is 1000 bytes, the bottleneck link capacity in dumbbell topology is configured with 100 Mbps, and the buffer size is 1 Mbytes (approximately 1000 packets).

Experiment 1: Transient Behavior in the Presence of Burst Traffic under Dumbbell Topology

The convergence and transient behavior of the protocols are examined in the presence of burst traffic under dumbbell topology in this experiment. Flow 1 with RTT of 400 ms starts at $t = 0$ second, and additional 9 flows with RTT of 10 ms join together at $t = 50$ seconds. The simulation runtime is 100 seconds.

Figure 11-6 presents per-flow throughput of each flow and the total throughput of all flows. Note that the Y-axis of RCP is on a logarithmic scale because of its high capacity overshoot. The stability of XCP is related with RTT, as a result, XCP exhibits unstable throughput trajectory. The total sending rate of RCP overshoots link capacity by approximately 9 times which will certainly result in surge of packet losses in transient time. The reason is that RCP source directly applies feedback and flow 1 with long RTT, however, does not release its consumed bandwidth quickly enough after other flows join the network. ARROW-TCP can eliminate capacity overshooting by virtual of the employment of "Propose-Approve" approach which forces those flows which want to increase their sending rates to be approved by the intermediate routers.

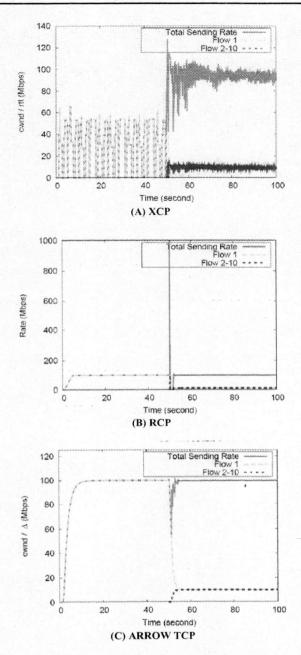

Figure 11-6. Experiment 1: Transient behavior in the presence of burst traffic under dumbbell topology.

Experiment 2: Stability in the Presence of Mice Flows under Dumbbell Topology

In this experiment, we investigate the stability of elephant flows which are affected by the random arrival/departure mice flows and examine the metric of packet loss rate. Flow 1 with RTT of 400 ms and flow 2 with RTT of 100 ms start transmission at $t = 0$ second and $t = 10$ seconds, respectively. From $t = 20$ seconds, 300 mice flows join. The inter-arrival time of mice flows follows an exponential distribution with mean value of 0.8 seconds and the duration of each flow is drawn from a log-normal distribution with mean value of 1.2 seconds.

The simulation runtime is 200 seconds. The number of active flows at any instant time is plotted in Figure 11-7(a). The simulation results, as shown in Figure 11-7, show that RCP and XCP suffer in packet losses, measured every 100 ms, in the presence of random mice flows. Although RCP exhibits stable control of sending rate, as the result of capacity overshooting, it leads to burst of packet losses which can be as high as 40%. The packet loss rate of XCP is even higher than that of RCP in most of times due to its inability to stabilize the window evolutions. ARROW-TCP obtains satisfactory stability and the two elephant flows can converge to the same throughput trajectory. Moreover, we do not observe packet losses for ARROW-TCP in the whole simulation runtime.

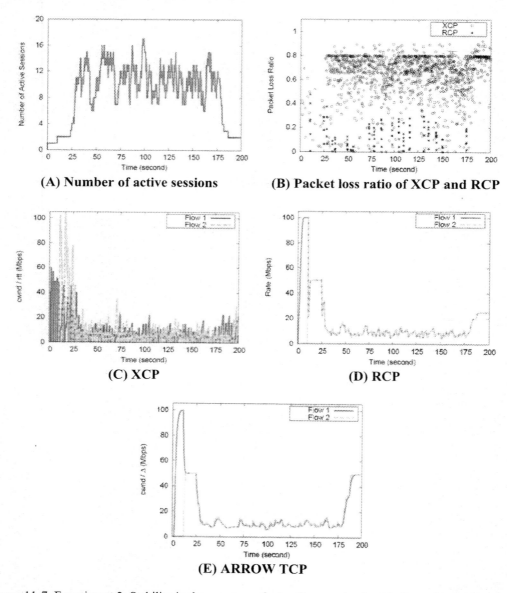

Figure 11-7. Experiment 2: Stability in the presence of mice flows under dumbbell topology.

Experiment 3: Stability and Max-Min Fair Allocation under Branch Topology

Linear topology has been considered as one of the multibottleneck network scenarios in Figure 11-5(a). In this experiment, the stability and fair allocation are tested in another multi-bottleneck scenario, i.e., branch topology shown in Figure 11-8(a). To reduce the transient packet losses, the router buffer size is set to be sufficient large (at least equals to 1 BDP). Flow 1 with RTT of 202 ms initially starts at $t = 0$ second, and flows 2-9 with same RTT of 2 ms start transmission after 50 seconds. The simulation results are shown in Figure 11-8. As the throughput trajectories of flow 2-9 are almost overlapped each other in both RCP and ARROW-TCP, the same line type is used to illustrate their throughput evolutions. From Figure 11-8, it can be seen clearly that XCP and RCP are inclined to instability after flows 2-9 join the network. The reason is that XCP and RCP are locally stable and their stability criterions are derived in the assumption that all flows are with the same bounded delay. As a result, XCP and RCP overshoot the link capacity in a different extent, queue will be built up and the average RTT computed by router may not reflect the correct delay of flows that are being controlled by the router, which adds up the adverse impact on their stability. ARROW-TCP obtains stable control of window evolutions and achieves max-min fairness by exploiting the useful bottleneck membership management. Although the bottlenecks of ARROW-TCP flows 2-9 initially switch to link 1, with the increasing of their sending rate, their bottlenecks will quickly shift to link 2 and hold the right bottleneck assignment for each flow.

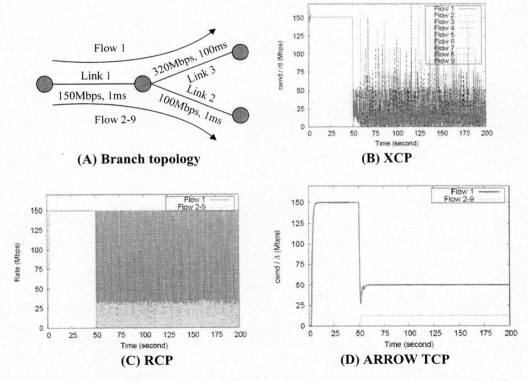

(A) Branch topology **(B) XCP**

(C) RCP **(D) ARROW TCP**

Figure 11-8. Experiment 3: Stability and max-min fair allocation under branch topology.

11.7. CONCLUSION

In this chapter, a novel distributed congestion control protocol, named ARROW-TCP, is developed based on the explicit rate assignment. ARROW-TCP consists of source algorithm and router algorithm, which are the key mechanism for the stability and convergence. Each source utilizes the fair rate calculated by its bottleneck router to update the window size and employs link price to manage bottleneck membership. Theoretical analysis and simulation demonstrate that ARROW-TCP achieves exponentially convergence to efficiency and fairness. Moreover, ARROW-TCP outperforms XCP and RCP in terms of stability in multi-bottleneck link topology scenarios. Meanwhile, ARROW-TCP avoids the capacity overshooting behavior and obtains the ideal performance of zero queueing delay and free packet loss.

Chapter 12

TCP CONGESTION CONTROL PROTOCOL BASED ON COOPERATION MODE IN HIGH BANDWIDTH-DELAY PRODUCT NETWORKS

12.1. INTRODUCTION

TCP is a reliable data transfer protocol used widely over the Internet for numerous applications, since it was proposed in 1980s [3]. The TCP congestion control mechanism has been evolving over time from TCP Tahoe to NewReno that is used widely in realistic networks. But with the development of the gigabit networks, wireless networks, wireless sensor networks and satellite networks, the traditional TCP faces a number of new challenges. Especially, TCP congestion control mechanism has been shown to be a limit factor for the effective utilization over emerging high Bandwidth-Delay Product networks. In these network environments, with the increase of the bandwidth and delay, the traditional TCP protocol itself becomes the bottleneck of the performance.

TCP increases its congestion window by AIMD mechanism. But in high BDP networks, the mechanism limits the link bandwidth utilization [40]. For example, over 83,333/2 RTTs are required for TCP to increase its window from half utilization to full utilization of 10Gbps with 1500-byte packets, approximately 1 hour with 100 ms RTT. This requires that no packet is to be lost within 1 hour. In other words, it means, the number of lost packets cannot be more than 1 per 2,600,000,000 packets, which is less than the theoretical limit of the network's bit error rates [41]. In traditional networks, TCP also has undesirable fairness properties when flows with different RTTs are competing over a shared link. But in high BDP networks, this problem becomes more serious and the RTT bias is enlarged.

In the last few years several high speed protocols have been proposed [134]. According to the methods of adjusting congestion windows, they can be broadly classified into three categories: purely loss-based congestion avoidance algorithms, e.g. HSTCP [40], BIC-TCP [41], CUBIC [107], STCP [101], H-TCP [108], Compound TCP [120], delay-based congestion avoidance algorithms, e.g. Astart [45], FAST TCP [89], YeAH-TCP [233], TCP-Fusion [234] and ECN-like feedback algorithms, such as AECN [88] and XCP [47], EMKC [50], JetMax [51]. Although these protocols can increase the utilization of link bandwidth in high BDP networks, they also bring some other limitations as stated below:

(1) Low TCP-friendliness

Any new protocol to be deployed which dominates either the myriad of existing Reno flows will not find acceptance due to the Internet's philosophy of providing best effort for all. In this scenario, how to improve the throughput of new protocol flow effectively while not decreasing the bandwidth of traditional TCP flow dramatically is an essential factor for TCP enhancement. Some protocols such as HSTCP, BIC-TCP have a significant effect on the throughput achieved by the traditional TCP flow, which starve the Reno flows. This phenomenon can be found in the simulations shown in Section 12.3.

(2) Severe RTT unfairness

The average throughput ratio of two flows is roughly inversely proportional to their RTT. Competing flows with different RTTs may consume vastly unfair bandwidth shares. Existing schemes, (e.g. HSTCP, STCP) have a severe RTT unfairness problem because the increasing rate of congestion window gets larger with the growth of congestion window [41].

(3) Losing Packet Frequently

While it is good for protocols to quickly reach nearly full capacity after a congestion event, actually reaching full capacity will also quickly induce the next congestion event. So at one time the new protocols enhanced the link utilization, they also increased the packet drop rates, just like HSTCP [40].

(4) Reflecting Network Events Ineffectively

How to detect the congestion events quickly and effectively in high BDP networks is an important problem for TCP enhancement. Some protocols, such as Tahoe and NewReno, just use the packet loss signal to judge the occurrence of congestion. But research results show that the loss event is only a weak signal for reflecting the networks state in high BDP networks [45, 42]. To deal with the problem, some modified protocols, such as Astart and Fast TCP, attempt to control the send-window of TCP sender based on RTT measurements. However, recent studies [117, 85] have shown that there is little correlation between increased delays and congestive losses, and indicated that noise in RTT samples leads to degraded throughput by guiding TCP to reduce window at wrong times (when there is no loss). The detection method using delay signals is also not exact in some scenarios. Moreover, delay-based algorithms are proved that they are not competitive to loss-based protocols in some scenario [235]. On the other side, explicit rates feedback could also detect the congestion of networks, just like XCP. However, these schemes are hard to deploy in nowaday Internet as they require a non-trivial number of bits, which are not available in the IP headers, to encode the rate.

In this chapter, a novel TCP congestion control protocol based on cooperation mode (CCP) is proposed. CCP just uses 1 bit routers' explicit feedback predicted information and RTT delay signals to adjust the congestion windows appropriately. It can efficiently improve the bandwidth utilization, TCP-friendliness and RTT fairness in High BDP Networks.

The rest of the chapter is organized as follows. Section 12.2 describes the congestion control algorithm in detailed. Section 12.3 discusses and analyzes the simulation results. Finally, concluding remarks for this chapter are presented in Section 12.4.

12.2. THE COOPERANT CONGESTION CONTROL PROTOCOL

In order to detect the occurrence of congestion, CCP uses 1 bit routers' explicit feedback predicted information and RTT delay signals, which can help CCP to adjust the congestion windows appropriately.

CCP provides a joint design of end-systems and routers. CCP sender computes the RTT of the whole path by monitoring the ACK packets. Then according to RTT information, the sender estimates the RTT congestion state and keeps it in CCP sender's buffer. On the other side, CCP router computes the traffic rates of a certain interval and uses a predictor to predict the future traffic rates in the next interval. Then depending on this predicted traffic rates and export link bandwidth, CCP router calculates the load factor in the next interval and also keeps it in the head of sending packets. During packet transmitting, each router computes a network path state with its own load factor information and the original information in head of packets by using an "OR" operation. In the following, router replaces with the new network path state into the head of transmitting packets. When the packet arrived at the destination, the network path state is piggybacked to the sender by ACK packet. Finally, by the combination of RTT and network path state information, CCP sender gets four cases which reflect four kinds of networks congestion states. Based on these four states, CCP senders adopt appropriate rules for adjusting congestion window to improve the efficiency and reliability of networks. There are five key aspects that need to be addressed in the design of CCP.

12.2.1. Congestion State Relativity of Network Path

How to detect the network congestion events effectively in high BDP networks is an important issue for TCP enhancement. The whole network is made up by a lot of end-to-end network transmitting paths. So CCP protocol adopts the congestion state of path as the basis of adjusting the congestion window. The relativity of network path congestion state is analyzed in the following.

In next τ interval, the predicted load factor LF_i of any node i in end-to-end path is:

$$LF_i = \frac{r_i}{C_i}$$

(12-1)

where r_i is the predicted arrival rates in the next interval and C_i is the bandwidth of export link. The value of LF_P is the maximum of the all nodes' predicted load factor in this path $P=\{1,2,\ldots\ldots,i,\ldots,m\}$.

$$LF_P = \max\{LF_i \mid i \in P\} = \max\left(\frac{r_i}{C_i} \mid i \in P\right)$$

The sum of data packets QL_{CP} for Connection C in all routers' queue in path P is:

$$QL_{CP} = \sum_{i=1}^{m} \tilde{q}_i$$

where $\tilde{q}_i$ is the estimated number of queueing packets in router i.

LF_P reflects the predicted congestion state of bottleneck nodes in the whole path, which is determined by the connections sharing path P. Nevertheless QL_{CP} mostly considers the congestion state of a single connection in the path which is determined by the sending rate of only one connection. Due to the complexity of networks, a novel congestion control protocol should consider not only the global load states by all connections but also the fair bandwidth sharing of a single flow in order to treat the congestion fairly. They are not an independent process but a constrained and coactive behavior.

So the global factor LF_P and local factor QL_{CP} are considered together to determine the congestion state CS_P in path P, which can be described as follows,

$$CS_P = f(LF_P, QL_{CP}) = f\{\max(\frac{r_i}{C_i} \mid i \in P), \sum_{i=1}^{m} \tilde{q}_i\} \qquad (12\text{-}2)$$

In CCP protocol, according to the two path congestion information LF_P and QL_{CP}, the protocol estimates the network congestion state, and then adjusts the congestion window appropriately. In the following, two congestion detecting methods are introduced in detail.

12.2.2. The Delay Metric

For CCP sender, the value of QL_{CP} means the variance of RTT delay detected by the sender. So in CCP protocol, the sender uses the RTT delay metric to estimate congestion states of network path. The estimation is based on the TCP Vegas algorithm [42] which uses the following formula:

$$QL_{CP} = \sum_{i=1}^{m} \tilde{q}_i \approx \frac{cwnd * (sRTT - baseRTT)}{sRTT} \qquad (12\text{-}3)$$

where $sRTT$ is the exponentially smoothed high accuracy RTT estimate kept by the CCP sender and $baseRTT$ is the minimal RTT kept by the flow, which is roughly equal to the path propagation delay. The quantity $(sRTT-baseRTT)$ gives an estimate of the queueing delay of the network. Since CCP maintains an average sending rate of $cwnd/sRTT$ packets per second, $cwnd*(sRTT-baseRTT)/sRTT$ is an estimate of the number of packets that the protocol currently has in the congestive route's queue.

CCP uses S_1 to keep the congestion state which is obtained by the delay metric. The threshold α determines how sensitive the protocol is to delay signals. When QL_{cp} is large than α, which means the sending rate is so aggressive that cause the extra queue in the bottleneck router, $S_1=1$. On the contrary, the sending rate is conservative and S_1 value is set to 0. α is set to 3 in TCP Vegas. According to above analysis, it can be obtained that:

$$\begin{cases} S_1 = 1 & QL_{CP} \geq \alpha \\ S_1 = 0 & QL_{CP} < \alpha \end{cases}$$

12.2.3. 1 Bit Explicit Congestion Feedback

On the other hand, in CCP protocol, each router computes a load factor and uses this factor to classify the level of load into two regions: low-load and high-load. The router encodes the level of load in the ECN [236] bits of packet head.

The load information used in CCP is the load factor which is defined as the ratio of periodically measured arrival rates and service rates (service rates is the link bandwidth). Firstly, the arrival rate is measured periodically (every τ ms time). Then a predictor is used to predict the future arrival rates in the next interval. So the load factor in the next interval can be calculated.

The predicted load factor LF_i in router i is calculated by using (12-1). According to the LF_i and a threshold β, the state of flag S_2 can be gotten as following, which shows the load of router by using 1 bit. If $LF_i > \beta$, then $S_2=1$, else $S_2=0$. In a word, it can be described as:

$$\begin{cases} S_2 = 1 & LF_i > \beta \\ S_2 = 0 & LF_i \leq \beta \end{cases}$$

The mechanism of conveying S_2 state value from the router to the sender is similar to the ECN mechanism [236].During packet transmission, each router computes a network path state with its own load factor information and original information in head of packets by using an "OR" operation. In the following, router replaces the load factor information with the new network path state into the head of transmitting packets. When the packet arrived at the destination, the network path state is piggybacked to the sender by ACK packet.

In the detection of congestion, the most important task is to predict the arrival rates in the next interval. To select a good predictor, two criteria have to be considered: one is the accuracy of the predictor and the other is the simplicity of the predictor, because the predictor will be run online. Finally MMSE is selected as the predictor of CCP path routers. A detail description of MMSE is given in the following subsection.

12.2.4. The Traffic Predictor

A number of recent empirical studies of traffic measurements from a variety of working packet networks have convincingly demonstrated that network traffic is self-similar or long-range dependent (LRD) in nature [189, 191]. Considering the LRD nature of network traffic, the best traffic predictors are FBM [186] and FARIMA [187]. Unfortunately, FBM and FARIMA include lots of complex calculation, so they are improper for online predictions.

Recently, studies of real traffic traces indicate that the Hurst parameter rarely exceeds 0.85 (Hurst parameter is an indicator of LRD) [189, 191]. Under this circumstance, the MMSE predictor shows performance as good as FBM or FARIMA.

The following is the description of MMSE.

Let $\{X_t\}$ denote a linear stochastic process and suppose that the next value of $\{X_{t+1}\}$ can be expressed as a linear combination of the current and previous observations. That is:

$$X_{t+1} = WX' + \varepsilon_t$$

where,

$$W = (w_m, w_{m-1}, ..., w_1)$$
$$X = (X_t, X_{t-1}, ..., X_{t-m+1})$$

m is the order of regression.

Let $\hat{W}$ denotes the estimated weight vector, and $\hat{X}_{t+1}$ denote the predicted value of X_{t+1}. While minimizing the mean square error, i.e., minimizing $E[e_t^2] = E[(X_{t+1} - \hat{X}_{t+1})^2]$, it is can be obtained:

$$\hat{W} = [\rho_m \quad \cdots \quad \rho_1] \times \begin{bmatrix} \rho_0 & \rho_1 & \cdots & \rho_{m-1} \\ \rho_1 & \rho_0 & \cdots & \rho_{m-2} \\ \cdots & \cdots & \cdots & \cdots \\ \rho_{m-1} & \rho_{m-2} & \cdots & \rho_0 \end{bmatrix}^{-1}$$

where, $\rho_k = \dfrac{1}{m} \sum_{t=k+1}^{m} X_t X_{t-k}$

The benefit of using MMSE is the simplicity of implementation. There are only some matrix manipulations that can readily be implemented in hardware and software at a very high speed. So the MMSE is chosen for estimating the load factor in CCP protocol to detect the congestion states of routers. The detail of network traffic prediction is presented in [78].

12.2.5. Updating Window Rules

In CCP protocol, the updating rules of congestion window are divided into *"slow-start"* and *"fast-comeback"* two modes. In *slow-start* mode, CCP employs a response function that matches TCP-Reno's behavior, i.e. increasing the congestion window by 1MSS/RTT. During data transmission, if the CCP flow suffers a loss event, the protocol enters the *fast-comeback* mode.

Table 12-1. CCP Congestion Window Change Rules during *fast-comeback*

S_1	S_2	Network state	Window rules
0	0	Low load	w=w*k
0	1	High load, but this problem is not cause by this flow	w=w+1
1	0	Low load, but this flow sending rate is too high	w=w+1/w
1	1	High load, congestive	w=w-1

In *fast-comeback* mode, according to the description in subsection *12.2.2* and *12.2.3*, the CCP sender can get two state values S_1 and S_2. By the combination of S_1 and S_2, four cases can be gotten. The four cases according to different S_1 and S_2 can reflect four kinds of networks congestion states. Based on these four states, CCP senders adopt appropriate updating rules of congestion windows. The updating window rules are shown in Table 12-1, where w is the size of congestion window and k is a constant, which is set to 1.01. Furthermore, when packet loss occurred, the congestion window reduces it by half.

The updating rule of CCP congestion window is shown in Figure 12-1.

```
The fast-comeback mode
Receiving acknowledgement packet p
if p return a drop information
the congestion window W=W/2;
else {
if (S₁ = 1) {
if (S₂ =1) W=W-1;
else W=W+1/W;
} else {
if (S₂ =1) W=W+1;
else  W=W*k;
}
}
```

Figure 12-1. Pseudo code of CCP updating rule during *fast-comeback*.

Figure 12-2 gives a closer look at dynamic *cwnd* of CCP. CCP consists of four kinds of congestion window adjusting phases during *"fast-comeback"* mode. Thus, CCP sender can adjust appropriate *cwnd* according to the network state, especially as *cwnd* approaches the limit of bandwidth. This prevents the temporary queue from building up too fast, and thus, prevents a sender from overflowing router's buffer. From Figure 12-2, it is clear that *cwnd* increase in CCP follows is a smooth fluctuant curve when it is close to the limit of bandwidth.

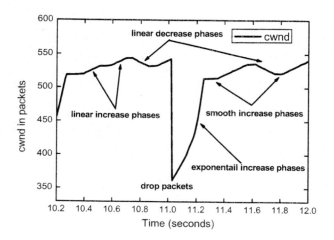

Figure 12-2. A closer look at dynamic *cwnd* of CCP during "*fast-comeback*" phase.

12.3. SIMULATIONS AND ANALYSIS

In this section, extensive simulations are used to evaluate the performance of CCP in high BDP networks. HSTCP, BIC-TCP, CUBIC, FAST, Astart and H-TCP are also chosen as comparative protocols.

The following series of experiments were performed using ns2, version 2.28. As a base configuration, the simulation uses a dumb-bell topology in which many flows share a single bottleneck link, as shown in Figure 12-3. In all simulations, a small amount of Poisson UDP traffic, roughly at 5% bottleneck utilization, was added to the links to simulate a very lightly utilized flow. The simulation tests lasted 480 seconds. As shown in Table 12-2, the parameters in protocols are set

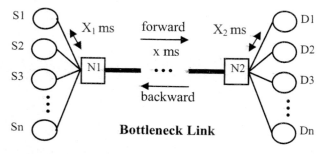

Figure 12-3. Simulation Network Topology.

Table 12-2. The Protocol Parameters Settings

The Protocols	Parameters Settings
BIC-TCP	*Smax*=32, *Smin*=0.01, *beta*=0.125
CUBIC	*MaxIncrement*=160
HSTCP	*LowWindow*=38
H-TCP	*DeltaL* = 1, 0.5 < *beta* < 0.8
FAST	*alpha*=312, *mithresh*=0.75
CCP	*alpha*=3, *beta*=0.8, *k*=1.01, *τ*=200

12.3.1. Link Utilization

In order to determine whether a high-speed protocol uses available bandwidth effectively in high BDP networks, the bandwidth utilization of 2.5Gbps bottleneck is measured firstly. Each test consists of two high-speed flows of the same type and two long-lived TCP Reno flow. In each test, the total utilization of all the flows including background traffic are measured. Among the simulations, except CCP protocol, the other protocols choose drop-tail or RED router in the test.

Table 12-3 shows that the link utilization of CCP is very close to that of other protocols in Drop-tail routers, but the CCP's utilization is higher than that of protocols in RED routers. The reason is that Drop-tail router allows flows to fill up the network buffers, but RED does not.

Table 12-3. Link Utilization

Protocol	Utilization	
CCP	97.1%	
	Drop-tail	RED
BIC-TCP	97.0%	95.3%
CUBIC	97.1%	95.8%
HSTCP	97.2%	92.1%
FAST	96.8%	95.1%
Astart	96.1%	95.2%
H-TCP	97.2%	95.7%

12.3.2. TCP Friendliness

In this scenario, the friendliness of CCP towards TCP Reno is evaluated. There are two classes of end hosts. One uses a high-speed protocol, and the other uses traditional TCP Reno. Both of them have 1Gbps access links, and 1ms path propagation delay. Following the aforementioned dumbbell configuration, the bandwidth of the bottleneck link was set to 622 Mbps, with a delay of 80 ms.

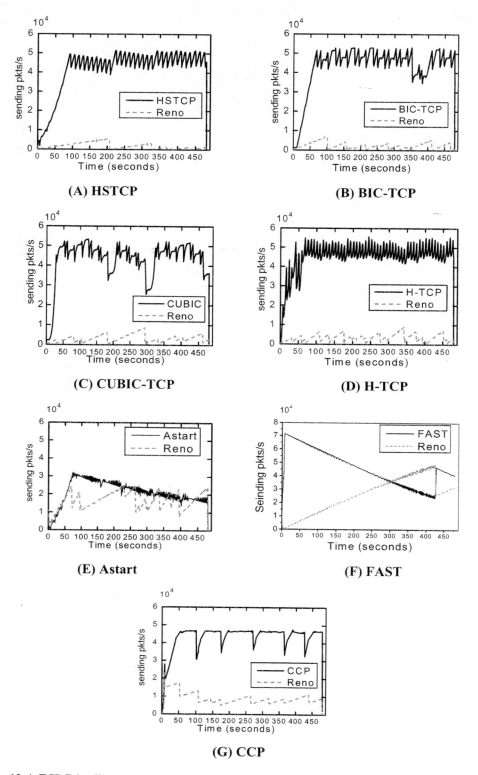

Figure 12-4. TCP Friendliness.

As one can see in Figure 12-4(a), HSTCP has a significant effect on the throughput achieved by the TCP-Reno flow, resulting in nearly starvation. The packet drop rate of HSTCP is also quite high. In BIC-TCP experiment, Figure 12-4(b) shows that BIC-TCP also brings the TCP-Friendliness problem. Reno flow can't achieve enough bandwidth allocation. The high-speed flows also have a large oscillation. CUBIC and H-TCP improve TCP friendliness than BIC-TCP and HSTCP, but only a little, which can be seen in Figure 12-4(c) and 12-4(d). On the other hand, Astart performs better TCP-Friendliness. In this simulation, from Figure 12-4(e), Reno gets the highest throughput than in other environment. But, it can be seen that instead of Reno flow obtaining high bandwidth, the throughput of Astart decreases over time continuously, even was lower than that of Reno in the end. It is mainly because of the conservative characteristic of pure delay-based protocols when sharing the links with loss-based protocols. This disadvantage of pure delay-based protocols is also illustrated in [85]. So it violates the requirement of new protocol for improving throughput performance in high BDP networks. Figure 12-4(f) illustrates that FAST achieves residual bandwidth in a few several RTT and reduces the throughput of TCP Reno immediately, which attributes to its aggressive increasing function. However, FAST employs a "*precautionary decongestion*" approach to react congestion in advance of packet losses. Therefore, Reno reclaims its fair share finally as a result of its "*greedy*" behavior, but in a very slow rate owing to its conservative additive increase rule. Actually, bandwidth sharing between FAST and Reno depends much on network parameters in heterogeneous networks and exhibits intricate behaviors [238].

CCP, however, has a minimal effect on the Reno flow, as shown in Figure 12-4(g). Both CCP and Reno flows achieve the bandwidth allocation appropriately. The ratio of CCP traffic to Reno traffic is roughly 5:1. CCP performs steadily through simulations, and the drop rate is low. The reason is that the delay and explicit feedback mechanism in CCP prevents CCP flow from holding extra queue buffer in bottleneck routers and the Reno flow can use some other queue buffer to increase its sending rate, which ensures CCP's TCP Friendliness.

12.3.3. RTT Fairness

In this experiment, two high-speed flows with a different RTT share the bottleneck. The RTT of flow 1 is 30ms. The RTT of flow 2 is varied among 30ms, 60ms, 90ms, 180ms. The bottleneck link has a capacity of 622Mbps, and a delay of 5ms. This setup allows the protocols to be tested for RTT unfairness with different window sizes.

Table 12-4 gives the throughput ratio of different protocols. As discussed in Section 12.1, there is a serious fairness problem with flows of different round trip times for BIC-TCP and HSTCP. The flow with short RTT quickly dominates the connection, starving out the other flow. In [41], the authors proposed that the RTT fairness could be improved when RED router is applied. As shown in Table 12-4, BIC-TCP in RED can get better fairness than BIC-TCP in Drop-tail and so can HSTCP. But both BIC-TCP in RED and HSTCP in RED do not obtain satisfied fairness, which is also illustrated in [237]. The window growth function of CUBIC and H-TCP are governed by a gain function in terms of the elapsed time since the last loss event. And the gain function provides a good stability and scalability in different RTT paths. So CUBIC and H-TCP perform better fairness than BIC-TCP and HSTCP, which can be seen in Table 12-4.

As shown in Table 12-4, the CCP flows and Astart flows share the bandwidth roughly proportional to their RTT. It is obvious that the RTT fairness of CCP and Astart are better than that of other protocols (either in Drop-tail router or RED router). The reason why CCP and Astart can achieve such excellent RTT fairness properties is that both of them choose the RTT delay information as their criterion of congestion and the delay mechanism has effect on limiting the aggressiveness of the dominant flows. Especially in CCP protocol, the flows that have a higher rate are more sensitive to the measured queuing delays. Thus, they enter their wincing window mode sooner than the flow with long RTT. While the flow with short RTT is in wincing mode, and the flow with long RTT is in its increased mode. So it ensures the CCP RTT fairness.

Table 12-4. The throughput ratio of protocols

Inverse RTT Ratio	1	3	6
CCP	1.022341	2.031433	8.922543
BIC-TCP in Drop-tail	1.033434	9.696173	30.431100
BIC-TCP in RED	1.164987	5.674582	24.454215
CUBIC in Drop-tail	1.054760	3.165610	15.245755
CUBIC in RED	1.011454	2.782637	9.545876
HSTCP in Drop-tail	0.942102	92.844748	384.833044
HSTCP in RED	1.155956	60.578422	248.157821
FAST in Drop-tail	1.125487	1.009883	19.543154
FAST in RED	1.102548	7.697454	18.597397
Astart in Drop-tail	1.117415	5.152478	10.845742
Astart in RED	0.998451	2.654214	7.912541
H-TCP in Drop-tail	0.999774	3.011015	8.477749
H-TCP in RED	1.028451	2.289412	7.053216

12.3.4. Convergence

The convergence time to the fair bandwidth share is also an important issue to the new protocols. In this experiment, there are 4 high-speed flows with RTT 100 ms. Two flows start earlier randomly in [0, 60] seconds, and the other two flows start later randomly in [100, 160] seconds. The total simulation time is 600 seconds. The bottleneck link bandwidth is 622 Mbps. For this experiment, the fairness index [97] is measured at each 50 seconds interval, and samples are only taken after the first 100 seconds.

As seen in Figure 12-5, FAST achieves the best convergence and is much more stable than other protocols as time evolves. Except that HSTCP has a little oscillation around the fair share, the other flows all have fast convergence rate.

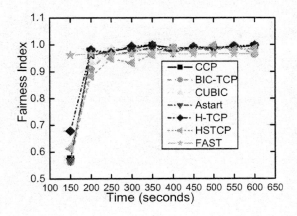

Figure 12-5. Fairness index over various time scales..

12.3.5. Protocol Adaptation

In this experiment, it is investigated how quickly CCP can adapt to changing network conditions. The bottleneck link has a capacity of 622Mbps, and the flow is experiencing a minimum round trip time of 84ms. After 160s, a CBR UDP flow at 300Mbps is started, then, at 320s, the UDP flow is stopped.

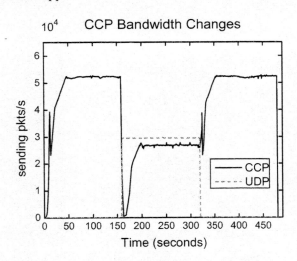

Figure 12-6. CCP adaptation.

As shown in Figure 12-6, CCP quickly reduces its bandwidth in response to the UDP flow. After the UDP flow terminates, CCP quickly re-enters its high speed mode, and quickly utilizes the newly freed bandwidth. Because of adapting Vegas-like congestion window updating rule in CCP steady state, the protocol performs stably in whole simulation.

12.4. CONCLUSION

In this chapter a simple and effective TCP enhancement protocol, called CCP, is proposed, which allows the senders to update the congestion window based on the load of networks and RTT delay information appropriately. The simulation results show that CCP protocol can achieve significant throughput gains, favorable TCP friendliness, and excellent RTT fairness in high BDP networks. It is easy to implement as the complexity of the protocol is just like ECN protocol, and the scheme does not require the routers to maintain per-flow state.

PART IV. TCP IN MIXED WIRED AND WIRELESS NETWORK

Chapter 13

A CROSS-LAYER TCP FOR PROVIDING FAIRNESS IN WIRELESS MESH NETWORKS

13.1. INTRODUCTION

Wireless Mesh Networks (WMN) is a key technology of wireless Internet access. In wireless Mesh Networks, nodes are comprised of mesh routers and mesh clients. Mesh routers have minimal mobility and act as BSs (Base Station), which provide network access for mesh clients. As the combination of multi-hop wireless networks and wired networks, mesh routers are responsible for network management and packets forwarding. Therefore, WMNs enable integration of various existing networks such as cellular networks and wireless Ad Hoc networks. To some extent, it has the centralized management features of traditional cellular networks, while maintaining the flexibility of Ad Hoc networks [239, 240].

However, WMNs are facing some practical problems. The existing wireless standards related to WMNs, such as IEEE 802.11 (Wi-Fi), IEEE 802.15 (Bluetooth and Zigbee) and IEEE 802.16 (WiMAX), are always hard to be standards of network schemes in practical [241]. One of the important reasons is the unfair phenomena. When one node is more than a hop away from the BS, its average bandwidth becomes lower, and the chance of successful access will decrease accordingly. If there are more nodes, the frequency reuse technology can be employed to alleviate this problem. However, in a single frequency channel, allocated bandwidth of a node can only reach between $1/2m$ and $1/m$ (m is the number of hop from the current node to BSs) [242]. As a result, serious unfairness problem exists between "near" nodes and "far" nodes.

To solve the unfairness problem among different TCP flows in multi-hop wireless networks, there are some improved methods in the network layer or MAC layer. For example, Nandiraju, N.S. et al. proposed weighted queue management for nodes [243], Min Cao et al. proposed an adaptive method that nodes adjust their exponent values with priority [244]. These methods improved the fairness among different TCP flows to some extent. However, they need many modifications on protocols, so they are difficult to be deployed. The latest research on this problem is from the Rice Networking Group, which deploys the TFA network platform in Houston (an operational mesh network that provides Internet access) to examine the starvation phenomena when a one-hop TCP flow is in competition with two-hop TCP flows. At the same time, a solution based on the IEEE802.11e is proposed [245].

The problem of these solutions mentioned above is that the interaction between MAC layer and TCP protocols has been overlooked. Thus, they can't simultaneously guarantee fairness and efficiency of resource distribution. This chapter analyzes this problem in NS2 and proposes a "Counter Cross-Layer ECN" (CCLE), which can improve fairness among TCP flows based on congestion control mechanism with priority.

13.2. "COUNTER STARVATION" PROBLEM

The "Counter Starvation" problem is an unfair problem among TCP flows with different hops away from the BS. It has been shown in [246] that starvation phenomenon also exists with longer chain topology, different package size or upload/download traffic. The typical topology, which is shown in Figure 13-1, is only considered in this chapter. Methods and conclusions in this chapter can be easily applied into other similar scenarios.

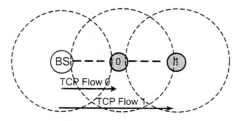

Figure 13-1. Typical topology of WMN.

Figure 13-1 shows a common situation in WMNs. There are two mesh nodes, 0 and 1, which are located one hop and two hops away from the BS respectively. Mesh nodes 1 and BS are hidden from each other. Both node 0 and node 1 receive TCP flows from the BS at the same time. The typical WMN topology is built in NS2, in which TCP0 and TCP1 flows are transmitted from BS to nodes 0 and node 1 respectively. The throughputs, congestion windows and delays of two TCP flows are compared, which are shown in Figure 13-2 and Figure 13-3.

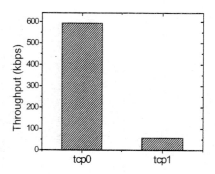

Figure 13-2. Comparison of TCP throughput in Typical Topology.

Figure 13-2 and Figure 13-3 show the occurrence of severe starvation. The average congestion window of TCP1 is only 26% of that of TCP0, while its average delay is 2 times more than that of TCP0. Subsequently the throughput of TCP1 is less than 10% of TCP0's .

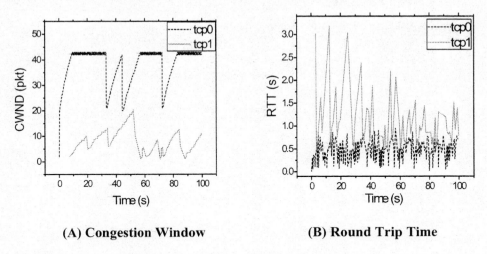

(A) Congestion Window	**(B) Round Trip Time**

Figure 13-3. Performance comparisons of TCP0 and TCP1 in Typical Topology.

The reason of "Counter Starvation" is analyzed as follows:

(1) Unfairness Induced by Different Hops

As shown in Figure 13-4, the bottleneck in typical topology is node 0, which not only receives TCP0 traffic, but also forwards TCP1 traffic. Assume that traffic on nodes 0 is the same as that on node 1, which is described as G. Traffic on link BS-Node(0) and link Node(0)- Node(1) are $2G$ and G respectively. So the total traffic on node 0 will be: $G + 2G = 3G$. Since it is restricted by the conflict domain of capacity (virtual capacity at MAC layer, being described as B), there is $3G \leq B$. Then the offered load at nodes 1 and 0 are $B/3$ and $2B/3$ respectively.

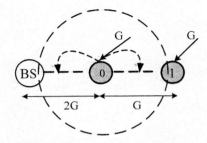

Figure 13-4. Traffic Distribution in typical topology.

(2) **Unfairness Induced by MAC Protocol**

The fairness problem mainly comes from three aspects in MAC layer: the scope of sense and conflict are larger than that of transmission, the problem of hidden terminal/exposed terminal, and the binary exponential backoff mechanism.

An example is shown in Figure 13-5, which can be used to analyze the unfairness induced by MAC protocol. Assume that there are packets to be transmitted both in the BS and two-hop mesh node 1 and they have the same contend windows. Since the two senders (1 and BS) are hidden from each other, a transmission from one sender will be successful only when its RTS fits within the other's backoff interval. Note that the contention window of two senders is small at the beginning of transmission, so the probability of collision between the two senders is very high.

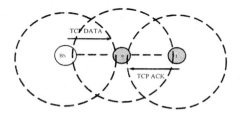

Figure 13-5. Access Competition in Typical Topology.

Without loss of generality, assume that node BS succeeds in transmitting a packet. BS resets its contention window back to its minimum size, while node 1 keeps a high contention window. In order to succeed in the next transmission attempt, node 1 must fit its packet in a small backoff interval of node BS, which is an unlikely event. After a resulting collision, it is difficult for node 1 to win the channel. Subsequently, the ability of accessing channel is strictly distinct between the two nodes.

In summary, due to the nodes with different hops away from the BS station and the inherent problems of MAC mechanism, severe unfairness and even complete starvation will occur in WMNs.

13.3. COUNTER CROSS-LAYER ECN

Jingpu Shi et al. show that the "Counter Starvation" problem is inevitable and serious in WMNs [246]. When TCP flows with different hops away from BS exist, only a one-hop TCP flow in competition with two-hop TCP flows is sufficient to induce starvation of the two-hop TCP flows.

To solve the unfairness problem, "Minimum Contention Window" policy is proposed [245]. Different from prior methods, "Minimum Contention Window" does not require any hardware or software modification. The policy just lets the BS's one-hop neighbors increase their minimum contention window to a value significantly greater than that of other neighbors. The neighbors with more than one hop away from BS should decrease their backoff window (CW_{min} for 16) to ensure a higher priority, while one-hop neighbors increase their backoff window (CW_{min} for 128, 512, 1024). In this way, the transmission probability of the one-hop neighbors decreases and the fairness is improved. However in "Minimum Contention Window", it is hard to set the value of CW_{min} of wireless node to achieve good tradeoff between fairness and efficiency. If CW_{min} of one-hop neighbors is too small, the unfairness problem will still be serious. If CW_{min} of one-hop neighbors is too large, the total throughput decreases excessively. Table 13-1 shows the simulation results of "Minimum Contention Window".

To obtain the total throughput in Table 13-1, the calculating method in [245, 246] is employed, by which two-hop nodes' throughput is counted twice. All parameters in this simulation are the same as these in [245]. As shown in Table 13-1, when CW_{min} is set to 128 for node 0, the fairness index is close to 0.5 and the overall throughput decreases by 10%. With the increasing of node 0's CW_{min}, the improvement of unfairness is not significant while the overall throughput deceases a lot. When the value of CW_{min} increases to 512, the overall throughput decreases even by 42%.

The above problem will be more serious when the sending rate of TCP flow is high and the network traffic increases. Since all TCP flows go through the one-hop neighbors, all flows will get low throughputs when the transmission probability of the one-hop neighbors decreases. It is clear that adjusting the parameters of MAC layer only is not the best way to solve the "Counter Starvation" problem.

Table 13-1. Throughput Comparison of Two TCP Flow by Using "Minimum Contention Window" in the typical topology

CW_{min}	TCP0 (kbps)	TCP1 (Mbps)	Total Throughput (Mbps)
32	593.53	57.51	708.55
64	495.51	89.29	674.09
128	330.87	155.75	642.37
256	366.13	110.87	587.87
512	315.57	91.91	499.39

In fact, the essential cause of the "Counter Starvation" problem is the cross-layer interaction between TCP and MAC mechanism in WMNs. The improper adjustment of TCP sending rate will cause more conflict and congestion in the wireless channel. The inappropriate access control at MAC layer will lead to the increase of TCP retransmission and delay. Therefore, the overall performance should be improved by the joint optimization of TCP and MAC layer.

Based on these analyses, the "Counter Cross-Layer ECN" (CCLE) method is proposed, which includes the following properties:

1) CCLE uses the RTS as the cross-layer congestion metric to detect the congestion in wireless channel.
2) CCLE implements congestion control on the one-hop TCP flows with high priority and the other TCP flows with low priority, thus the fairness can be improved.

3) The priority congestion control is based on the "cross layer ECN" scheme. In detail, when detecting congestion in wireless channel, CCLE calculates the ECN marking probability for each TCP flow. The "near" TCP flows are assigned with a higher marking probability. Thus, CCLE ensures the fair congestion control on TCP flows in WMNs.

Figure 13-6 shows the instruction of CCLE method.

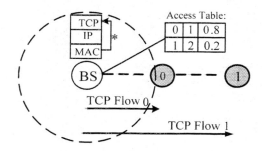

Figure 13-6. Counter Cross-Layer ECN.

13.3.1. Cross-layer Congestion Detect

Cross-layer design is a promising approach to promote the performance of wireless networks. Using the RTS (retry counter) in MAC layer, CCLE implements congestion detection on wireless channels.

ECN scheme is deployed in intermediate routers, which can provide the congestion information to TCP senders. The ECN scheme has been proven to be an effective mechanism to enhance the performance of TCP in wired networks. In CCLE, ECN scheme is extended to the MAC layer. If the number of RTS from MAC exceeds a given threshold, TCP sender will trigger congestion control to decrease its sending rate by ECN feedback. As shown in Figure 13-6, the part with "*" can be described as: *if (RTS > Threshold) Marking CE bit* .

In this way, the cross-layer ECN scheme can detect congestion from MAC layer effectively in wireless networks and maintain existing TCP congestion control in wired networks.

13.3.2. Priority Congestion Control based on Distance

To allocate the bandwidth fairly between TCP flows, CCLE marks the ECN bit in "near" TCP flows with high priority and "far" TCP flows with low priority.

As shown in Figure 13-6, CCLE is deployed in Base Station (BS). BS maintains a "Marking Probability Table" (for simplicity of presentation, it will be named as "Marking Table" in Figure 13-6) to specify the ECN marking probability of each TCP flow. As shown in Table 13-2, "Marking Table" includes the ID, the hop counter from BS and the ECN marking probability of TCP Flow. The value of ID and the hop counter are written directly as soon as the routing table is built. At the same time, the marking probability can be assigned based on the hop counter. For example, Table 13-2 shows that the marking probability of one-hop TCP flows is 0.8, and the probability of two-hop TCP flows is 0.2.

Table 13-2. Format of Marking Table

Flow ID	Counter	P[Counter]
i	C_i	$P[C_i]$
j	C_j	$P[C_j]$

In the following, how to assign the marking probability for achieving the fairness between TCP flows will be discussed.

According to the TCP throughput formula, the ratio of the average throughput of TCP flow i and flow j can be given as:

$$\frac{T_i}{T_j} = \frac{RTT_j * \sqrt[2]{P_j}}{RTT_i * \sqrt[2]{P_i}} \tag{13-1}$$

where T, RTT and P are each flow's throughput, delay and packet loss rate (be equal to ECN marking probability) respectively. From (13-1), it is clear that the TCP fairness can be achieved by adjusting the probability of ECN marking. Assume $T_i = T_j$, it is can be obtained:

$$\frac{P[C_i]}{P[C_j]} = \begin{cases} 1 & if(C_i = C_j) \\ (RTT_{C_j} / RTT_{C_i})^2 & else \end{cases} \tag{13-2}$$

From (13-2), the conclusion can be made that TCP flows with the same hops away from BS have the same marking probability, otherwise the marking probability is determined by delay.

When the flow reaches node i, its delay D_i can expressed as:

$$D_i = \sum_{n=1}^{C_i} d_n = \sum_{n=1}^{C_i} (d_n^t + d_n^q + d_n^c) \tag{13-3}$$

where d_n^t, d_n^q and d_n^c are transmission delay, queuing delay and contention delay that a packet experiences at node n. C_i is the hop number of node n.

For simplicity of presentation, assume that packet sizes are fixed. Then the transmission delay d_n^t is a constant. Therefore,

$$\sum_{n=1}^{C_i} d_n^t = C_i * d_1^t \tag{13-4}$$

where d_1^t is transmission delay of wireless node with one hop away from BS.

Based on queuing theory, d_n^q is determined by the packet reaching time A_n and service time X_n. Since $X_n = d_n^c + d_n^t$, D_i is determined by d_n^c if A_n follows a uniform distribution.

To calculate d_n^c, it is necessary to understand the different states of node, which are mainly determined by characteristic that the neighbor nodes contend for channel. Node states consist of busy state, idle state and backoff state. Backoff state is always less than 0.2 ms, far below the busy state and idle state [247]. Thus the backoff state can be neglected. The delay of busy state and idle state is denoted as d_n^b and d_n^f respectively.

According to MAC protocol, d_n^f can be obtained as:

$$d_n^f = DIFS \tag{13-5}$$

If a packet k reaches node n during busy state, the queue of node n either has packets waiting to send, or is empty. If the queue is empty, node n will be immediately send RTS frame. As the channel is busy, packet k will be send after a backoff time. If the queue is not empty, packet k will wait until all the packets in the queue are sent completely. During this period, each packet, including packet k, will experience a backoff time. Therefore, d_n^b can be expressed as:

$$d_n^b = DIFS + w_n \varepsilon + m_n T_d + m_n^c T_c' \tag{13-6}$$

where w_n is the number of backoff slots, ε is the backoff slots, T_d is the period number of sending packets successfully, T_c is the period number of collision, m_n is the number of data packets transmitted during node i's backoff process, and m_n^c is the number of collision periods during node i's backoff process.

By (13-5) and (13-6), d_n^c is determined by the distribution of w_n, m_n, m_n^c and probability p_n^b that packet k reaches at node during the busy state. In [248], the authors have proved that the probability of the neighbors of node i sending packets at the same time only dependent on distributing of their reaching packets, and are independent of their contention window size. This means that node 1 and BS receive packets with the same rate because they are hidden nodes for each other in the typical topology. Under this consideration, p_n^b is a fixed value. The designed cross-layer ECN mechanism is corresponding to it. In the same way, the distribution of w_n, m_n and m_n^c are also determined by the mode that packets reach nodes. Hence, d_n^c is a certain value which is independent of node's location. Thus,

$$\sum_{n=1}^{C_i} d_n^c = C_i * d_1^c \tag{13-7}$$

Similarly,

$$\sum_{n=1}^{C_i} d_n^q = C_i * d_1^q \tag{13-8}$$

By (13-4), (13-7) and (13-8), (13-3) can be expressed as:

$$D_i = i * (d_1^t + d_1^q + d_1^c) \tag{13-9}$$

By (13-2), it is can be obtained

$$\frac{P_{c_i}}{P_{c_j}} = (\frac{D_{C_j}}{D_{C_i}})^2 = (\frac{C_i}{C_j})^2 \tag{13-10}$$

As for flows going through the BS, their counters (distance from BS) can be got from centralized routing table, and their corresponding marking probability should meet the following requirements:

$$\begin{cases} p_1 : p_2 : \cdots : p_N = 1 : \dfrac{1}{2^2} : \cdots : \dfrac{1}{N^2} \\ \quad p_1 + p_2 + \cdots + p_N = 1 \end{cases} \tag{13-11}$$

Taking the typical topology shown in Figure 13-5 as an example, it can be obtained that the marking probability of two flows: $p_1=0.8$, $p_2=0.2$.

13.3.3. Protocol Design

```
RetransmitRTS( pktTx ):
assert(pktTx_);
assert(pktRTS_);
ssrc_ += 1;   //RTS counter increasing by 1
if (ssrc_ >threshold)
   fid=pktTx->flowid();
      calculation p[i] according to fid;
      Marking CE bit with p[i];
endif;
```

Figure 13-7. Pseudo code of CCLE.

BS is responsible for counting the number of RTS when a packet is successful in transmission. If the number exceeds a given thresh, BS will mark the ECN bit. Different flows will be marked with different probabilities. In this way, the channel distribution can be adjusted on the basis of congestion control. Hence, fairness of TCP flows can be achieved. Because the structure of wireless mesh network is generally less than three layers, one hop node's sense for RTS can reflect the overall channel state. Therefore it is feasible to employ the BS to detect and control congestion.

13.4. PERFORMANCE ANALYSIS

This chapter proposes a solution based on congestion control mechanisms. The comparison results of whether to employ CCLE or not are given by repeating the experiment in Section 13.2.

It is shown in Figure 13-8 that CCLE can improve the fairness of TCP flows. Especially when RTS threshold is set to 2, fairness index of two TCP flow almost reaches 1.

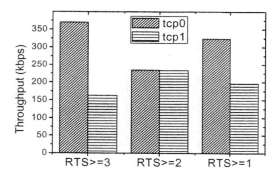

Figure 13-8. Fairness comparison of TCP0 and TCP1 by using CCLE.

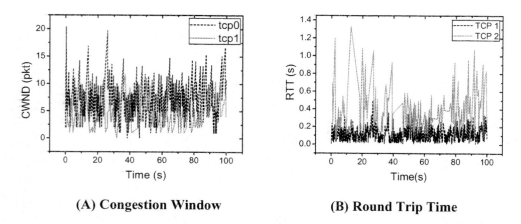

(A) Congestion Window   (B) Round Trip Time

Figure 13-9. Performance of Two TCP Flow by Using CCLE.

As an example, the comparison of congestion window and RTT while RTS threshold being set to 3 is shown in Figure 13-9. Compared to Figure 13-3, it is obvious in Figure 13-9 that the disparity in congestion window and RTT between two TCP flows becomes small. By using CCLE, the competition ability of TCP1 is remarkably improved in the process of adjusting congestion windows.

Detailed description of TCP performance is shown in Table 13-3. Compared to "Minimum Contention Window" in Table 13-1, it can be concluded that CCLE can obtain better performance in both throughput and fairness. The performance can be analyzed as following:

1) Employing congestion marking with priority, CCLE decreases the send window ratio of TCP0 and TCP1 from 3.8 to 0.1, which significantly improved fairness between the two TCP flows. When RTS is set to 2, TCP fairness is close to 1. At the same time, the overall throughput is maintained.

2) Delay decreases more than 3-4 times by using CCLE. By detecting the congestion in wireless channel, TCP decreases the delay. Especially in large-scale WMNs, more the nodes are, the greater the overall delay will be. Actually some applications, such as voice or streaming media application, have delay requirement. Therefore, CCLE is very helpful in decreasing communication delay.

Table 13-3. Comparison of TCP Performance with/without CCLE in the typical topology

Parameters	Fairness (-)	Total Throughput (kbps)	Sending Window		RTT	
			TCP0 (pkt)	TCP1 (pkt)	TCP0 (s)	TCP1 (s)
noECN	0.595	695.09	38.529	10.31	0.437	1.067
RTS≥3	0.868	701.58	7.755	18.576	0.121	0.668
RTS≥2	0.999	701.58	3.640	18.974	0.061	0.685
RTS≥1	0.943	715.75	2.121	18.500	0.032	0.560

To further analyze the "Counter Starvation" problem, another topology with two branches is considered. In Figure 13-10, a new TCP flow traverses through the other branch {BS, node 2} besides TCP0 and a TCP1. In this case, the two one-hop TCP flows and a two-hop TCP flow will contend for channel access together.

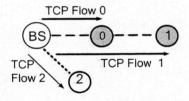

Figure 13-10. the Topology of Two Branches in WMNs.

The fairness and throughput among three TCP flows are examined in this two-branch scenario. Then the result of employing "Minimum Contention Window" and CCLE are analyzed respectively. The results are shown in Table 13-4 and Table 13-5.

Table 13-4. Comparison of TCP Performance by Using "Minimum Contention Window" in the two-branch scenario

CWmin	TCP0 (kbps)	TCP1 (kbps)	TCP2 (kbps)	Total Throughput (kbps)
32	407.49	12.71	285.88	717.79
64	267.51	43.79	349.05	704.14
128	267.93	34.52	353.67	690.64
256	244.00	50.76	285.06	630.58
512	219.45	46.39	269.72	581.59

From the comparison of Table 13-4 and Table 13-5, it is obvious that fairness improvement of "Minimum Contention Window" highly depends on the value of CW_{min}. In the best situation under "Minimum Contention Window" (CW_{min} =64), fairness and total throughput are worse than the worst situation under CCLE (RTS=3). When RTS is set to 1 in CCLE, the fairness probability is closed to 1 and the overall throughput increased by 23.6% compared to the default value that CW_{min} is set to 16 in IEEE 802.11b.

Table 13-5. Comparison of TCP Performance by Using CCLE in the two-branch scenario

RTS Threshold	TCP0 (kbps)	TCP1 (kbps)	TCP2 (kbps)	Total Throughput (kbps)
1	242.60	205.56	251.07	904.79
2	297.01	167.56	235.37	867.50
3	340.86	132.98	226.22	833.04

13.5. CONCLUSION

This chapter investigates the "Counter starvation" problem among TCP flows with different hops away from the BS. A priority-based congestion control method based on cross-layer ECN is proposed. Analysis and simulation results illustrate that this method can improve the fairness among TCP flows in WMNs. Compared with the solution based on IEEE 802.11e in [246], the solution has two characteristics:

1) By regulating cross-layer ECN marking probability, the bandwidth can be accurately assigned to meet requirements of QoS, such as proportional fairness;
2) It can be easily applied to all MAC protocols with RTS/CTS scheme.

The key idea of this method is that it builds on congestion control mechanisms and considers the interaction between TCP and MAC. Thus the "Counter starvation" problem among TCP flows can be solved without impact on TCP performance.

Chapter 14

AN ECN-BASED CONGESTION CONTROL ALGORITHM FOR TCP ENHANCEMENT IN WIRELESS LOCAL AREA NETWORKS

14.1. INTRODUCTION

Based on the IEEE 802.11 protocol, WLANs (Wireless local area networks) are widely deployed in cafes, schools, hotels, and other hot spot areas [249]. As one of the core protocols of the Internet, however, TCP is facing some problems in WLAN connected with Internet.

In WLAN connected with Internet, AP (Access Point) plays an important role for connecting wired and wireless networks. Because of the narrow bandwidth, high latency and high bit-error-rate characteristics of the wireless channel, the APs are prone to be the TCP congestion bottleneck in the downlink direction (from wired network to wireless network) [250].

While the MAC layer protocol provides all the wireless nodes with equal opportunity for media access, it does not guarantee fairness at the TCP layer. In fact, the greedy closed loop control nature of TCP congestion control, the long-term equal channel access probabilities guaranteed by MAC layer protocol, and the performance anomaly of wireless channel lead to the significant unfair bandwidth distribution between TCP flows and low network efficiency [251, 198].

To address the TCP congestion and fairness problems, an ECN-based congestion control algorithm, called APCC (AP congestion control), is proposed. By using both wireless channel load and buffer length as the compound congestion indicator, APCC brings more stable and higher efficient TCP congestion control. Taking into account the direction and the wireless channel rate of each TCP flow, APCC achieves the time fairness between the up/down TCP flows and high total network goodput.

The rest of the chapter is organized as follows. The related works are introduced in Section 14.2. APCC algorithm is presented In Section 14.3. Simulation results are shown in Section 14.4. The chapter is concluded in Section 14.5.

14.2. RELATED WORKS

In the last few years, extensive studies have been carried out to address the TCP congestion and fairness issues in WLAN connected with Internet.

Several congestion control algorithms have been proposed. In [195], RED algorithm is deployed on AP as the congestion control policy to achieve low delay, low packet loss rate and high goodput. However, the main purpose of RED algorithm is not to improve the fairness among flows. To resolve this problem, RA-Snoop [252] fairly calculates window feedback of each single TCP flow based on the bandwidth delay product estimation. Then it conveys the feedback information on the advertised window in the ACKs. In this way, RA-Snoop achieves the goodput fairness between TCP flows.

Pilosof et al. observed that the goodput of uplink TCP is much higher than that of downlink TCP, and pointed out that the greedy closed loop control nature of TCP is the essential cause of this up/down TCP unfairness problem [251]. Pilosof et al. also proposed a TCP rate limiting scheme that manipulates the advertised windows of the ACKs. By setting the advertised windows to $\lfloor B/n \rfloor$ (where B is the buffer size and n is the TCP flow number), this scheme limits the sending rates of the uplink and downlink TCP flows. VQRED [196] is an AQM (Active Queue Management) algorithm on AP. VQRED treats all the uplink and downlink TCP flows fairly. By setting the same drop threshold for the queue lengths of all uplink and downlink TCP flows, VQRED achieves the up/down TCP fairness.

In multi-rate wireless network, for transmitting the packet with the same size, wireless nodes with low transmission rate will take more time than nodes with higher transmission rate, which leads to the reduction of channel utilization [198]. To provide the time fairness, some novel MAC layer protocols give the high-rate nodes with high priority to access the wireless channel [253, 254, 255]. By allocating more network bandwidth to high-rate nodes, these protocols improve the overall system efficiency. However, these solutions, which implicitly assume that every node is always involved in the MAC layer contention, do not consider the congestion control of TCP layer. In fact, the TCP congestion control scheme has impact on the opportunity that each node contends for resources in MAC layer. Thus, the time fairness between TCP flows cannot be obtained successfully just by improving the MAC layer protocol.

Although these algorithms can increase the efficiency or the fairness of TCP, they also bring some other limitations as follows.

1) Detecting Network Congestion Ineffectively

How to detect the congestion events quickly and effectively is an important issue for congestion control. While the length of buffer queue is a good measure for the wired network, it cannot be directly applied to wireless networks. The large queue length may indicate that severe congestion has already happened in wireless channel. Thereby it is too late for the network to control the congestion. In wireless channel, although the number of retries from MAC layer [256] and the channel utilization [257] are good congestion indicators, these wireless measures cannot reflect the degree of buffer congestion in AP.

2) Severe TCP Unfairness

Most congestion control algorithms neglect the TCP unfairness problems in the following two cases. Firstly, while most current congestion control algorithms only limit the rate of TCP flows in downlink direction, the uplink TCP flows consume vastly unfair shares of network resource. Secondly, the object of the current fair congestion control schemes is to guarantee the goodput fairness between TCP flows. When goodput fairness is provided in multi-rate wireless network, however, wireless nodes with low transmission rate degrade the channel utilization.

To overcome these shortcomings, an ECN-based congestion control algorithm (APCC) is proposed in this chapter. By using a novel compound metric to measure the congestion, APCC detects the network congestion more effectively. Since APCC sets the ECN marking probability based on the direction and the wireless channel rate of each TCP flow, the time fairness between the up/down TCP flows and network efficiency are achieved.

14.3. AP CONGESTION CONTROL

Deployed in intermediate routers, ECN (Explicit Congestion Notification) scheme provides the explicit congestion notification to the TCP sender [46]. The ECN scheme has been proven to be an effective mechanism to enhance the performance of TCP [236, 258]. Based on the ECN scheme, a novel congestion control algorithm is proposed, whose main characteristics are introduced in the following.

1) APCC detects the network congestion based on the compound congestion indicator, which uses both the load of wireless channel and the length of buffer queue.
2) In the downlink buffer of AP, APCC marks the ECN bit in the DATA packets of downlink TCP flows and the ACK packets of uplink TCP flows. In this way, APCC provides the bi-direction congestion control.
3) Based on the ECN congestion control model, APCC calculates the ECN marking probability for each TCP flow with different wireless transmission rate. Thus, APCC achieves the time fairness and high network goodput.

14.3.1. Compound Congestion Indicator

The utilization U_c of wireless channel is used to measure the congestion of wireless channel, which is defined as

$$U_c = \frac{T_{interval} - T_{idle}}{T_{interval}} \tag{14-1}$$

where $T_{interval}$ is the length of the measurement period, T_{idle} is the channel free time during $T_{interval}$, and $T_{interval} - T_{idle}$ includes the channel time of transmitting, receiving, carrier sensing busy and virtual carrier sensing busy (e.g. deferral to RTS, CTS etc.).

To measure the degree of congestion in AP's buffer, the buffer's utilization U_b is defined as

$$U_b = \frac{Q}{B} \qquad (14\text{-}2)$$

where Q is the current number of packets (including the TCP DATA packets of downlink TCP and TCP ACK packets of uplink TCP) in the downlink buffer of AP, and B is the size of the downlink buffer .

Since AP connects the wired and wireless network, it is reasonable to combine the length of buffer queue and the load of wireless channel as the congestion indicator. In APCC, the utilization U_c of wireless channel and the buffer's utilization U_b are combined to measure the degree of congestion in AP. The probability P of ECN marking is defined as

$$P = \alpha U_c + (1 - \alpha)U_b \qquad (14\text{-}3)$$

where α is a multiplicative factor, U_c and U_b are normalized.

In APCC, using the metric U_c can be a benefit for detecting congestion in AP more early. Using the length of buffer queue as the congestion indicator, APCC can make the congestion control more stable, which can reduce the sensitivity to the metric U_c in AP.

14.3.2. Fair ECN Marking

In TCP congestion avoidance cycle, upon receipt of the ACK packet with its ECN-bit being marked, TCP sender halves the congestion window. Then the congestion window of the TCP flow keeps increasing linearly from $W/2$ to W periodically, where W is the maximum value of the congestion window. RTT is round trip time of TCP. According to the saw-tooth variation of the TCP congestion window [16], the average goodput R of TCP can be calculated by using the following formula.

$$R = \frac{\int_{W/2}^{W} w\,dw}{RTT \times W/2} = \frac{3W}{4RTT} \qquad (14\text{-}4)$$

Then, the total number T of packets delivered per congestion avoidance cycle is

$$T = \frac{R \times W \times RTT}{2} = \frac{3W^2}{8} \qquad (14\text{-}5)$$

Since there is one ECN-marked packet in these T packets, the probability p of marking ECN bit is

$$p = \frac{1}{T} = \frac{8}{3W^2} \tag{14-6}$$

Assume that the downlink buffer of AP is the network bottleneck and most of the delay of downlink and uplink TCP flows is due to waiting in the downlink buffer of AP. Since the delay that is caused for waiting in buffer is the main part of RTT, the average RTT of all TCP flows are almost equal.

From (14-4) and (14-6), the goodput ratio R_i/R_j of flow i and flow j is determined by the probability of ECN marking p_i and p .

$$\frac{R_i}{R_j} = \frac{RTT_j \times \sqrt{p_j}}{RTT_i \times \sqrt{p_i}} = \sqrt{\frac{p_j}{p_i}} \tag{14-7}$$

From (14-7), it can be concluded that TCP fairness can be achieved by adjusting the probability of ECN marking. In the following, two ECN marking methods is presented to achieve the up/down and time fairness between TCP flows.

14.3.3. Up/down Fairness

In the downlink buffer of AP, the DATA packets of downlink TCP flows and the ACK packets of uplink TCP flows are waiting for transmission. When APCC detects the congestion, APCC sets the Congestion Experienced (CE) bit in TCP DATA packets and the ECE (ECN-Echo) bit in TCP ACK packets. The probability of setting the CE bit in TCP DATA packets is the same as that of setting the ECE bit in TCP ACK packets. In this way, APCC can provide the bi-direction congestion control to achieve the up/down TCP fairness.

14.3.4. Time Fairness

In the multi-rate wireless network, the goodput fairness between flows will bring about the time unfairness problem and low network efficiency. Thus, it is more reasonable to guarantee the time fairness in the multi-rate wireless network.

Firstly, assume that a single packet of flow i is transmitted. If the propagation time is neglected, the overall transmission time t_i is composed of packet transmission time and a protocol-specific overhead:

$$t_i = \frac{s_i}{r_i} + t_{ov}, \tag{14-8}$$

where s_i is the packet length in bits, r_i is the wireless transmission rate. Since all flows get through the AP, r_i can be gotten form the lower layer by cross-layer communication. The overhead t_{ov} is composed of the backoff time, the transmission time of RTS, CTS, PHY header, MAC ACK and the associated inter-frame delay of SIFS and DIFS.

Assume that no collision with another frame occurs and the backoff time is chosen from a uniform distribution. As described in the standard [259], the overhead t_{ov} based on the IEEE 802.11 system parameter can be calculated by using the following formula:

$$t_{ov} = \frac{CW_{min} \times Slottime}{2} + DIFS + 3 \times SIFS + \frac{RTS + CTS + ACK + PHY_{header}}{Basic\ rate} \tag{14-9}$$

To guarantee the time fairness, the goodput ratio of flow i and flow j should be

$$\frac{R_i}{R_j} = \frac{t_j}{t_i} = \left(\frac{s_j}{r_j} + t_{ov}\right) \Big/ \left(\frac{s_i}{r_i} + t_{ov}\right) \tag{14-10}$$

By using (14-7), it is clear that the probability ratio of ECN marking is

$$\frac{P_i}{P_j} = \left(\frac{s_i}{r_i} + t_{ov}\right)^2 \Big/ \left(\frac{s_j}{r_j} + t_{ov}\right)^2 \tag{14-11}$$

14.3.5. ECN Marking Probability for Single TCP

Assume that n uplink and downlink TCP flows are getting through the AP. In the downlink buffer, the number of packets of TCP flow i is q_i, and the number of packets of all TCP flows is Q. Then it can be obtained

$$PQ = \sum_{i=1}^{n} p_i q_i \tag{14-12}$$

where P can be obtained from (14-3). Finally, the ECN marking probability p_i can be gotten for TCP flow i from (14-11) and (14-12).

14.3.6. Description of APCC Algorithm

Figure 14-1 shows the pseudo-code of APCC algorithm. APCC calculates P according to the congestion degree of AP during last time period $T_{interval}$. When a new packet of flow i arrives, p_i is computed according to the wireless transmission rate and the buffered packet number of flow i. Finally, APCC sets the CE bit in DATA packet or the ECE bit in ACK packet with the probability p_i.

```
for each T_interval
{ calculate U_c;
   calculate P with equation (14-3);
}


on receiving packet s of flow i
{ If (the downlink buffer is full) drop packet s ;
   else
   { calculate p_i with formula (14-11) and (14-12);
      if (random(0,1) < p_i)
      { PacketType = classify(s);
         if (PacketType==DATA) s.CE=1;
         if (PacketType==ACK) s.ECE=1;
      }
      enque s;
   }
}
```

Figure 14-1. Pseudo-code of APCC.

14.4. PERFORMANCE EVALUATION

To verify the effectiveness of APCC algorithm, a simulation study is conducted by using NS2 simulator [173]. The simulation topology is given in Figure 14-2. Each wired/wireless node only sends or receives one TCP NewReno flow (the size of TCP DATA packet is 1500 bytes). The capacity of the wired links is 100Mbps and their propagation time is 2ms. The size of the AP's downlink buffer is 100 packet. Each wireless node, including the AP, uses the NO Ad-Hoc Routing Agent (NOAH) routing protocol [200]. The MAC protocol uses RTS-CTS access mechanism, which conforms to the IEEE 802.11b specification (Table 14-1).

Table 14-1. IEEE 802.11 System Parameters

Parameter	Parameter Value	Parameter	Parameter Value
PHY header	192 bits	SIFS	$10 \mu s$
RTS frame	352 bits	DIFS	$50 \mu s$
CTS frame	304 bits	CW_{min}	31
ACK frame	304 bits	Basic rate	1Mbps
Slot time	$20 \mu s$		

Since the wireless channel is shared by wireless nodes, there exists background traffic in many scenarios such as multi-AP network. The background traffic occupies the wireless channel and makes interference in the wireless channel. To simulate the background traffic, two TCP flows are set between wireless nodes, which do not associate with the AP. Although the two TCP flows do not get through the AP, they increase the utilization of wireless channel.

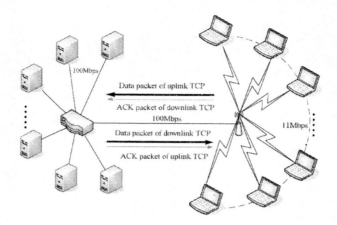

Figure 14-2. Simulation topology.

The performances of APCC together with that of the other three algorithms: Droptail, RED, and VQRED are evaluated. Droptail is the current default algorithm. RED and VQRED are the congestion control algorithms on the AP. The simulation time is 50 second. The default parameter settings for these algorithms are listed in Table 14-2.

Table 14-2. Algorithm Parameters

Parameter	
RED	min_{th}= 20, max_{th}= 70, w_p= 0.002, max_p= 0.1
VQRED	min_{th}= 20, max_{th}= 50, w_p= 0.002, max_p= 0.1
APCC	$T_{interval}$= 0.01s, α= 0.5

14.4.1. Congestion Control

In order to evaluate the performance of congestion control, three metrics, which are the packet loss rate, the mean length of buffer queue and the total network goodput, are used. Wireless transmission rate of all TCP flows is 11 Mbps. The number of downlink TCP flows varies from 3 to 15.

The packet loss rate of the four algorithms is shown in Figure 14-3. The packet loss rate of APCC is much lower than that of the other three algorithms. In APCC, the load of wireless channel is used to detect congestion, which leads to the lowest packet loss rate. In VQRED, the number of flow and the drop threshold are used to calculate the drop probability of each flow. With the increasing of flow number, the drop probability of each flow increases. When the number of TCP flows is larger than 12, the packet loss rate of VQRED is even higher than 10%.

Figure 14-4 shows that APCC gets the lower value of mean queue length than that of Droptail and RED, which means that APCC can maintain the smaller queuing delay. This is because APCC effectively controls the queue length through using the compound congestion indicator. Among the four algorithms, the packet loss rate of APCC is the lowest and its queuing delay is also very small. Thus, it is clear that APCC can obtain high network goodput. Figure 14-5 shows that APCC can achieve the highest total network goodput of the four algorithms.

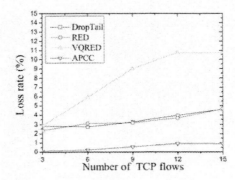

Figure 14-3. Loss rate.

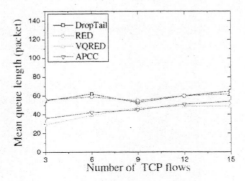

Figure 14-4. Queue length.

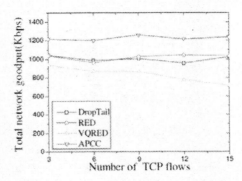

Figure 14-5. Total network goodput.

14.4.2. Up/down Fairness

In this scenario, the up/down TCP fairness of the four algorithms are evaluated. It is investigated whether or not APCC can guarantee the up/down TCP fairness when the number of downlink TCP flows is more than that of uplink TCP flows. The number of downlink TCP flows increases from 1 to 10, and the number of uplink TCP flows is fixed to 1.

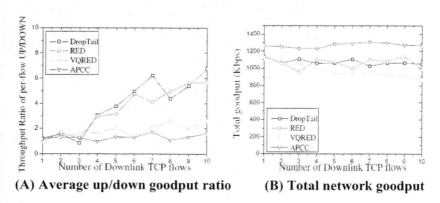

(A) Average up/down goodput ratio   **(B) Total network goodput**

Figure 14-6. Up/down fairness.

Figure 14-6(a) shows that the average goodput ratio of the single up/down TCP flow. In Droptail and RED, when the number of downlink flows is larger than 3, the goodput of uplink flows is much higher than that of downlink flows. Thus, Droptail and RED bring the serious up/down unfairness problem between TCP flows. This phenomenon can be explained by the TCP-unfriendly behavior of TCP ACK packet. When congestion happens in AP, if a DATA packet of downlink TCP flow is dropped, the congestion window of the wired node is reduced to half. However, if an ACK packet of uplink TCP flow is dropped, the cumulative ACK scheme lets uplink TCP flow tolerate the loss of TCP ACK packet. If the next ACK packet with the higher sequence number is delivered timely to the wireless node, the next ACK packet can make up for the loss of the previous ACK packet. Thus, the uplink TCP window size will not decrease. In this way, the goodput of the uplink TCP is much higher than that of the downlink TCP. Since VQRED and APCC use the bi-direction congestion control, the sending rates of uplink and downlink TCP flows are limited and the up/down TCP fairness is achieved. Figure 14-6(b) shows that, while APCC adjusts the bandwidth allocated for the uplink and downlink TCP flows, APCC also achieves the highest total network goodput of the four algorithms.

14.4.3. Time Fairness

In this section, the performance of APCC and other three algorithms is evaluated by using time fairness in multi-rate wireless networks. There are four downlink TCP flows TCP1 ~ 4, and one uplink TCP flow TCP5. The wireless nodes are initially connected to the AP with wireless transmission rates of 11Mbps. While the simulation is running, the wireless transmission data rate of TCP5 decreases successively from 11 Mbps to 5.5 Mbps, 2 Mbps and 1 Mbps.

As shown in Figure 14-7(a) and Figure 14-7(b), if Droptail or RED is used, the goodput of the uplink TCP flow TCP5 is much higher than that of the uplink TCP flows TCP1 ~ 4. Figure 14-7(c) shows that VQRED can guarantee the throughout fairness between TCP flows. However, if there are different transmission rates in the wireless channel, VQRED, RED and Droptail all bring about the problem of the low network efficiency. In Figure 14-7(a)~ (c), when the wireless transmission data rate of TCP5 decreases, the goodputs of other four TCP flows and the total network goodput also decrease. This is because TCP5 occupies more and more channel time with the decreasing of transmission date rate. Thus, the channel time allocated for other TCP flows is decreased and the total network efficiency is degraded.

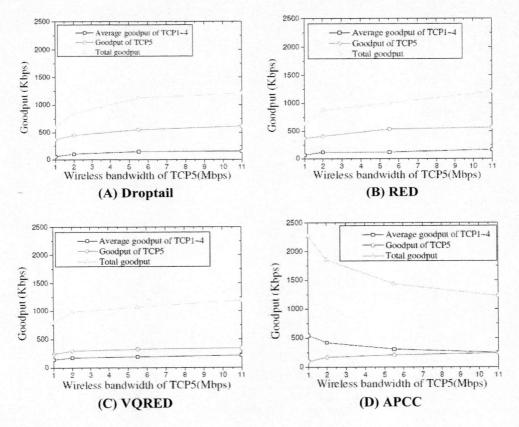

Figure 14-7. Time fairness.

As shown in Figure 14-7(d), while using APCC as the congestion control algorithm, the goodput of each TCP flow is differentiated and dependent on the channel transmission rate. When the wireless transmission rate of TCP5 decreases, the goodput of the other flows are protected. Furthermore, the decreased data rate of TCP5 means a decrease of the number of packets served by TCP5. As the number of packets served by TCP5 decreases, the time consumed by channel contention becomes a free resource and is reallocated to all other flows. Therefore, the goodput of other flows increases. As shown in Figure 14-7, compared with Droptail, RED and VQ-RED, APCC obtains the 280%, 260%, 185% increase in total goodput respectively when the wireless transmission data rate of TCP5 is 1 Mbps.

14.5. CONCLUSION

In this chapter, a simple and effective ECN-based congestion control algorithm, called APCC, is proposed in WLAN connected with Internet. Compared with the other algorithms, APCC has the following properties:

1) Based on the load of wireless channel and the length of buffer queue, APCC achieves low packet loss rate, low mean queue length, and high total network goodput.
2) APCC improves the up/down fairness by considering the direction of TCP flow.
3) APCC achieves higher total network goodput by saving more wireless channel resource for the flows with the higher channel transmission rate.

Chapter 15

A CHANNEL-AWARE SCHEDULING ALGORITHM FOR IMPROVING TCP FAIRNESS

15.1. INTRODUCTION

Based on IEEE 802.11 protocol, wireless local area networks (WLANs) are widely deployed in hotels, schools, offices, and other hot spot areas. While the IEEE 802.11 protocol provides all the competing nodes with equal opportunity for wireless channel access, it does not guarantee the fairness at the transport layer. In fact, the greedy closed loop control nature of TCP and the performance anomaly of wireless channel leads to the up/down and time unfairness problems between TCP flows.

When the uplink and downlink TCP flows coexist in WLAN, the DATA packets of the downlink TCP flows and the ACK packets of the uplink TCP flows compete in the downlink buffer of AP. However, the uplink and downlink TCP flows react to the buffer overflow in different ways. If a data packet of the downlink TCP is lost, the downlink TCP reduces its congestion window size. However, if an ACK packet is lost, the cumulative ACK mechanism lets the uplink TCP tolerate the loss of ACK packet as long as the next ACK packet with a higher sequence number is delivered timely to the sender. Then, the uplink TCP flow does not reduce its congestion window. Due to the greedy closed loop control nature of TCP, the throughput of the uplink TCP becomes much higher than that of the downlink TCP, and the downlink TCP tends to starve [251].

Recently, the multi-rate WLAN, such as IEEE 802.11a, 802.11b, and 802.11g, which supports high bandwidth in wireless hotspot areas, is widely employed. Such WLANs match their data transmission rates to the channel conditions [260, 194]. Berger et al indicate that, when a flow with a low data transmission rate captures the channel, it takes more time than a flow with a higher transmission rate, and hence the utilization of the channel is degraded [198].

Thus, the Up/Down Time Fair LAS (UDTFLAS) scheduling algorithm is proposed to achieve the up/down time fairness between TCP flows. By considering the multiple data rates, UDTFLAS sets different scheduling probability for each uplink and downlink TCP flow going through the AP. Analysis and simulation results show that, compared with throughput fair algorithms, UDTFLAS achieves the up/down time fairness, per-flow throughput protection, and 70% increase in total throughput.

15.2. RELATED WORK

Pilosof et al. firstly observed the unfairness problem between the uplink TCP flows and downlink TCP flows and proposed a TCP rate limit scheme (ModifyACK) [251]. By setting the advertised windows of ACK packet to $\lfloor B/n \rfloor$ (where B is the buffer size and n is the TCP flow number), ModifyACK limits the sending rates of the uplink and downlink TCP flows. However, since AP needs to manipulate the TCP headers of all packets, this scheme is very complex to be implemented.

To resolve the up/down TCP unfairness problem, some packet scheduling algorithms are proposed. The per-flow scheduling algorithm proposed in [261] deploys multiple queues for all the uplink and downlink TCP flows. The AP serves these queues with different probability to guarantee the up/down throughput fairness. The scheduling scheme is also very complex to be implemented for using per-flow scheduling. For solving the problem, a dual queue scheduling algorithm is proposed in [262], which uses two queues for TCP DATA and ACK packet respectively. Unlike these two multiple queues scheduling schemes, LAS (Least Attained Service) scheduling algorithm deploys only one queue [66]. LAS gives the priority to the flow that has received the least amount of service. In this way, LAS provides the uplink and downlink flows with the same throughput. However, the up/down TCP throughput fair schemes all neglect the time unfairness problem. It is clear that these throughput fairness schemes will bring about the time unfairness problem and low network efficiency.

To provide the time fairness, some novel MAC layer protocols are proposed to give the high transmission rate node with higher priority to access the wireless channel [254, 263, 253]. By allocating more network bandwidth to high-rate nodes, the overall system efficiency improves. However, these solutions, which implicitly assume that every node is always involved in the MAC layer contention, do not consider the congestion control of TCP layer. In fact, the TCP congestion scheme controls the wireless node's opportunity for MAC layer contention [264]. Thus, the time fairness between TCP flows can not be obtained successfully just by improving the MAC layer protocol.

15.3. THE UDTFLAS ALGORITHM

15.3.1. The Basic Idea of UDTFLAS

To achieve the up/down TCP fairness, LAS maintains the downlink buffer of AP as a single priority queue and inserts each incoming TCP DATA and TCP ACK packet at its appropriate position in that queue. The less service a connection has received so far, the closer to the head of the queue its arriving packets will be inserted. When a packet arrives and the queue is full, LAS first inserts the arriving packet at its appropriate position in the queue and then drops the packet that is at the end of the queue. Thus, LAS provides the same sending rate for TCP DATA packets of downlink TCP and TCP ACK packets of uplink TCP. Because of the self-clock function of TCP ACK packet, the uplink TCP gets the same sending rate as that of the downlink TCP.

However, the throughput fairness degrades the total network efficiency in the multi-rate WLAN. UDTFLAS scheduling algorithm is proposed to achieve the up/down TCP time fairness. Different with LAS, UDTFLAS sets the different block-factor for each TCP flow. The higher block-factor is set for the flow with the lower channel transmission rate. When the incoming packet is inserted into the queue, UDTFLAS determines the inserted position by the product of the block-factor and the received service of the flow. Thus, the flow with the higher channel transmission rate will be scheduled with the higher probability.

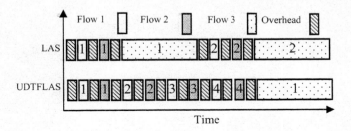

Figure 15-1. LAS and UDTFLAS scheduling.

Figure 15-1 illustrates the examples of the order in which packets are scheduled by LAS and UDTFLAS. Here, the contention overhead time of all packets is 1 sec (for illustration purposes), and the size of all packets is 10 bytes. There are three flows 1 ~ 3. The wireless channel transmission rates of flow 1 and flow 2 are all 10 byte/sec and that of flow 3 is 1.5 byte/sec. As shown in the scheduled order of LAS, LAS can guarantee the throughput fairness between the three flows. The total network throughput of LAS is 2.5 byte/sec. For UDTFLAS, since the wireless channel transmission rates of flow 3 is lower than that of the other flows, the block-factor of flow 3 is set to 4. In this way, UDTFLAS achieves the time fairness between the three flows. By protecting the TCP flows with the fast wireless channel transmission rate, UDTFLAS achieves much higher total network throughput, which increases by 52% to 3.8 byte/sec.

15.3.2. Description of UDTFLAS Algorithm

```
on receiving packet P
{ i = classify (P);
  key_i = key_i + 1;
  Mark_key (P, key_i);
  b_i = estimate_block_factor (i);
  j = 0;
  while ( j <Buffer_size && P_j.key >b_i*key_i) j ++;
  if (j == Buffer_size) Drop (P);
  else
    { Insert (P, P_j);
      If (queue is full) Remove_tail( ) ; }
}
```

Figure 15-2. Pseudo-code of UDTFLAS.

Figure 15-2 shows the pseudo-code of UDTFLAS algorithm. It explains the operations performed when a new packet P of flow i arrives. The inserted position of the packet P of flow i is computed as the block factor of flow i and the number of packets received in flow i.

15.3.3. Calculate the Block-Factor

The total wireless channel time of a packet (TCP DATA or ACK) comprises two parts, namely, the transmission time of the payload packet, and a constant protocol-specific overhead.

$$t_{channel} = \frac{s_i}{r_i} + t_{ov} \tag{15-1}$$

where s_i is the frame length in bits, r_i is the data rate. The constant protocol overhead t_{ov} is obtained by summing all the timing components that accompany the transmission of a packet. These time components include the transmission times for RTS, CTS, MAC, PHY, MAC ACK and the associated inter-frame delays SIFS and DIFS. Asume that no collision with another data packet occurs and the backoff time is chosen from a uniform distribution, the contention overhead time can be calculated based on the IEEE 802.11 system parameter:

$$t_{ov} = \frac{CW_{min}}{2} + DIFS + 3 \times SIFS + \frac{RTS + CTS + ACK + PHY_{header}}{Basic\ rate} \tag{15-2}$$

Since most data are transferred by TCP protocol, the channel time utilized by a TCP flow should take into account the time consumed by TCP DATA and TCP ACK packets.
Then the channel usage time T_i of flow i can be calculated as

$$T_i = \left(\frac{sdata_i + sack}{r_i} + 2t_{ov}\right) \times \frac{1}{block\_factor_i} \times N \tag{15-3}$$

where $sdata_i$ and $sack$ are the frame lengths of TCP DATA and ACK packet respectively, and N is the number of all packets. To guarantee the time fairness, the $block\_factor$ should be proportional to $\frac{sdata_i + sack}{r_i} + 2t_{ov}$. The $block\_factor$ of the flow with the highest channel transmission rate is set to 1. Therefore

$$block\_factor_i = \left(\frac{sdata_i + sack}{r_i} + 2t_{ov}\right) \bigg/ \left(\frac{sdata_{base} + sack}{r_{base}} + 2t_{ov}\right) \tag{15-4}$$

where $sdata_{base}$ and r_{base} are the TCP DATA frame length and the data rate of the packet of the flow with the highest channel transmission rate.

15.3.4. Fairness Bound Analysis

In this subsection, the relative fairness bound of UDTFLAS is analyzed. With UDTFLAS, the two flows i and j have a fairness bound, $FB(i,j)$, which is the upper limit of the difference between the channel usage times of the two flows.

Figure 15-3 illustrates the worst-case scheduling scenario when using UDTFLAS. Flow i and j are continuously back-logged. Flow i starts to serve the first packet after time $t1$, and finish serving the mth packet before time $t2$. Flow j starts to serve the first packet after the time flow i finishes serving the first packet, and finishes serving the nth packet after time $t2$.

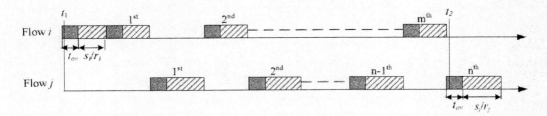

Figure 15-3. Fairness bound of UDTFLAS.

It is clear that the maximum channel usage time of flow i is $(m+1)(t_{ov} + s_i/r_i)$, and the minimum channel usage time of flow j is $(n-1)(t_{ov} + s_j/r_j)$. Thus the fairness bound, $FB(i,j)$, can be calculated as

$$FB(i,j) = (m+1)(t_{ov} + s_i/r_i) - (n-1)(t_{ov} + s_j/r_j) \tag{15-5}$$

Since UDTFLAS can guarantee the time fairness, $m : n$ equals to $(t_{ov} + s_j/r_j) : (m+1)(t_{ov} + s_i/r_i)$. Thus, it can be obtained

$$FB(i,j) = 2t_{ov} + s_i/r_i + s_j/r_j \tag{15-6}$$

Then, when using UDTFLAS, the difference in the channel usage times between flow i and flow j is bounded by $2t_{ov} + s_i/r_i + s_j/r_j$.

15.4. PERFORMANCE EVALUATION

The performance of the UDTFLAS algorithm is evaluated together with that of the other three algorithms: Droptail, ModifyACK and LAS. As reference points, Droptail is chosen as the default scheme and ModifyACK and LAS are chosen as the up/down throughput fairness algorithms.

All simulations are run on the NS-2 simulator [173] with the simulation topology given in Figure 15-4. There are three downlink TCP flows TCP1 ~ 3, and one uplink TCP flow TCP4. Nodes $A \sim D$ are initially connected to the AP with data rates of 11 Mbps. While the simulation is running, the data rate of node D changes successively from 11 Mbps to 5.5 Mbps, 2 Mbps and 1 Mbps. All wired bandwidths are set to 25 Mbps. The downlink buffer queue is located between the LL and the MAC protocol. The buffer size of the downlink buffer is 100 packets. Each wireless node, including the AP, uses the NO Ad-Hoc Routing Agent (NOAH) routing protocol [200]. The MAC protocol used conforms to the IEEE 802.11b specification, which is shown in Table 15-1.

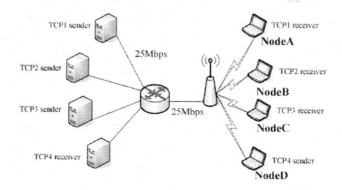

Figure 15-4. simulation topology.

Table 15-1. IEEE 802.11 System Parameters

Parameter	Parameter Value	Parameter	Parameter Value
PHY header	192 bits	SIFS	10 μs
RTS frame	352 bits	DIFS	50 μs
CTS frame	304 bits	CW_{min}	31
ACK frame	304 bits	Basic rate	1Mbps
Slot time	20 μs		

15.4.1. Individual TCP Throughput

Firstly, the individual throughput is examined. Figures 15-5 ~ 15-8 show the individual TCP throughput of the four algorithms. As the channel transmission rate of TCP4 decreases, these figures show that the throughputs of the four TCP flows change over time.

Figure 15-5 shows that when Droptail is used, the throughput of the uplink TCP flow TCP4 is much higher than that of the downlink TCP flows TCP1 ~ 3. This comparison between the throughputs of uplink and downlink TCP flows shows obviously the up/down unfairness problem. When the time is larger than 40 second, the throughput of TCP4 becomes lower with the decreasing of the channel transmission rate. The throughputs of other three TCP flows also decrease because TCP4 occupies more and more channel usage time and degrades the throughput of the other TCP flows.

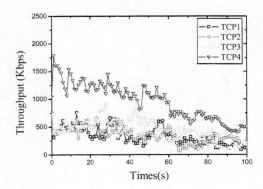

Figure 15-5. Per-flow throughput of Droptail.

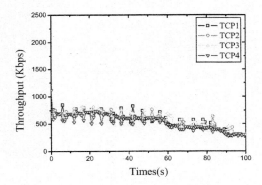

Figure 15-6. Per-flow throughput of LAS.

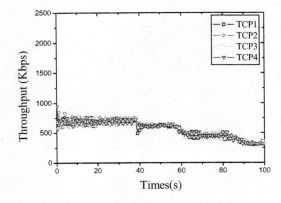

Figure 15-7. Per-flow throughput of ModifyACK.

Figure 15-6 and Figure 15-7 show that, since LAS and ModifyACK can guarantee the up/down TCP throughput fairness, the throughputs of all four TCP flows are almost the same. However, when the channel transmission rate of TCP4 becomes lower, the throughputs of all four TCP flows are all reduced because the TCP flow with the lowest data rate degrades the throughputs of the other TCP flows. This phenomenon shows the tradeoff between the throughput fairness and total network efficiency in the multi-rate wireless network.

In Figure 15-8, using UDTFLAS as the scheduling algorithm, the throughput of each TCP flow is differentiated and dependent on the channel transmission rate. As shown in Figure 15-8, when the channel transmission rate of TCP4 decreases, the throughputs of the other flows remain almost unchanged and are protected. Since UDTFLAS takes into account the data rate of each flow, the throughputs of TCP1 ~ 3 are stable and the per-flow protection of throughput is guaranteed.

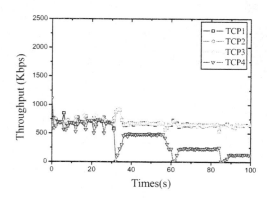

Figure 15-8. Per-flow throughput of UDTFLAS.

15.4.2. Total Network Efficiency and Fairness

This subsection evaluates the overall performance of the four algorithms: Droptail, LAS, ModifyACK and UDTFLAS. Figure 15-9 shows that, compared with the other algorithms, UDTFLAS achieves 70% average increase in total throughput. This is explained by the fact that UDTFLAS can protect the throughputs of the TCP flows with the higher channel transmission rate, thus can achieve the higher total network throughput.

A fairness index is defined, which represents the relative time fairness achieved for the uplink and downlink flows. It is calculated by measuring the amount of channel time that each flow has used for its transmissions.

$$Up/down\ time\ ratio = \frac{average\ time\ of\ uplink\ TCP}{average\ time\ of\ downlink\ TCP} \qquad (15\text{-}7)$$

Figure 15-10 shows the up/down time ratio of the four algorithms. Droptail shows the most severe TCP unfairness problem. When the time is larger than 80 seconds, the channel usage time of TCP4 can even be about 18 times as larger as that of downlink TCP flows in Droptail. This means that TCP4 occupies most of the wireless channel. For LAS and ModifyACK, the time fairness ratios increase a lot when the channel transmission rate of TCP4 becomes lower. As shown in Figure 15-10, when using UDTFLAS, the time fairness ratio remains about to 1, which means that the uplink and downlink TCP flows receive almost the same channel usage time.

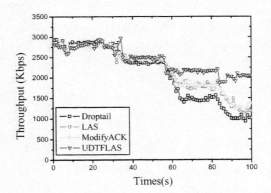

Figure 15-9. Total network throughput.

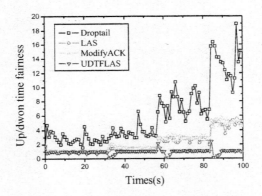

Figure 15-10. Up/down time ratio.

15.5. CONCLUSION

In this chapter, the UDTFLAS algorithm is proposed to improve the up/down time fairness of TCP flows. By setting the block factors for the TCP flows, UDTFLAS achieves per-flow throughput protection, up/down time fairness, and an increase in total throughput.

Compared with the other algorithms, UDTFLAS has the following properties:

1) UDTFLAS improves the up/down time fairness by considering the multiple transmission rates.
2) UDTFLAS achieves higher total network throughput by saving more wireless channel resource for the flows with the higher channel transmission rate.

3) UDTFLAS is only deployed on AP without any change to the wireless nodes.
4) UDTFLAS works at the flow level, which involves no change to the underlying MAC protocols.

Chapter 16

AN IMPROVED TCP WITH CROSS-LAYER CONGESTION NOTIFICATION OVER WIRED/WIRELESS HYBRID NETWORKS

16.1. INTRODUCTION

With the increasing application of mobile equipments, new techniques such as Wireless LAN, Ad Hoc Network, and Wireless Sensor Network are used in many occasions. However, how to syncretize these wireless networks into traditional Internet is becoming more and more important. In Ad Hoc Network, people require to download data from the Internet and update real-time information. In Wireless Sensor Network, the data collected from sensor nodes will be timely aggregated to relevant center nodes. There are many great applications as mentioned above. Thus, a big problem comes up to design a TCP protocol in order to ensure efficient transmission over multi-hop wireless/wired hybrid networks.

This chapter is organized as follows. Section 16.2 analyzes TCP protocol of wireless network and concludes that requirement of cross-layer design is totally different from that of wired networks. In Section 16.3, a TCP model is proposed by using cross-layer congestion notification over wireless/wired hybrid networks. And its particular design and implementation are also described. Simulations are shown in Section 16.4, which indicate that network performance over wireless/wired hybrid networks is improved by using the proposed TCP model.

16.2. CROSS-LAYER DESIGN OF TCP OVER WIRELESS NETWORKS

Currently, the prime method of congestion control over wired network is an optimization framework based on utility functions. However, this method is unable to be applied into wireless network, because metrics such as queue length on routers, sending rate of links can't characterize congestion price due to the immanent interference of wireless links. By simulations, V. Raghunathan and P.R.Kumar manifest that the method fails in wireless networks [265], because there is an oscillatory throughput behavior that its order of magnitude is worse than the corresponding wired networks. Thereby, the authors use a model of "interference matrix" to characterize the interference of wireless links. Only if this model being coupled with the method based on utility functions, it can become successful in controlling congestions of wireless networks. As a result, TCP should be modified in wireless networks. Concretely, cross-layer design of wireless TCP and MAC is needed to explicitly account for effects of the interference nature in wireless links.

Similarly, L. Chen proposes Flow Contention Graph and Contention Matrix to establish the model of link-layer state for the first time [266], by which resource allocation is formulated as a utility maximization problem with constraints that arise from contention of channel access. Suppose that the network is shared by a set S of sources. The aim of congestion control is to select a sending rate $x_s(t)$, by which $\underset{x_s \geq 0}{Max} \sum_s U_s(x_s)$ can be satisfied with restriction: $FRx \leq \varepsilon$, whose meaning is that total slots each link occupied according to Contention Matrix is less than the maximal flow of Flow Contention Graph. The congestion control algorithm based on shadow price could be described as: $x_s = k_s(U_s^l(x_s(t)) - q_s(t)), s \in S$. Aggregated rate $q_s(t)$ is the feedback of source, which reflects competition degree of all source paths, and it can be defined as $q_s = \sum_{nl} \lambda_n(z_n) F_{nl} R_{ls}$, where $\lambda_n(z_n)$ is equal to the congestion price of competition degree of ring n when the normalize rate is z_n. And it will be evaluated to be a given function in the MAC algorithm.

It is concluded that wireless TCP should be cross-layer designed following optimization framework based on utility functions and combined with shadow price of MAC layer.

16.3. CROSS-LAYER DESIGN FOR TCP IN WIRELESS/WIRED NETWORKS

This section firstly introduces metrics from MAC layer that can be treated as congestion price for TCP. Then, a cross-layer ECN scheme is proposed to syncretize the cross-layer design into existing TCP protocols in hybrid networks.

16.3.1. Selection of Congestion Metric from MAC Layer in Wireless Networks

There has been some congestion metrics from MAC layer in wireless networks, which can be cited as following:

Joint Metric

$\alpha \cdot \dfrac{T \cdot B}{n+1} - \beta \cdot Q_{ifq} - \zeta \cdot \mathrm{Re}\, try_{avg}$ [267], where the three items are available bandwidth, interface queue (IFQ) length and average link layer retransmission (ALR) respectively. Parameters α, β and ζ are weighted values of the three items. The joint metric illustrates that available resource can be calculated by subtracting occupied bandwidth at IP and MAC layer from available bandwidth. With the decrease of this value, congestion probability will increase. It is an accurate method for rate control in TCP. However, the problem of non-compatibility comes up due to too much modification.

Frame Service Delay

The interval of a sender between the interception for channel access and successful receiving an ACK frame from next hop, which is the sum of conflicting cycle and sending cycle [268]. Actually it is the RTT (Round trip Time) of MAC layer. Dong.Y etc. investigate that FSD is the best indication of congestion state in MAC layer [269]. However, it is difficult to apply FSD into cross-layer design because the change of this metric is of complexity.

Channel Busyness Ratio

The ratio of time intervals when the channel is busy due to successful transmission or collision to the total time [270]. It can reflect the condition of MAC contention and collision since it indicates the available bandwidth of wireless channel. But its calculation depends on the simple interval in MAC transmitting process, in which the number of connection station must be considered, as well as TCP sending rate, the packet size and so on.

RTS Retry Count

RTS retry count is most widely used as a metric for congestion in MAC layer. Zh.h.Fu et al. firstly draw an important conclusion that congestion states appear to be the block of access competition in MAC rather than the increase of queue length on routers as wireless hops increasing [256]. Subsequently, Link RED, a virtual packet drop mechanism, is proposed by using this metric. LRED improves TCP throughput by adjusting their backoff slots adaptively. But the routing failure and competition collision will increase due to this virtual drop mechanism.

In the following, the correlation between this metric and the congestion state in MAC layer is analyzed by experiments.

As shown in Figure 16-1, there is a TCP/Reno connection from $n0$ to $n1$, whose packet size is 1000bit. The buffer size of node $n0$ and $n1$ are 10 packets. At the same time, neighbor nodes of $n0$ or $n1$ are forwarding UDP flow, which acts as cross flows. More UDP flows being injected will mean more congestion. The simulation lasts for 300ms.

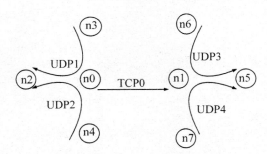

Figure 16-1. Topology for congestion metric analysis.

RTS retry count (RTS), Frame Service Delay (FSD) and Channel Busyness Ratio (R_b) are the main metrics for evaluate the congestion in wireless MAC layer. The three metrics are counted at $n0$. In Table 16-1, RTS(%) is the ratio of RTS counter being large than 2 to the total RTS counter, which is counted just based on TCP0 packets. FSD is the average value of frame service delay of TCP0's packets. R_b is sampled in every certain interval. Since idle time is easy to be summed up, R_b of the channel $n0$-$n1$ is the ratio of idle time to the interval.

Table 16-1. RTS counter, FSD, R$_b$ with different UDP flows

	TCP+ 1UDP	TCP+ 2UDP	TCP+ 3UDP	TCP+ 4UDP
RTS (%)	0.1349	0.1688	0.2068	0.2109
FSD(ms)	20.234	21.289	23.560	24.395
R$_b$	0.66237	0.69409	0.71038	0.72191

As shown in Table 16-1, RTS ratio will increase with the increasing of the number of UDP flows, as well as the average value of FSD and R$_b$. Therefore, these metrics can describe congestion from MAC layer. In the following section, RTS counter is selected for more discussion.

16.3.2. The Model of Cross-layer Design for TCP Protocol

The result of the experiments is according to the design of TCP in [271], which firstly applied RTS retry count into TCP congestion control, whose main scheme is as following:

$$wnd_{max} = \begin{cases} [wnd_{max}/2], rts\_retry > 2 \\ wnd_{max} + 2, 0 < rts\_retry \leq 2 \end{cases}$$

(16-1)

As shown in (16-1), the TCP window is still adjusted by the additive increase and multiplicative decrease (AIMD) scheme. But the problem is: (1) notifying window is only a limitation to sending rate, so its impact on TCP rate is not large enough; (2) the AIMD scheme is not advocated in the view of decreasing TCP sending rate and delay jitter in wireless networks, which is especially in multi-hop networks. FeW (Fractional increment of TCP congestion window) scheme proposed by K. Nahm et al has been proved to be efficient to provide more stability rate and higher throughput [272]. By and large, it is important for congestion control to adjust TCP sending rate appropriately according to congestion metrics from MAC layer. Actually, it draws more attention that redesign of wireless TCP should syncretize with existing wired TCP protocols, by which exiting schemes of TCP rate control can still be effective. And the cross-layer design in wireless networks should be a supplement or modification.

Based on the previous works [273], this chapter proposes the TCP model with cross-layer congestion notification over wired/wireless hybrid networks, which is shown in Figure 16-2. It is mostly distinguished from other TCP variants by taking into account the congestion induced by access competition in wireless link, in which cross-layer ECN (Explicit Congestion Notification) is the key supplement to original TCP model.

TCP protocol by using this model can be described as following:

(1) Routers in Wired Network

All routers in wired network count the queue length. Then they mark packets with congestion according to queue length.

(2) Routers in Wireless Network

All routers in wireless network will count the number of RTS retrying times when they send packets. Then if it is larger than one given threshold, they will mark the arriving packet with congestion flag.

(3) TCP Receiver

When a packet is arriving, TCP receiver will check its head to obtain the information about congestion in network path, which will be inserted into the corresponding ACK packet.

(4) TCP Sender

When a ACK packet is arriving, TCP sender will check it head to judge whether its congestion flag (CE) is 1 or not. If CE=1, TCP sender will trigger congestion control, otherwise it will do the same work as the sender of TCP Reno.

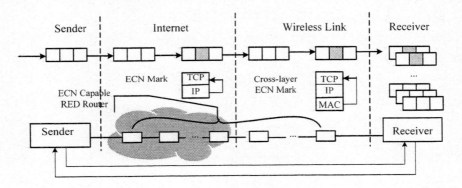

Figure 16-2. TCP model with Cross-layer ECN over wired/wireless Hybrid Networks.

16.3.3. Cross-layer Design for TCP Protocol

In this chapter, ECN scheme will mark packets according to RTS Retry counts, whose threshold is specified to 2 by the experiments and analysis therein before. As all known, IEEE 802.11 is the standard protocol for wireless Ad Hoc, which offers two options for access: basic scheme and RTS / CTS scheme. Since RTS / CTS scheme is more widely used in Ad Hoc networks than the basic scheme, it is the only consideration in this chapter, but the design can be also applied to basic scheme.

In RTS / CTS scheme, each node maintains a variable *ssrc* to record the retransmit count of RTS frame in the current node. When a node fails to transmit RTS frame, it will retransmit this RTS frame and increase *ssrc* by 1 at the same time. If the value of *ssrc* reaches 7, the sender in MAC will report a link failure notification to network layer, discard the RTS frame and the Data frame to be transmitted together, reset *ssrc* to an initial value of 0. Once the node successfully transmits the RTS frame, it will also refresh *ssrc* with an initial value of 0. In this way, when a node starts to transmit a new RTS frame, regardless of whether the initial RTS was successfully transmitted or abandoned, *ssrc* will be the initial value of 0. Obviously, the node would not know the RTS retry count of the last frame for its resetting, result in unknowing about its channel state.

In order to solve this problem, the value of *ssrc* is recorded when each RTS frame is retransmitted. Once it exceeds the given threshold "2", the packet to be transmitted will be marked "1" in its CE (congestion experience) bit, which indicates an imminent congestion in ECN mechanism.

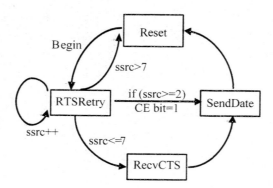

Figure 16-3. State transit of wireless nodes with cross-layer ECN.

Figure 16-3 gives the state transit of wireless nodes and indicates how the cross-layer ECN scheme works. In fact, the cross-layer information is stored in the expansion of the first IP Packet and then it is transferred among the packet heads. This is a simple way of in-band information transfer [274], and the transfer channel of original ECN mechanism only exists between TCP layer and IP layer. In the following, ECN signal will be extended to MAC layer.

Moreover this method can be easily extended, and be of both good compatible and less costly. The most important is that the combination of ECN methods and AQM mechanisms has been proven to be effective for TCP Congestion Control. The method of cross-layer ECN is an expansion of their congestion control mechanism in wireless networks, which combining the two mechanisms seamlessly. Therefore, the TCP model shown in Figure 16-2 is worthy to be referred to TCP research in hybrid networks.

16.4. SIMULATIONS AND ANALYSIS

The MAC of 802.11b module is modified to simulate cross-layer ECN shown in Figure 16-2 [173], whose performance is evaluated in the multi-stream wireless LAN and multi-hop wireless/wire hybrid networks.

16.4.1. Performance Analysis in Wireless LAN

Figure 16-4 shows the simulated scenario that a wireless network accesses to the Internet, in which several TCP flows send from $W(i)$ to wireless nodes $N(i)$ through the BS. Suppose the bandwidth between $W(10)$ and BS is large enough to shield congestion on routers. Thus, in this case, network congestion can be only reflected by the competition of MAC layer Channel.

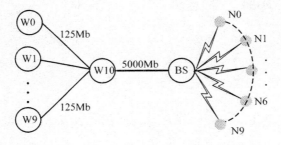

Figure 16-4. Simulation Topology 1.

Table 16-2. Parameter settings in topology 1

Parameter	Value
Prop	TwoRayGround
Mac	802_11
Ifq	DropTail/PriQueue
Ifqlen	20
adhocRouting	DSDV

Table 16-2 shows the parameter settings of the wireless network in scenario 1, and the remaining parameters without special statement employ the default value of NS2. The simulation time is 300 s.

Table 16-3. Throughput and fairness with different numbers of TCP flows

TCP Number	Throughput (kbps)		Fairness (-)	
	ECN	noECN	ECN	noECN
5	**826.95**	822.89	**0.973**	0.972
8	**763.42**	763.31	**0.977**	0.869
10	**615.46**	611.35	**0.811**	0.520

Table 16-3 shows the performance analysis in scenario 1 with TCP flows traversing the hybrid network. With the increase of flows number, the total TCP throughput and TCP fairness decreased by 34% and 46.5% respectively, which is the result of MAC layer competition being intensified and the channel state being deteriorated. By using the cross layer ECN, TCP fairness only decreased by 16.6% because of the sender's deceleration in advance.

Figure 16-5 shows throughput comparison of each TCP flow in case of 8 TCP flows concurrence. As shown in Figure 16-5(a), the throughput of seventh flow almost decreases to zero, which is the result of channel competition of multi TCP flows in hybrid networks.

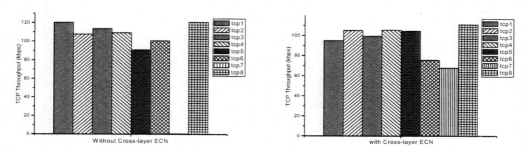

(A) TCP Throughput Without Cross-layer ECN (B) TCP Throughput With Cross-layer ECN

Figure 16-5. TCP Throughput Comparison in topology 1.

By using the cross-layer ECN, TCP flows that access channels will decelerate initiatively as soon as receiving congestion notifications, which makes these starved TCP flows have opportunity to participate in competition. As shown in Figure 16-5(b), multi TCP flows remain relatively fair throughput.

The experimental results show that total TCP throughput has not been increased. That is because there are no hidden nodes in networks, so each node can detect the transmission of other nodes and the RTS/CTS scheme in MAC can effectively control channel access of nodes. So the sender's window size does not affect the TCP throughput.

In summary, the cross-layer ECN scheme can adjust TCP sending rate based on the competition degree in wireless channel. Therefore the channel conflict is alleviated in the precondition of keeping the total throughput. As a result, the unfair phenomenon of multi-flow competition can be mitigated.

16.4.2. Performance Analysis of Multi-hop Wireless/Wired Hybrid Networks

Figure 16-6 shows the scenario of multi-hop wireless network access to the Internet, in which a TCP flow sending from $W(0)$ to wireless $Node(4)$. The distance between any two wireless nodes is 200m and the transmission distance of each node is 250m. During the simulation period (300s), two UDP flows join into $Node(1)$ and $Node(2)$ respectively in the periods of 50s ~ 250s and 100s ~ 200s, whose send interval is 0.02s. The size of UDP packet is 1460byte and other parameters are the same as that of scenario 1.

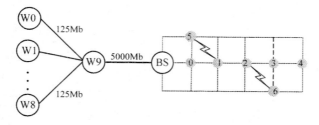

Figure 16-6. Simulation Topology 2.

As shown in Figure 16-6, these are hidden terminals when a TCP flow is transmitted over this multi-hop wireless hybrid network. The two UDP flows will also aggravate the impact of hidden terminal *Node*(1) and *Node*(2). However, the receiver only depends on whether there is packet dropping or not to regulate the window size and knows nothing about congestion induced by channel access. It will lead to more conflict at intermediate nodes, especially on *Node*(1) and *Node*(2), as well as increases competition and channel deterioration.

However TCP Reno with ECN function in MAC can apperceive congestion from changes of RTS Retry, regulate window size according to explicit feedback in MAC, change the number of packets being transmitted into networks, and reduce the probability of congestion collapse. Eventually it can improve the total throughput of hybrid networks.

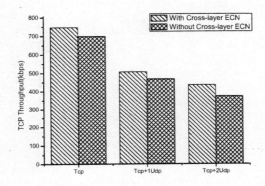

Figure 16-7. Throughput Comparison in topology 2.

Figure 16-7 shows the comparison of TCP throughputs in three cases corresponding to "one TCP flow", "one TCP flow and one UDP flow concurrence", "one TCP flow and two UDP flows concurrence" in scenario 2.

As shown in Figure 16-7, TCP throughput increases from 6.92% to 16.76% while the number of UDP is increasing and the problem of hidden terminal being prominent. The reason is that an improved TCP with cross-layer congestion notification can alleviate the impact of hidden terminal to some extent.

16.5. CONCLUSION

This chapter proposes an improved TCP with cross-layer congestion notification over Wired-wireless hybrid networks. Being different from some existing TCP protocols, it takes into account the congestion of channel competition in MAC layer. The most important is that this model is built on the ECN scheme, which have been proven to be effective on congestion control and widely supported in many situations [275, 276, 236]. So the model is of good feasibility and scalability. Simulation results show that it is an effective supplement.

Chapter 17

A PREDICTION METHOD FOR CONGESTION PROBABILITY BASED ON ECN OVER WIRED-WIRELESS HYBRID NETWORKS

17.1. INTRODUCTION

Different from the Internet, wireless networks have characteristics of higher bit error rate, lower bandwidth, longer delay, frequent mobility and so on. So there are packets dropping frequently in wireless network. However, traditional TCP protocols assume that all packet loss is the result of network congestion and decrease its sending rate, which leads to the performance degradation in wired/wireless hybrid networks. Therefore, TCP protocols need to exclude impact of non-congestion loss on congestion control mechanism [277] [203].

Currently, TCP enhancements over wired/wireless hybrid networks have mainly focused on differentiating packet losses. In fact, reasons of packet dropping are more complicated in hybrid networks, including link disconnection, routing change and handoff, and so on. It is becoming more and more difficult to shield TCP layer from non-congestion losses. Therefore, finding a more precise scheme to aware congestion and/or distinguish state is the best way to improve TCP performance in such long and leaky TCP pipes.

ECN is always been applied extensively since it was proposed by S.Floyd [46]. Microsoft Vista and netBSD have specially designed to support this mechanism [236] [276]. At the mean time, many research focused on improvement of congestion control mechanism based on ECN [275] [48] [92]. So it is a most simple and most effective approach that ECN is used to mark congestion and control TCP behavior accordingly.

In hybrid networks, congestion aware schemes based on ECN are mainly applied to control TCP behavior while packet loss occurring. Wireless ECN, named as WECN, is proposed by F. Peng and S.d. Cheng [278]. By using WECN, the packet loss will be judged as error induced if its CE (Congestion Explicit) bit is 1. Otherwise it will be judged as congestion induced. WECN have been applied in TCP protocols such as TCP Jersey, TFRC etc [279-281].

However some research results point out that ECN mechanism can't differentiate losses efficiently because its ability mostly depends on how accurate ECN mechanism can aware congestion [282,283]. With respect to this problem, Rain J. etc proposed Wireless WMECN [285] based on MECN [284]. In WMECN, different weight values are assigned to CE bits feedback by ACKs in the latest period, their weighted sum is calculated and partitioned into 4 congestion degrees as the judgement of TCP rate control. The method is other than previous congestion control methods based on single ECN feedback. However the improvement of TCP performance rather depends on threshold values. Moreover, there is less emphasis on changes of network states.

This chapter mainly focuses on how TCP sender should response to congestion signal feedback by ECN if error losses and congestion losses are coexisting in hybrid networks. There are two aspects which should be considered:

1) The delay in hybrid networks should not be overlooked. It is prominent in hybrid networks that feedback delay is large and uncertain. Simulations by V. Raghunathan and P. R. Kumar manifest that there are oscillatory throughput behavior that is orders of magnitude worse than the corresponding wired networks, as well as that of RTT (round trip time)[265]. As a result, even if congestion state can be notified by ECN perfect correctly, the feedback with uncertain delay may do nothing good for congestion control. So it is one of the problems how to alleviate non-real-time effects on congestion aware schemes.

2) No matter how the routers intend to aware congestion, information of ECN feedback just indicates the imminent congestion, not congestion already occurring. Since the state of network changes dynamically, the congestion loss may occur or not in the next interval, i.e. the congestion may either become true if packets are discarded continually, or clear up if link state is recovered in a short period. So it is not suitable for congestion control protocols to respond to such non-exactness feedback information.

In light of the two observations, it can be concluded that ECN feedback information cannot be used to adjust the TCP control behavior directly, but should be utilized in an efficient manner. Aiming at mitigating the impact of large delay and reducing accuracy requirements of congestion metrics, this chapter proposes a congestion aware scheme named as CPECN (Congestion Probability based on Explicit Congestion Notification). The method to control the sender's behavior based on CPECN is more reasonable than previous methods based on single loss event or single ECN feedback. Simulation results show that CPECN can be easily extended to existing TCP variants and improve TCP performance in hybrid networks.

The rest of the chapter is organized as follows. Section 17.2 presents *CP* and investigates the correlation between *CP* and network states. Section 17.3 describes TCP protocol with CPECN in detail. Section 17.4 discusses and analyzes the simulation results. Finally, concluding remarks for this chapter are presented in Section 17.5.

17.2. CPECN: CONGESTION PROBABILITY BASED ON ECN

The key idea of CPECN is to analyze the distribution of CE bit from ECN feedbacks and predict congestion states by the correlation between feedback serials.

17.2.1. Calculation of Congestion Probability

Single ECN feedback only reflects the network state at some earlier point in time, thus several ECN feedbacks can reflect the dynamic change of network state at several intervals. So it is more reasonable to respond to several ECN feedbacks together in an appropriate way.

In order to characterize serial ECN feedbacks, a new conception of CP (*Congestion Probability*) is introduced. Assume that there are m-1 ACK packets before the ith ACK packet arrives, which is $ACK[m-1]$, $ACK[m-2]$, ..., $ACK[1]$. When the ith ACK packet arrives, named $ACK[0]$, CP at this moment can be calculated as follows.

$$CP[i] = \frac{1}{m} \times \sum_{j=0}^{m-1} w_j \times Ack[j].ecnecho \qquad (17\text{-}1)$$

where $ACK[j].ecnecho$ is the value of CE bit in $ACK[j]$, w_j is the weight of $ACK[j]$ and $\sum_{i=0}^{m-1} w_j = 1$. $CP[i]$ is calculated based on m ACKs, which includes itself and m-1 ACKs before it. To be concise, $ACK[j].ecnecho$ is expressed as $ACK[j]$ in this following.

The sender always gathers CE bit from ACK and calculates the current CP value by using EWMA (Exponentially Weighted Moving Average) predictor shown in (17-1). The m ACKs are divided into several segments and each ACK will be assigned with a weight. The weights of ACKs in the same segment are equal, which means that the ACKs in the same segment have the same impact on the judgement of network state. By this way, the role of one single ACK is decreased and that of all ACKs in one segment is increased. So the judgement of network state is built on the change trends of ECN feedback.

If the last m ACKs are divided into n segments, then $CP[i]$ can be calculated as following:

$$CP[i] = \sum_{j=1}^{n} w_j \times \frac{n}{m} \times \sum_{i=\frac{m}{n}(j-1)}^{\frac{m}{n}j-1} ACK[i] \qquad (17\text{-}2)$$

where

$$\sum_{j=1}^{n} w_j = 1 \qquad (17\text{-}3)$$

Generally, the weight of the new ACK is larger than that of the old one. So the weights of the ACKs in each segment are assigned as following:

$$w_j = \alpha \times w_{j-1}, \alpha \in (0,1) \qquad (17\text{-}4)$$

In traditional TCP protocol, the sender enters the slow-start mode after receiving three duplicate ACK packets. So four ACK packets is chosen to compose one segment, i.e:

$$m = 4n \tag{17-5}$$

By using (17-3), (17-4), (17-5), (17-2) can be rewritten as following:

$$CP[i] = \sum_{j=1}^{n} w_j \times \frac{1}{4} \times \sum_{i=4(j-1)}^{4j-1} ACK[i], i \in [1, m] \tag{17-6}$$

which can be expanded to

$$CP[i] = w_1 \times \frac{1}{4} \times \sum_{i=0}^{3} ACK[i] + \frac{w_1}{\alpha} \times \frac{1}{4} \times \sum_{i=4}^{7} ACK[i] + \ldots + \frac{w_1}{\alpha^{n-1}} \times \frac{1}{4} \times \sum_{i=4(n-1)}^{4n-1} ACK[i] \tag{17-7}$$

When $CP[i+1] > CP[i]$, the congestion probability is increasing. Meanwhile, the congestion probability may be decreasing when $CP[i+1] < CP[i]$. Therefore, the change of CP value can be used to judge the network state.

Let $\Delta CP = CP[i+1] - CP[i]$, it can be obtained:

$$\Delta CP = \frac{w_i}{4} \times ((ACK[4] - ACK[0]) + \frac{1}{\alpha} \times (ACK[8] - ACK[4]) + \ldots$$

$$+ \frac{1}{\alpha^{n-1}} \times (ACK[4n] - ACK[4n-4]))$$

$$= \frac{w_i}{4} \times (-ACK[0] + (1 - \frac{1}{\alpha}) \cdot ACK[4] + (\frac{1}{\alpha} - \frac{1}{\alpha^2}) \cdot ACK[8] + \ldots$$

$$+ (\frac{1}{\alpha^{n-1}} - \frac{1}{\alpha^n}) \times ACK[4n]) \tag{17-8}$$

From (17-8), it is very clear that ΔCP is just related to $ACK[4i]$, which is the last ACK of each segment. The value of ΔCP lies in a discrete set that contains 2^{n+1} elements. If CE bit of the last ACK in the last segment is 0, the value of ΔCP will be in $[-1, 0]$. In general, it can be concluded that the congestion probability is decreasing, which has the same meaning with one single *ECN* feedback. On the contrary, if the CE bit of the latest arriving ACK is 1, the value of ΔCP will belong to $[-1, 1]$. In this case, it cannot be determined whether the network is going to become congested or not. Whatever the CE bit of the new arriving ACK is, $\Delta CP \leq 0$ always indicates that the network congestion may be relieved.

For simplicity, the last m ACKs are divided into 2 segments, that is $n = 2$ and $m = 8$. Let $w_1 = 0.25 * w_2$. By using (17-3) and (17-4), it can be obtained that $w_1 = 0.2$ and $w_2 = 0.8$. All these parameters are used in the following simulations. Figure 17-1 is the pseudo code of calculating CP.

```
CP[i-1]=CP[i];

int ecnecho=hdr_flags::access(pkt)→ecnecho();

int w1,w2;

for i=1 to m − 1

ACK[i − 1] = ACK[i];

ACK[m − 1] = ecnecho;

u₁= ACK[m − 1] + … + ACK[m/2];

u₂= ACK[m/2 − 1] + … + ACK[0];

CP[i]=w1× u₁+w2×u₂;

return CP[i];
```

Figure 17-1. Pseudo code of calculating *CP*.

17.2.2. Analysis of Congestion Probability

In this subsection, the correlation of *CP* and network states is analyzed by simulations. The network topology for simulation is the same as that used in [283], which is a typical topology for wire/wireless hybrid network (which is also shown in Figure 17-7). One TCP Reno flow traverses along a bottleneck link and a wireless terminal. When the sender receives the signal of packet dropping or the ACK packet in which the CE bit is 1, it regulates the sending window size according to TCP Reno. Packets on routers will be marked if the average queue length exceeds the given threshold.

In Figure 17-2, the size of TCP sending window, the queue length of bottleneck link and *CP* are shown while the loss rate of wireless link is 0 and 0.001. As shown in Figure 17-2(*a*), the size of TCP sending window varies very regularly because of no loss in wireless link. While there exists packet loss in wireless link, the size of TCP sending window changes frequently and irregularly, which is shown in Figure 17-2(*b*). From Figure 17-2(*a*) and Figure 17-2(*b*), it is obvious that the average size of the sender window without packet loss is larger than that with packet loss.

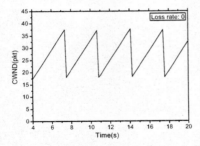

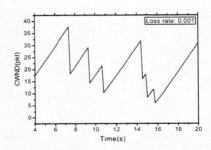

(A) TCP window without link loss   **(b) TCP window with link loss**

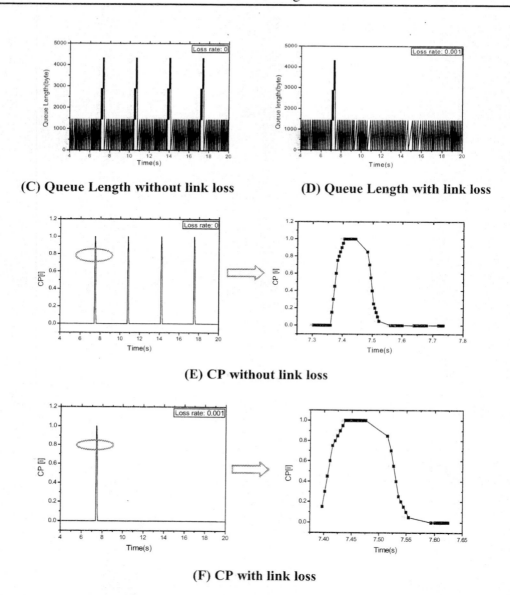

(C) Queue Length without link loss   (D) Queue Length with link loss

(E) CP without link loss

(F) CP with link loss

Figure 17-2. Correlation between CP and network state.

The queue length of bottleneck link is shown in Figure 17-2(c) and Figure 17-2(d). As shown in Figure 17-2(c), there are 4 periods in which the queue length is larger than the given threshold. In this case, the router will mark the packet and the sender will receive the ACK packet with CE=1. It is clear that the changes of the sending window are consonant with that of the queue length. In Figure 17-2(d), there is only one period in which the queue length is larger than the given threshold. But the sending window does not change according to the queue length because there are packets losses in wireless link.

The statistics of CP under different situation are shown in Figure 17-2(e) and Figure 17-2(f) respectively. It is indicated that the trend of CP changing is consistent with that of queue length. So network states can be captured according to ΔCP. The detailed figures show how CP value ranged in one of the period, which show that CP can sense congestion accurately and characterize congestion particularly. Compared with end-to-end metrics or single ECN feedback, *CP* can provide more accurate and richer information about network states.

17.3. TCP PROTOCOL WITH CPECN

TCP sender with CPECN responds to loss events based on CP values. While receiving an ACK packet, TCP sender will recalculate CP. If ACK arrived is a new ACK, TCP sender operates the same as TCP NewReno does. If ACK arrived is duplicate ACK and $\Delta CP > 0$, TCP sender concludes that the congestion occurs and adjusts its sending rate. If ACK arrived is duplicate ACK and $\Delta CP \leq 0$, TCP sender only retransmits this data packet.

By using CPECN, TCP sender's behavior is modified according to ΔCP when there are packet losses. This is the important distinguishing feature of the modified TCP with respect to other TCP variants. For example, the sender of Westwood will trigger **RateControl** without caring about the situation of mid routers. The sender of Westwood modified by ECN or WECN will decide whether to do **RateControl** just by single ECN signal.

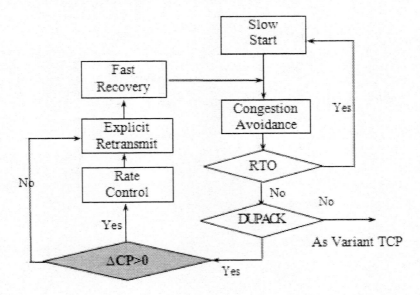

Figure 17-3. State Transition Graph of TCP Sender with CPECN.

Figure 17-3 is the transition graph of TCP Sender modified by CPECN, which indicates how TCP variants with CPECN work.

There are two scenarios to show the advantage of TCP with CPECN in hybrid networks.

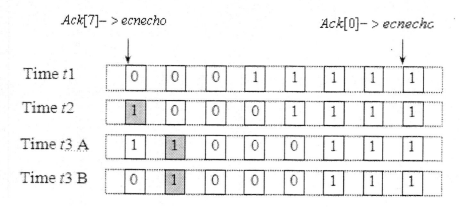

Figure 17-4. The first scenario.

As shown in Fig 17-4, the CE lists at t_1, t_2 and t_3 are given, where t_2 is the time when the sender receives the first ACK packet after t_1, and t_3 is after t_2. At t_1, the CE list of the latest 8 ACK packets is 00011111. At t_2, the sender receives a **duplicate** ACK in which CE=1. So the CE list of the latest 8 ACK packets is 10001111 at t_2. In TCP with WECN, the sender will trigger congestion control. However, By using CPECN, the calculating result is $CP[1] = CP[2] = 0.4$, which means that probability of congestion occurred in time t_2 is not increased. So TCP sender does not invoke **RateControl** procedure at t_2.

At t_3, if the sender receives a duplicate ACK in which CE=1 and gets $CP[3] = 0.55$. Due to $CP[3] > CP[2]$, the sender predicts that congestion would occur soon and triggers the congestion control mechanism at the moment. On the contrary, if the sender receives a duplicate ACK in which CE=0 and gets $CP[3] = 0.35$. Due to $CP[3] < CP[2]$, TCP sender does not trigger the congestion control mechanism. Subsequently by using CPECN, network throughput can be improved by increasing the link occupancy.

The second scenario describes the handling process in TCP protocol with CPECN while non-congestion losses occur successively.

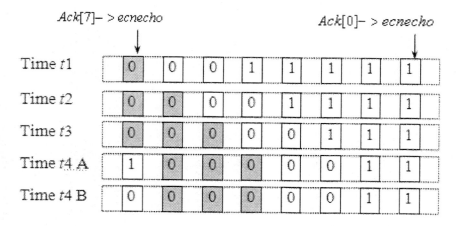

Figure 17-5. The second scenario.

As shown in Figure 17-5, assume that the sender received the duplicate ACK packets with CE=0 at three successive interval t_1, t_2, t_3. It implies that three successive loss events may be caused by link error. Due to $CP[2] < CP[1]$ and $CP[3] < CP[2]$, the sender did not decrease its sending rate immediately. The sender decreased its sending rate only when receiving the ACK packet with CE=1 at t_4 because of $CP[4] > CP[3]$. On the contrary, as long as $CP[4]$ is less than $CP[3]$, the sender will not decrease the sending rate.

It is obvious that by using CPECN, even if the sender receives duplicate ACKs caused by several errors, as long as the queue length does not exceed the threshold or the congestion probability does not increase, the TCP sender will not decrease its sending rate. Contrarily, even if there is only one duplicate packet arrival, the sending rate might decline because of CP value being increased.

As a whole, by deducing the congestion probability, TCP with CPECN can protect TCP connection from short-term, recoverable, non-congestive packet losses, and enhance its performance in hybrid network eventually.

17.4. PERFORMANCE EVALUATION

Method of ECN mark has not been mentioned hereinbefore. There are two methods of probability mark and threshold mark. Since TCP sender needs to predict network state by tracking change of queue length, routers with CPECN should use threshold marking. Concretely, CE bit will be marked with 1 when EWMA value of average queue length exceeds a given threshold. With this marking method, routers can provide determinate information to end hosts in minimal cost.

In order to describe a simple and reasonable model for analyzing the dynamic change of queue length, assume that:

1) Sender always has data to send and will send as many as their windows allow;
2) Receiver windows are large enough;
3) There are no delayed ACK;
4) All packets have the same length.

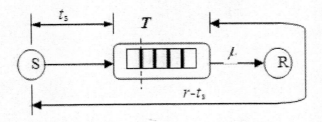

Figure 17-6. Queue model of single TCP flow.

Along the path with only one TCP connection, if the bottleneck link bandwidth is u packet/second, then the downstream packet inter-arrival time and the acknowledgement inter-arrival time on the reserve link must be greater than or equal to $1/u$ [286]. Based on this statement, the analytical model shown in Figure 17-6 is used. The notations in Figure 17-6 are described as follows:

$w(t)$: The sender's window size at time t.

r: Round Trip Time(RTT).

u: Bandwidth of the bottleneck link.

t_s: The time a packet needs to traverse from the sender to the router.

T: The threshold of RED router.

The queue length at the congestion router is: $Q(t) = w(t - t_s) - ru$.

The maximum queue length in slow start phase is $2T+ru+1$. The maximum queue length in the congestion avoidance phase is $T+1$; the minimum queue length is $\dfrac{T - ru + 1}{2}$. The optimal threshold for the RED queue should let the bottleneck link be fully utilized and queue delay be zero, i.e., $\dfrac{T - ru + 1}{2} \leq 0$, which means $\hat{T} \leq ru - 1$.

Similar to the discussion in single TCP flow, the optimal threshold for multi TCP flow should be described as $u - m \leq \hat{T} \leq ru - 1$.

It is obvious that the optimal threshold of ECN mark is dynamic. In order to decouple the effect of ECN mechanism, TCP performance will be evaluated under different threshold of ECN mark. In this manner, it is to be manifested that no matter what kind of marking method ECN schemes employ, TCP performance can be improved with comparison to primary TCP variants by using CPECN.

The simulation environment is depicted in Figure 17-7, which is published by TCP Westwood for TCP performance evaluation over hybrid networks [109]. As shown in Figure 17-7, one TCP flow is sent from R0 to R3. R1 to R2 is a simulation of long delay Internet traversed by some routers, and the last hop is a wireless link with error model. Concretely, the bandwidth of access link is 100Mbps with 3ms delay, bandwidth of wireless link is 10Mbps with 3ms delay. The bandwidth of bottleneck is 5Mbps with 40ms delay. The buffer of bottleneck is set to be 30 packets based on "Rule of thumb". The rest of the parameters are set as NS2 default. The simulation tests last for 100s.

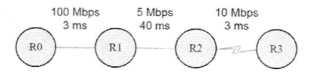

Figure 17-7. Network Topology 1.

17.4.1. Throughput Analysis without Link Loss

The throughput without link losses are shown in Figure 17-8, in which ECN, WECN, CPECN are labeled as TCP throughput with variant ECN schemes and 1/4, 1/2, 3/4 (* buffer size of bottleneck) are labeled as TCP throughput with variant ECN mark threshold. It is obvious from Figure 17-8 that the throughputs of TCP Reno with three ECN schemes are similar. Meanwhile TCP throughput is increasing with the increasing of marking threshold. When marking threshold is equal to 3/4 buffer size of bottleneck bandwidth, TCP throughput with CPECN is a bit higher than other ECN schemes.

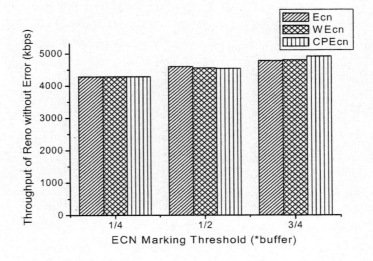

Figure 17-8. Throughput Comparison of Reno Without Link Loss.

TCP throughput of Westwood is shown in Figure 17-9, which has the similar trend with that of TCP Reno. However, TCP throughput with WECN is decreased a bit. This is because WECN depending on single ECN feedback is so sensitive and link utilization is decreasing with delicious rate control of Westwood. This problem can be avoided with CPECN.

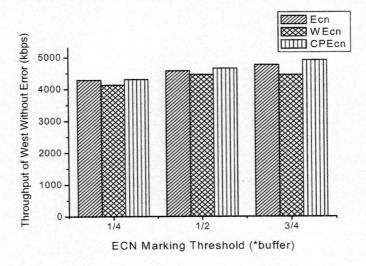

Figure 17-9. Throughput Comparison of Westwood Without Link Loss.

17.4.2. Throughput Analysis with Link Loss

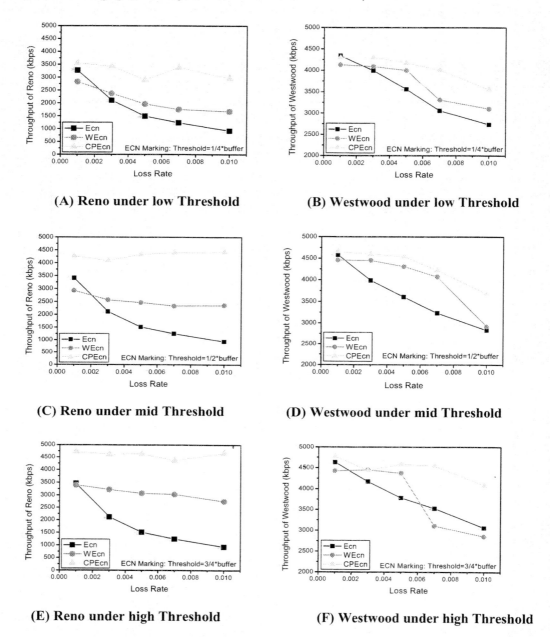

Figure 17-10. Throughput Comparison with link loss.

In this section, the random link error rate at the wireless bottleneck link varies from 0.001 to 0.1, which is created by a simple union error model.

With link loss rate ranging from 0.001 to 0.01, TCP throughput of Reno and Westwood are shown in Figure 17-10, in which effect of CPECN is becoming more and more distinct as link loss rate is increasing. It is shown in Figure 17-10(a) that improvement of TCP throughput is also becoming salience as marking threshold is increasing. For example, when with the link loss rate is 0.005 and the marking threshold is 1/4 of buffer size, the throughput of TCP Reno with CPECN outperforms that of Reno with WECN by 1.13. Whereas when the marking threshold is 3/4 of buffer size, the corresponding value is 2.16.

Figure 17-10(d) shows the throughput of Westwood when the link loss rate is 0.005. At this point, the throughput of TCP Westwood with ECN is increased by 22.8% when the marking threshold is 1/4 of buffer size. When the marking threshold is 3/4 of buffer size, the corresponding value is 18.4%. The results show that: (1) The improvement of TCP Westwood with CPECN is limited; (2) The marking threshold on router is of less affect on TCP Westwood with CPECN. This is because that rate adjustment of TCP Westwood is flexible to lost link in some degree.

17.4.3. Fairness and Friendliness Analysis

Fairness is an important metric for evaluating TCP protocol. Multiple connections of the same TCP scheme must cooperate fairly. As shown in Figure 17-11, there are 10 same TCP flows with 1000Mbps total bandwidth. They share a 20Mbps long delay bottleneck link. Description in detail for the scenario is labeled. In the following experiments, Jain's fairness index is used to justify the fairness of TCP variants [287].

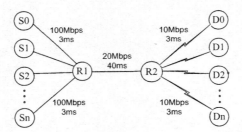

Figure 17-11. Network topology 2.

(1) Fairness and Friendliness of Reno with CPECN

As shown in Table 17-1, fairness of TCP Reno decreases as loss rate increases. This is because the flows suffering error loss will decelerate and compete for channel again, so short term unfairness exists in some extent. However simulation results of Table 17-1 show that this impact is not serious. At the same time, fairness of TCP Reno with CPECN approximates to that of TCP Reno with other two ECN schemes.

Table 17-1. Fairness Comparison of 10 Same Reno Flows

Loss Rate	ECN	WECN	CPECN
0	0.98	0.992	0.999
0.001	0.999	0.997	0.979
0.005	0.990	0.983	0.993
0.01	0.994	0.985	0.992

The experiment of friendliness partitions ten flows into two parts, one uses TCP Reno with CPECN, and the other uses TCP Reno with traditional ECN.

Table 17-2 gives the change of mean throughput when there are 10 pairs of connections, of which m are Reno with ECN connections and n are Reno with CPECN connections. The mean throughput of Reno with ECN and CPECN is calculated by summing up the throughput of the same ECN scheme and dividing the result by the number of connections. It is observed that the mean throughputs of two kinds of connection are approximated in case of no link losses, which indicates that bandwidth allocation of TCP Reno connection with different ECN schemes is close to its fair at bottleneck bandwidth link. When loss rate is 0.01, mean throughput of Reno with CPECN is 10% higher than that of ECN, which is within a tolerate range.

Table 17-2. Friendliness Performance of CPECN with TCP Reno

ECN:CPECN	No loss		Loss Rate: 0.001		Loss Rate: 0.005		Loss Rate: 0.01	
	ECN (kbps)	CPECN (kbps)	ECN (kbps)	CPECN (kbps)	ECN (kbps)	CPECN (kbps)	ECN (kbps)	CPECN (kbps)
3: 7	1440	**1437**	1327	**1440**	1001	**1220**	566	**944**
5: 5	1283	**1291**	1245	**1396**	972	**1190**	553	**945**
7: 3	1057	**1237**	1093	**1241**	941	**1121**	545	**913**

(2) Fairness and Friendliness of Westwood with CPECN

Fairness comparison of 10 same TCP Westwood flows is shown in Table 17-3. The simulation results show that the fairness of TCP Westwood with CPECN is favorable.

Table 17-3. Fairness Comparison of 10 Same Reno Flows

Loss Rate	ECN	WECN	CPECN
0	0.935	0.962	**0.997**
0.001	0.998	0.999	**0.999**
0.005	0.999	1.0	**1.0**
0.01	0.999	0.998	**0.999**

The experiment of friendliness partitions ten flows into two parts, one uses TCP Westwood with CPECN, and the other uses TCP Westwood with traditional ECN. Table 17-4 gives the change of mean throughput when there are 10 pairs of connections, of which m are Westwood with ECN connections and n are Westwood with CPECN connections. The simulation results show that CPECN scheme can coexist with Westwood when there exists a wireless link with packet loss.

It is concluded from the simulation results that TCP Westwood with CPECN performs satisfactory in the fairness and friendliness aspects. This is because Westwood already overcomes some limitations of traditional TCP protocol by the following characteristics. Firstly, available bandwidth estimate in Westwood is more eligible to control sending rate comparing with Reno. Secondly, WECN scheme decouples the error control and congestion control with the help of midway routers. CPECN scheme utilizes congestion notification in an efficient way based on the above two components, so its fairness and friendliness are satisfactory.

Table 17-4. Friendliness Performance of CPECN with TCP Westwood

ECN:CPECN	No loss		Loss Rate: 0.001		Loss Rate: 0.005		Loss Rate: 0.01	
	ECN (kbps)	CPECN (kbps)	ECN (kbps)	CPECN (kbps)	ECN (kbps)	CPECN (kbps)	ECN (kbps)	CPECN (kbps)
3:7	1162.00	**1174.85**	1161.33	**1174.14**	1289.66	**1314.85**	1099.00	**1186.57**
5:5	1316.80	**1331.40**	1312.80	**1329.40**	1294.80	**1319.80**	1269.80	**1352.2**
7:3	1519.28	**1536.66**	1511	**1539.00**	1485.28	**1508.33**	1388.14	**1506.00**

17.5. CONCLUSION

In this chapter a novel congestion control technology, named CPECN, is proposed. CPECN includes two key points: (1) adopting *CP* to predict network state from ECN series arrived in latest period; (2) modifying TCP behaviors upon occurring of loss events. By using CPECN, TCP sender will trigger the rate adjustment only when network state is judged as congestion. Simulation results show that CPECN can be extended to TCP variants easily and improve TCP throughput in wired-wireless network.

REFERENCES

[1]   D. Bertsekas, R. Gallager. *Data networks*. Prentice Hall, 2nd edition, 1992.

[2]   S. Keshav. *An engineering approach to computer networking: ATM networks, the Internet, and the telephone network*. Addison-Wesley, 1st edition, 1997.

[3]   V. Jacobson, "Congestion avoidance and control", *Proceedings of ACM Conference of the Special Interest Group on Data Communication (SIGCOMM)*, 1988, 314-329.

[4]   R. Braden, D. Clark, S Shenker, "Integrated Services in the Internet Architecture: An Overview", *http://www.ietf.org/rfc/rfc1633.txt*, 1994.

[5]   R. Jain, "Congestion Control in Computer Networks: Trends and Issues", *IEEE Network*, 1990, 4(3):24-30.

[6]   S. Keshav, "A control-theoretic approach to flow control", *Computer Communication Review*, 1991, 21(4):3-15.

[7]   D. Tse, M. Grossglauser, "Measurement-based Call Admission Control: Analysis and Simulation", *Proceedings of IEEE Conference on Computer Communications (INFOCOM)*, 1997, 981-989.

[8]   S. Jamin, P. Danzig, S. Shenker, L. Zhang, "A Measurement-based Admission Control Algorithm for Integrated Services Packet Networks", *ACM/IEEE Transactions on Networking*, 1997,5(1):56-70.

[9]   S. Jamin, S. Shenker, P. Danzig, "Comparison of Measurement-based Admission Control Algorithms for Controlled-Load Service", *Proceedings of IEEE Conference on Computer Communications (INFOCOM)*, 1997, 973-980.

[10] D. Clark, S. Shenker, L. Zhang, "Supporting real-time applications in an integrated services packet network: Architecture and mechanism", *Proceedings of ACM Conference of the Special Interest Group on Data Communication (SIGCOMM)*, 1992, 14-26.

[11] D. Ferrari, D. Verma, "A scheme for real-time channel establishment in wide-area networks", *IEEE Journal on Selected Areas in Communications*, 1990, 8(5):368-379.

[12] M. Grossglauser, S. Keshav, D. Tse, "RCBR: A simple and efficient service for multiple time-scale traffic", *Proceedings of ACM Conference of the Special Interest Group on Data Communication (SIGCOMM)*, 1995, 219-30.

[13] T. Anderson, S. Owicki, J. Saxe, C. Thacker, "High-speed switch scheduling for local-area networks", *ACM Transactions on Computer Systems*, 1993, 11(4):319-352.

[14] A. Demers, S. Keshav, S. Shenker, "Analysis and simulation of a fair queueing algorithm", *Internetworking: Research and Experience*, 1990, 1(1):3-26.

[15] S. Golestani, "A self-clocked fair queueing scheme for broadband applications", *Proceedings of IEEE Conference on Computer Communications (INFOCOM)*, 1994, 636-646.

[16] J. Padhye, V. Firoiu, D. Towsley, "Modeling TCP throughput: a simple model and its empirical validation", *Computer Communication Review*, 1998, 28(4):303-314.

[17] V. Misra, W. Gong, D. Towsley, "Stochastic differential equation modeling and analysis of TCP window size behavior", *Technical Report ECE-TR-CCS-99-10-01*, 1999

[18] V. Misra, W. Gong, D. Towsley, "Fluid-based analysis of a network of AQM routers supporting TCP flows with an application to RED", *Proceedings of ACM Conference of the Special Interest Group on Data Communication (SIGCOMM)*, 2000, 151-160.

[19] R. Jain, S. Routhier, "Packet Trains-Measurements and a New Model for Computer Network Traffic", *IEEE Journal on Selected Areas in Communications*, 1986, 4(6):986-995.

[20] W. Leland, M. Taqqu, W. Willinger, D. Wilson, "On the Self-Similar Nature of Ethernet Traffic", *Proceedings of ACM Conference of the Special Interest Group on Data Communication (SIGCOMM)*, 1993, 183-193.

[21] J. Postel, "Transmission Control Protocol", *http://www.ietf.org/rfc/rfc793.txt*, 1981.

[22] B. Braden, D. Clark, J. Crowcroft, "Recommendations on queue management and congestion avoidance in the internet", *http://www.ietf.org/rfc/rfc2309.txt*, 1998.

[23] R. Guerin, S. Kamat, V. Peris, "Scalable QoS provision though buffer management", *Proceedings of ACM Conference of the Special Interest Group on Data Communication (SIGCOMM)*, 1998, 29-40.

[24] S. Floyd, V. Jacobson, "Random early detection gateways for congestion avoidance", *IEEE/ACM Transactions on networking*, 1993, 1(4), 397-413.

[25] W. Feng, D. Kandlur, D. Saha, "The blue active queue management algorithms", *IEEE/ACM Transactions on networking*, 2002, 10(4):513-528.

[26] R. Pan, B. Probhakar, K. Psounis, "CHOKe: A stateless active queue management scheme for approximating fair bandwidth allocation", *Proceedings of IEEE Conference on Computer Communications (INFOCOM)*, 2000, 942-951.

[27] S. Athuraliya, S. Low, V. Li, "REM: Active queue management", *IEEE Network Magazine*, 2001, 15(3):945-949.

[28] C. Hollot, V. Misra, D. Towsley, "Analysis and design of controllers for AQM routers supporting TCP flows", *IEEE Transactions on automatic control*, 2002, 47(6):945-959.

[29] C. Wang, B. Li, Y. Hou, "LRED: A robust active queue scheme based on packet loss ratio", *Proceedings of IEEE Conference on Computer Communications (INFOCOM)*, 2004, 1-12.

[30] S. Kunniyurs, R. Srikant, "Analysis and design of an adaptive virtual queue (AVQ) algorithm for active queue management", *Proceedings of ACM Conference of the Special Interest Group on Data Communication (SIGCOMM)*, 2001, 123-134.

[31] A. Parekh, R. Gallager, "A generalized processor sharing approach to flow control in integrated services networks: the single-node case", *IEEE/ACM Transactions on Networking*, 1993, 1(3):344-357.

[32] D. Stiliadis, A. Varma, "Efficient fair queueing algorithms for packet-switched networks", *IEEE/ACM Transactions on networking*, 1998, 6(2):75-185.

[33] J. Nagle, "On packet switches with infinite storage", *IEEE Transactions on Communications*, 1987, 35(4):435-438.

[34] S. Lu, V. Bharghavan, R. Srikant, "Fair scheduling in wireless packet networks", *Proceedings of ACM Conference of the Special Interest Group on Data Communication (SIGCOMM)*, 1997, 63-74.

[35] P. Ramanalhan, P. Agrawal, "Adapting packet fair queueing algorithms to wireless networks", *Proceedings of ACM Conference on Mobile Computing and Networking (MOBICOM)*, 1998, 1-9.

[36] S. Lu, T. Vandagopal, V. Bharghavan, "Fair scheduling in wireless packet networks", *Computer Communication Review*, 1997, 27(4):63-74.

[37] M. Allman, V. Paxson, W. Stevens, "TCP congestion control", *http://www.ietf.org /rfc/rfc2581.txt*, 1999.

[38] W. Stevens, "TCP slow start, congestion avoidance, fast retransmit, and fast recovery algorithms", *http://www.ietf.org/rfc/rfc2001.txt*, 1997.

[39] M. Mathis, J. Mahdavi, S. Floyd, "TCP selective acknowledgement options", *http://www.ietf.org/rfc/rfc2018.txt*, 1996.

[40] S. Floyd S, "Highspeed TCP for large congestion windows", *http://www.ietf.org/ rfc/rfc3649.txt*, 2003.

[41] X. Lisong, H. Khaled, R. Injong, "Binary Increase Congestion Control (BIC) for Long Distance Networks", *http://netsrv.csc.ncsu.edu/twiki/bin/view/Main/BIC.html*, 2008.

[42] L. Brakmo, S. Malley, L. Peterson, "TCP Vegas: New techniques for congestion detection and avoidance", *Proceedings of ACM Conference of the Special Interest Group on Data Communication (SIGCOMM)*, 1994, 24-35.

[43] S. Mascolo, C. Casetti, M. Gerla, "TCP Westwood: Bandwidth estimation for enhanced transport over wireless links", *Proceedings of ACM Conference on Mobile Computing and Networking (MOBICOM)*, 2001, 287-297.

[44] C. Jin, D. Wei, S. Low, "FAST TCP: motivation, architecture, algorithms, performance", *Proceedings of IEEE Conference on Computer Communications (INFOCOM)*, 2004, 2490-2501.

[45] R.Wang, G. Pau, K. Yamada, "TCP Startup performance in Large Band-width Delay Networks", *Proceedings of IEEE Conference on Computer Communications (INFOCOM)*, 2004, 796-805.

[46] S. Floyd, "TCP and Explicit Congestion Notification", *Computer Communication Review*, 1994, 24(10):8-23.

[47] D. Katabi, M. Handley, C. Rohrs, "Congestion control for high bandwidth delay product networks", *Proceedings of ACM Conference of the Special Interest Group on Data Communication (SIGCOMM)*, 2002, 89-102.

[48] Y. Xia, L. Subramanian, I. Stoica, "One more bit is enough", *Proceedings of ACM Conference of the Special Interest Group on Data Communication (SIGCOMM)*, 2005, 37-48.

[49] B. Wydrowski, L. Andrew, M. Zukeman, "MaxNet: A congestion control architecture for scalable network", *IEEE Communications Letters*, 2003, 7(10):511-513.

[50] Y. Zhang, S. R. Kang, D. Loguinov, "Delayed stability and performance of distributed congestion control", *Proceedings of ACM Conference of the Special Interest Group on Data Communication (SIGCOMM)*, 2004.

[51] Y. Zhang, D. Leonard, D. Loguinov, "JetMax: scalable max-min congestion control for high-speed heterogeneous networks", *Proceedings of IEEE Conference on Computer Communications (INFOCOM)*, 2006.

[52] T. Karagiannis, M. Molle, M. Falout, "A non-stationary poisson view of Internet traffic", *Proceedings of IEEE Conference on Computer Communications (INFOCOM)*, 2004,1558-1569.

[53] Z. Sahinoglu, S. Tekinay, "On multimedia networks: Self similar traffic and network performance", *IEEE Communications Magazine*, 1999, 37 (1):48-52.

[54] J. Beran, R. Sherman, M. Taqqu, "Long range dependence in variable bit rate video traffic", *IEEE Transactions on Communications*, 1995, 43(2):1566 -1579.

[55] W. Willinger, V. Paxson, M. Taqqu, *Self similarity and heavy tails: Structural modeling of network traffic*, Birkhauser, 1998.

[56] K. Maulik, S. Resnick, "The Self-Similar and Multi-fractal Nature of a Network Traffic Model", *Stochastic Models*, 2003, 19(4):548-577.

[57] L. Ellen, Hahne, "Round-robin scheduling for max-min fairness in data networks", *IEEE Journal on Selected Areas in Communications*, 1991, 9(7):1024-1039.

[58] M. Katevenis, S. Sidiropoulos, C. Courcoubetis, "Weighted round-robin cell multiplexing in a general-purpose ATM switch chip", *IEEE Journal on Selected Areas in Communications*, 1991, 9(8):1265-1279.

[59] M. Shreedhar, Gvarghese, "Efficient fair queueing using deficit round robin", *IEEE/ACM Transactions on networking*, 1996, 4(3):37S-385.

[60] C. Guo, "SRR: An O(1) time complexity packet scheduler for flows in muti-service packet networks", *Proceedings of ACM Conference of the Special Interest Group on Data Communication (SIGCOMM)*, 2001,211-222.

[61] S. Ramabhadran, J. Paqquale, "Stratified round robin: a low complexity packet scheduler with bandwidth fairness and bounded delay", *Proceedings of ACM Conference of the Special Interest Group on Data Communication (SIGCOMM)*, 2003, 239-250.

[62] D. Stiliadis, A. Varma, "Efficient fair queueing algorithms for packet-switched networks", *IEEE/ACM Transactions on networking*, 1998, 6(2):175-185.

[63] L. Zhang, "Virtual clock: A new traffic control algorithm for packet switching networks", *Proceedings of ACM Conference of the Special Interest Group on Data Communication (SIGCOMM)*, 1990, 19-29.

[64] W. Gao, J. Wang, S. Chen, "A Novel Core Stateless Virtual Clock Scheduling Algorithm", *Proceedings of Third International Conference on Computer Network and Mobile Computing (ICCNMC)*, 2005, 662-671.

[65] J. Cobb, "Time-shift scheduling: Fair scheduling of flow in high-speed networks", *IEEE/ACM Transactions on networking*, 1998, 6(3):274-285.

[66] D. Ferrero, G. UrvoyKeller, "A size-based scheduling approach to improve fairness over 802.11 wireless networks", *Proceedings of ACM Conference of the Special Interest Group on Data Communication (SIGCOMM) Post session*, 2006.

[67] Y. Jiang, C. Tham, C. Ko, "A probabilistic priority scheduling discipline for high-speed networks", *Proceedings of IEEE International Conference on High Performance Switching and Routing*, 2001, 1-5.

[68] Y. Jiang, C. Tham, C. Ko, "A probabilistic priority scheduling discipline for mufti-service networks", *Proceedings of IEEE symposium on Computers and Communications*, 2001, 450-455.

[69] T. Anker, "Probabilistic Fair Queuing", *Proceedings of IEEE Workshop on HPSR*, 2001, 397-40l.

[70] M. Zhang, "Probabilistic packet scheduling: achieving proportional share bandwidth allocation", *Proceedings of IEEE Conference on Computer Communications (INFOCOM)*, 2002, 1650-1659.

[71] P. Kenney, "Stochastic fairness queueing", *Proceedings of IEEE Conference on Computer Communications (INFOCOM)*, 1990, 733-740.

[72] S. Floyd, R. Gummadi, S. Shenker, "Adaptive RED: an algorithm for increasing the robustness of RED's active queue management", *Available from http://www.icir.org/ floyd/papers.html*. 2001.

[73] J. Aweya, M. Ouellette, D. Montuno, "A control theoretic approach to active queue management", *Computer Networks*, 2001, 36(2):203-235.

[74] J. Teunis, T. Lakshman, H. Larry, "SRED: Stabilized RED", *Proceedings of IEEE Conference on Computer Communications (INFOCOM)*, 1999, 1346-1355.

[75] R. Pan, L. Breslau, B. Prabhakar, "Approximate fairness through differential dropping", *ACM Computer Communication Review*, 2003, 33(2):23-39.

[76] Stoica, "Core-stateless fair queue: Achieving approximately fair bandwidth allocations in high-speed networks", *IEEE/ACM Transactions on networking*, 2003, 11(1):33-46.

[77] B. Wydrowski, M. Zukerman, "GREEN: An active queue management algorithm for a self managed internet", *Proceedings of IEEE International Conference on Communications (ICC)*, 2002, 2368-2372.

[78] W. Gao, J. Wang, J. Chen, S. Chen, "PFED: a prediction-based fair active queue management algorithm", *Proceedings of IEEE International Conference on Parallel Processing (ICPP)*, 2005, 485-491.

[79] E. Park, H. Lim, K. Park, "Analysis and design of the virtual rate control algorithm for stabilizing in TCP Networks", *Computer Networks*, 2004, 44(1):17-41.

[80] Wang, L. Rong, Y. Liu, "A Robust Proportional Controller for AQM Based on Optimized Second-Order System Model", *Elsevier Journal of Computer Communications*, 2008, 31(10):2468-2473.

[81] Wang, L. Rong, Y. Liu, "Design of a Stabilizing AQM Controller for Large-Delay Networks based on Internal Model Control", *Elsevier Journal of Computer Communications*, 2008, 31(10):1911-1918.

[82] J. Sun, M. Zukerman, "RaQ: a robust active queue management scheme based on rate and queue length", *Elsevier Journal of Computer Communications*, 2007, 30(8):1731-1741.

[83] V. Cerf, Y. Dalal, C. Sunshine, "Specification of Internet Transmission Control Program". *http://www.ietf.org/rfc/rfc675.txt*, 1974.

[84] J. Andren, M. Hilding, D. Veitch, "Understanding End-to-End Internet Traffic Dynamics", *Proceedings IEEE Global Communications Conference (GLOBECOM)*, 1998.

[85] J. Martin, A. Nilsson, I. Rhee, "Delay-Based Congestion Avoidance for TCP", *IEEE/ACM Transactions on Networking*, 2003, 11(3):356-369.

[86] S. Biaz, N. Vaidya, "Is the Round-Trip Time Correlated with the Number of Packets in Flight?", *Proceedings Internet Measurement Conference (IMC)*, 2003, 273-278.

[87] C. Hollot, V. Misra, D. Towsley, W. Gong, "On Designing Improved Controllers for AQM Routers Supporting TCP Flows", *Proceedings of IEEE Conference on Computer Communications (INFOCOM)*, 2001, 1726-1734.

[88] S. Kunniyur, "AntiECN Marking: A Marking Scheme for High Bandwidth Delay Connections", *Proceedings of IEEE International Conference on Communications (ICC)*, 2003, 647-651.

[89] J. Wang, D. Wei, S. Low, "Modeling and Stability of FAST TCP", *Proceedings of IEEE Conference on Computer Communications (INFOCOM)*, 2005, 938-948.

[90] F. Kelly, A. Maulloo, D. Tan, "Rate Control for Communication Networks: Shadow Prices, Proportional Fairness and Stability", *Journal of the Operational Research Society*, 1998, 49(3):237-252.

[91] Massouli, "Stability of Distributed Congestion Control with Heterogeneous Feedback Delays", *IEEE/ACM Transactions on Networking*, 2002, 47(6):895-902.

[92] Qazi, T. Znati, "On the Design of Load Factor based Congestion Control Protocols for Next-Generation Networks", *Proceedings of IEEE Conference on Computer Communications (INFOCOM)*, 2008, 96-100.

[93] Dukkipati, M. Kobayashi, R. Zhang, N. McKeown, "Processor Sharing Flows in the Internet", *Proceedings of International Workshop on Quality of Service (IWQoS)*, 2005, 271-285.

[94] R. Jain, K. Ramakrishnan, Dah-Ming Chiu, "Congestion Avoidance in Computer Networks with a Connectionless Network Layer", *Technical Report, Digital Equipment Corporation DEC-TR-506*, 1988.

[95] L. Peterson, B. Davie. *Computer Networks: A System Approach*, Morgan Kaufmann Publishers, 2000.

[96] Jaffe. "Bottleneck Flow Control", *IEEE Transactions on Communication*, 1981, 29(7): 954-962.

[97] Dah-Ming Chiu, R. Jain, "Analysis of the Increase and Decrease Algorithms for Congestion Avoidance in Computer Networks", *Computer Networks and ISDN Systems*, 1989, 17(1):1-14.

[98] Luo Wangming, Lin Chuang, Yan Baoping. "A survey of congestion control in the Internet". *Chinese Journal of Computers*, 2001, 24(1): 1-18 (in Chinese with English abstract).

[99] Internet2. *http://www.internet2.edu/*

[100] NSFCnet. *http://www.nsfcnet.net/*

[101] T Kelly. "Scalable TCP: Improving performance in highspeed wide area networks". *ACM SIGCOMM Computer Communication Review*, 2003, 32(2): 83-91.

[102] S H Low, F Paganini, J Wang, S Adlakha, J C Doyle. "Dynamics of tcp/aqm and a scalable control". *Proceedings of IEEE Conference on Computer Communications (INFOCOM)*, 2002, 239-248.

[103] Ren Fengyuan, Lin Chuang, Ren Yong, Shan Xiuming. "Congestion control algorithm in Large-Delay networks". *Journal of Software*, 2003, 14(3):503-511 (in Chinese with English abstract).

[104] Zhang Miao, Wu Jianping, Lin Chuang. "Survey on Internet end-to-end congestion control". *Journal of Software*, 2002, 13(3):354-363 (in Chinese with English abstract).

[105] Huang Xiaomeng, Lin Chuang, Ren Fengyuan. "Recent Development of High Speed Transport Protocols". *Journal of Computers*, 2006, 29(11):1901-1908 (in Chinese with English abstract).

[106] Floyd, S, Henderson, T. "The NewReno Modification to TCP's Fast Recovery Algorithm". *RFC 2582*, 1999.

[107] I Rhee, L Xu. "CUBIC: A new TCP-friendly high-speed TCP variant". *Proceedings of International Workshop on Protocols for FAST Long-Distance Networks (PFLDnet)*, 2005.

[108] R N Shorten, D J Leith. "H-TCP: TCP for high-speed and long-distance networks". *Proceedings of International Workshop on Protocols for FAST Long-Distance Networks (PFLDnet)*, 2004.

[109] Gerla M, Sanadidi M, Wang R, Zanella A, Casetti C, Mascolo S. "TCP Westwood: congestion window control using bandwidth estimation". *Proceedings of IEEE Global Communications Conference (GLOBECOM)*, 2001, 1698-1702.

[110] Ryan King, Richard Baraniuk, Rudolf Riedi. "TCP-Africa: An Adaptive and Fair Rapid Increase Rule for Scalable TCP". *Proceedings of IEEE Conference on Computer Communications (INFOCOM)*, 2005, 1838-1848.

[111] S Floyd, "Quick-Start for TCP and IP", *Internet-draft*, 2006.

[112] Wang Jianxin, Gong Hao, Chen Jianer. "C3P: A Cooperant Congestion Control Protocol in High Bandwidth-Delay Product Networks". *Journal of Software*, 2008, 19(1):125-135 (in Chinese with English abstract).

[113] Michele C Weigle, Pankaj Sharma, Jesse R Freeman IV. "Performance of Competing High-Speed TCP Flows". *Proceedings of IFIP NETWORKING*, 2006, 476-487.

[114] Jianxin Wang, Liang Rong, Guojun Wang, Weijia Jia, Minyi Guo. "Design of a Stabilizing Second-Order Congestion Controller for Large-Delay Networks". *Proceedings of IEEE International Conference on Communications (ICC)*, 2007, 29.

[115] CISCO. "Interface and Hardware Component Commands". *http://www.cisco.com/ univercd/cc/ td/doc/product/software/ios123/123tcr/123tir/int_d1gt.htm#wp1049944*.

[116] Guido Appenzeller, Isaac Keslassy, Nick McKeown. "Sizing Router Buffers". *Proceedings of ACM Conference of the Special Interest Group on Data Communication (SIGCOMM)*, 2004, 281-292.

[117] Ravi S Prasad, Manish Jain, Constantinos Dovrolis. "On the Effectiveness of Delay-Based Congestion Avoidance". *Proceedings of International Workshop on Protocols for FAST Long-Distance Networks (PFLDnet)*, 2004.

[118] Mihaela Enachescu, Yashar Ganjali, Ashish Goel, Nick McKeown, Tim Roughgarden. "Routers With Very Small Buffers". *Proceedings of IEEE Conference on Computer Communications (INFOCOM)*, 2006.

[119] Ha S, Rhee I. "Hybrid Slow Start for High-Bandwidth and Long-Distance Networks". *Proceedings of International Workshop on Protocols for FAST Long-Distance Networks (PFLDnet)*, 2008.

[120] Sridharan M, Tan K, Bansal D, et al. "Compound TCP: A New TCP Congestion Control for High-Speed and Long Distance Networks". Seattle, USA: *Microsoft, Tech. Rep.*, 2007

[121] Konda V, Kaur J. "RAPID: Shrinking the Congestion-control Timescale". *Proceedings of IEEE Conference on Computer Communications (INFOCOM)*, 2009, 1-9.

[122] Qazi I A, Andrew L, Znati T. "Congestion Control using Efficient Explicit Feedback". *Proceedings of IEEE Conference on Computer Communications (INFOCOM)*, 2009, 10-18.

[123] Wang Jianxin, Rong Liang, Zhangy Xi, et al. "ARROW-TCP: Accelerating Transmission toward Efficiency and Fairness for High-speed Networks". *Proceedings of IEEE Global Communications Conference (GLOBECOM)*, 2009.

[124] Brown K, Singh S, "M-TCP: TCP for mobile cellular networks". *ACM Computer Communication Review*, 1997, 27(5):19-43.

[125] Wang K., Tripathi S. K., "Mobile-end transport protocol: An alternative to TCP/IP over wireless links", *Proceedings of IEEE Conference on Computer Communications (INFOCOM)*, 1998, 1046-1053.

[126] Balakrishnan H, Seshan S, Katz R H. "Improving Reliable Transport and Handoff Performance in Cellular Wireless Networks". *ACM Wireless Networks*, 1995, 1(4):469-481.

[127] Fu Cheng peng, Liew S. "TCP Veno: TCP enhancement for transmission over wireless access networks". *IEEE Journal of Selected Areas in Communications*, 2003, 21(2):216-228.

[128] Fonseca N, Crovella M. "Bayesian packet loss detection for TCP". *Proceedings of IEEE Conference on Computer Communications (INFOCOM)*, 2005, 1826-1837.

[129] Apone A, Fratta L, Martignon F. "Bandwidth Estimation Schemes for TCP over Wireless Networks". *IEEE Transactions on Mobile Computing*, 2004, 3(2):129-143 .

[130] Wang R, Valla M, Sanadidi M Y, et al. "Efficiency/Friendliness Tradeoffs in TCP Westwood". *Proceedings of IEEE Symposium on Computers and Communications (ISCC)*, 2002.

[131] Akyildiz Ian F, Morabito Giacomo, Palazzo Sergio. "TCP-Peach: A New Congestion Control Scheme for Satellite IP Networks". *IEEE/ACM Transactions on Networking*, 2001(19): 307-321.

[132] Caini C, Firrincieli R. "TCP Hybla: a TCP enhancement for heterogeneous networks". *International Journal of Satellite Communications and Networking*, 2004(22):547-566.

[133] Caini C, Firrincieli R. "End-to-End TCP Enhancements Performance on Satellite Links". *Proceedings of Seventh IEEE Symposium on Computers and Communications (ISCC)*, 2006, 1031-1036.

[134] Li Ee-Ting, Leith Douglas, Shorten Robert N. "Experimental evaluation of TCP protocols for high-speed networks". *IEEE/ACM Transactions on Networking*, 2007, 15:1109-1122.

[135] Wu Xiuchao, Chan Mun Choon, Ananda A L. "Effects of Applying High-Speed Congestion Control Algorithms in Satellite Network". *Proceedings of IEEE International Conference on Communications (ICC)*. 2008, 1925-1929.

[136] Andrew L, Marcondes C, Floyd S, et al. "Towards a Common TCP Evaluation Suite". *Proceedings of International Workshop on Protocols for FAST Long-Distance Networks (PFLDnet)*, 2008, 5-7.

[137] C. Villamizar and C. Song. "High performance TCP in ANSNET". *ACM SIGCOMM Computer Communications Review*, 1994, 24(5):45-60.

[138] A. Dhamdhere, H. Jiang, and C. Dovrolis. "Buffer Sizing for Congested Internet Links". *Proceedings of IEEE Conference on Computer Communications (INFOCOM)*. 2005, 2: 1072-1083.

[139] M. Enachescu, Y. Ganjali, A. Goel, N. McKeown, and T. Roughgarden. "Part III: Routers with very small buffers". *ACM SIGCOMM Computer Communication Review*, 2005, 35(3): 83-90.

[140] R. Morris. "Scalable TCP congestion control". *Proceedings of IEEE Conference on Computer Communications (INFOCOM)*. 2000, 3: 1176-1183.

[141] R. Stanojevic, R. N. Shorten, and C. M. Kellett. "Adaptive tuning of drop-tail buffers for reducing queueing delays". *IEEE Communications Letters*, 2006, 10(7): 570-572.

[142] A. Dhamdhere, C. Dovrolis. "Open issues in router buffer sizing". *ACM SIGCOMM Computer Communications Review*, 2006, 36(1): 87-92.

[143] A. Aggarwal, S. Savage, and T. Anderson. "Understanding the performance of TCP pacing". *Proceedings of IEEE Conference on Computer Communications (INFOCOM)*. 2000, 3: 1157-1165.

[144] N. Beheshti, Y. Ganjali, R. Rajaduray, D. Blumenthal, N. McKeown. "Buffer sizing in all-optical packet switches". *Proceedings of Optical Fiber Communication Conference and the 2006 National Fiber Optic Engineers Conference (OFC/NFOEC)*. 2006, 5-10.

[145] S. Gorinsky, A. Kantawala, and J. Turner. "Link buffer sizing: a new look at the old problem". *Technical Report WUCSE-2004-82*, 2004.

[146] R. S. Prasad, C. Dovrolis and M. Thottan. "Router buffer sizing revisited: the role of the output/input capacity ratio". *Proceedings of International Conference on emerging Networking EXperiments and Technologies (CoNEXT)*. 2007, 1-12.

[147] D. Barman, G. Smaragdakis and I. Matta. "The effect of router buffer size on highspeed TCP performance". *Proceedings of IEEE Global Communications Conference (GLOBECOM)*. 2004, 3: 1617-1621.

[148] Y. Ganjali, N. McKeown. "Update on buffer sizing in internet routers". *ACM SIGCOMM Computer Communication Review*, 2006, 36(5): 67-70.

[149] Theagarajan, G., Ravichandran, S., and Sivaraman,V. "An experimental study of router buffer sizing for mixed TCP and real-time traffic". *Proceedings of IEEE International Conference on Networks(ICN)*. 2006, 204-209.

[150] D. Wischik. "Buffer sizing theory for bursty TCP flows". *Proceedings of IEEE International Zurich Seminar on Digital Communications (IZS)*, 2006, 98-101.

[151] G. Raina, D. Wischik. "Buffer sizes for large multiplexers: TCP queueing theory and instability analysis". *Proceedings of the Next Generation Internet Networks (NGI)*. 2005, 173-180.

[152] K. Avrachenkov, U. Ayesta, A. Piunovskiy. "Optimal choice of the buffer size in the Internet routers". *Proceedings of IEEE Conference on Decision and Control, and the European Control Conference (CDC-ECC)*. 2005, 1143-1148.

[153] J. Auge, J. Roberts. "Buffer sizing for elastic traffic". *Proceedings of Next Generation Internet Design and Engineering (EuroNGI)*. 2006, 33-40.

[154] D.Y. Eun, X. Wang. "Performance modeling of TCP/AQM with generalized AIMD under intermediate buffer sizes". *Proceedings of IEEE International Performance, Computing, and Communications Conference (IPCCC)*. 2006, 367-374.

[155] R. N. Shorten and D. J. Leith. "On queue provisioning, network efficiency and the transmission control protocol". *IEEE/ACM Transactions on Networking*, 2007, 15(4): 866- 877.

[156] N.Hohn, D. Veitch, K. Papagiannaki and C. Diotet. "Bridging router performance and queuing theory". *ACM SIGMETRICS Performance Evaluation Review*, 2004, 32(1): 355-366.

[157] G.Appenzeller, "Sizing router buffers". PhD thesis, *Stanford* 2004.

[158] A. Odlyzko. "Current state and likely evolution of the Internet". *Proceedings of IEEE Global Communications Conference (GLOBECOM)*. 1999, 1869-1875.

[159] A. Odlyzko. "Data networks are lightly utilized, and will stay that way". *Review of Network Economics*, 2003, 210-237.

[160] D. Wischik and N. McKeown. "Part I: Buffer sizes for core routers". *Computer Communication Review*, 2005, 35(3): 75-78.

[161] M. Mathis, J. Semke, J. Mahdavi and T. Ott. "Macroscopic behaviors of TCP congestion control". *Computer Communication Review*, 1997, 27(3): 67-82.

[162] V. Firoiu, J-Y. L. Boudec, D. Towsley, and Z.-L. Zhang. "Theories and models for Internet quality of service". *Proceedings of the IEEE*, 2002, 90(9): 1565-1591.

[163] E. Altman, K. Avrachenkov, and C. Barakat. "TCP network calculus: the case of large delay-bandwidth product". *Proceedings of IEEE Conference on Computer Communications (INFOCOM)*. 2002, 417-426.

[164] P. Goyal, H. M. Vin, and H. Cheng. "Start-time fair queueing: a scheduling algorithm for integrated services packet switching networks". *IEEE/ACM Transactions on networking*, 1997, 5(5): 690-703.

[165] G. Raina, D. Towsley, and D. Wischik. "Part II: Control theory for buffer sizing". *Computer Communication Review*, 2005, 35(3): 79-82.

[166] S. Floyd. "Recommendations on using the gentle variant of RED". *http://www.aciri.org/floyd /gentle.html*, 2000.

[167] James Aweya, Michel Ouellette, Delfin Y. Montuno, Kent Felske. "Rate-based proportional- integral control scheme for active queue management". *International Journal of Network Management*, 2006, 16(3).

[168] C. Hollot, V. Misra, D. Towsley, W. Gong. "A control theoretic analysis of RED". *Proceedings of IEEE Conference on Computer Communications (INFOCOM)*, 2001, 1510-1519.

[169] F. Ren, F.Wang, Y. Ren, X. Shan. "PID controller for active queue management". *Journal of Electronics and Information Technology*, 2003, 25(1).

[170] H. Zhang, B. Liu, W. Dou. "Design of a robust active queue management algorithm based on feedback compensation". *Proceedings of ACM Conference of the Special Interest Group on Data Communication (SIGCOMM)*. 2003, 265-276.

[171] H. Jiang, C. Dovrolis. "Passive estimation of TCP round-trip times". *ACM Computer Communications Review*, 2001, 32(3): 75-88.

[172] Srinivas Shakkottai, R. Srikant, Nevil Brownlee, Andre Broido. "The RTT distribution of TCP flows in the Internet and its impact on TCP-based flow control". *http://www.caida.org/outreach/ papers/2004/tr-2004-02/tr-2004-02.pdf*, 2004.

[173] UCN/LBL/VINT. "Network Simulator-NS2", *http://www-mash.cs.berkeley.edu/ns*.

[174] Qi Wu. "Automatic control theory". *Tsinghua University Press*, 1990, 134-140.

[175] Fernando Paganini, Zhikui Wang, Steven H. Low, John C. Doyle. "A new TCP/AQM for stable operation in fast networks". *Proceedings of IEEE Conference on Computer Communications (INFOCOM)*, 2005, 96-105.

[176] Shao Liu, Tamer Basar, R. Srikant. "Exponential-RED: a stabilizing AQM scheme for low- and high-speed TCP protocols". *IEEE/ACM Transactions on Networking*, 2005, 13(5).

[177] Srisankar Kunniyur, R. Srikant. "End-to-End congestion control schemes: utility functions, random losses and ECN marks". *IEEE/ACM Transactions on Networking,* 2003, 11(5): 689-702.

[178] Yuping Tian. "Stability analysis and design of the second-order congestion control for networks with heterogeneous delays". *IEEE/ACM Transactions on Networking*, 2005, 13(5): 1082-1093.

[179] Fernando Paganini, Zhikui Wang, John C. Doyle, Steven H. Low. "Congestion control for high performance, stability, and fairness in general networks". *IEEE/ACM Transactions on Networking*, 2005, 13(1): 43-56.

[180] Jianxin Wang, Liang Rong. "AOPC: an adaptive optimized proportional controller for AQM". *Proceedings of the International Conference on Parallel Processing(ICPP)*, 2006, 164-174.

[181] [181] Carlos E. Garcia, Manfred Morari. "Internal model control. 1. A unifying review and some new results". *Industry and Engineering Chemical Process Design and Device*, 1982, 21: 308-323.

[182] O. J. M Smith. "A controller to overcome dead time". *ISA Journal* 6(2), 1959: 28-33.

[183] D.Lin, R.Morris. "Dynamics of random early detection". *Proceedings of ACM Conference of the Special Interest Group on Data Communication (SIGCOMM)*, 1997, 127-137.

[184] I. Stoica, and H. Zhang. "Providing guaranteed services without per flow management". *Proceedings of ACM Conference of the Special Interest Group on Data Communication (SIGCOMM)*, 1999.

[185] P. Whittle. "Prediction and regulation by linear least-square methods", *University of Minnesota Press*, 1983.

[186] P.J. Brockwell, and R.A. Davis. "Time series: Theory and methods", *Springer-Verlag*, 1991.

[187] Y. Shu, L. Wang, L. Zhang. "Internet traffic modeling and prediction using FARIMA models". *Journal of computers*, 2001, 24(1): 46-54.

[188] W. Willinger, M. S. Taqqu, R. Sherman, and D. V. Wilson. "Self-similarity through high-variability: Statistical analysis of Ethernet LAN traffic at the source level". *IEEE/ACM Transactions on Networking,* 1997, 5(1): 71–86.

[189] M. E. Crovella and A. Bestavros. "Self-similarity in world wide web traffic: Evidence and possible causes". *IEEE/ACM Transactions on Networking.* 1997, 5(6): 835–846.

[190] R. Ramachandran and V. R. Bhethanabotla. "Generalized autoregressive moving average modeling of the Bellcore data". *Proceedings of IEEE Conference on Local Computer Networks (LCN)*, 2000, 654–661.

[191] A. Sang, S. Li. "A predictability analysis of network traffic". *Computer Networks*, 2002, 39(2-3): 329-345.

[192] S. Haykin, "Adaptive Filter Theory", *4th ed. Prentice Hall*, 2002.

[193] P. S. R. Diniz. "Adaptive filtering: Algorithms and Practical Implementation", *2nd Edition, Kluwer academic publishers*. 2002.

[194] A. Kamerman, L. Monteban, "WaveLAN II: A high-performance wireless LAN for the unlicensed band", *Bell Labs Technical Journal*, 1997, 2(3): 118-133.

[195] H. Gavin, V. Nitin, B. Paramvir, "A rate-adaptive MAC protocol for multi-hop wireless networks", *Proceedings of the annual international conference on Mobile computing and networking (MOBICOM)*, 2001, 236-251.

[196] S. Yi, M. Kappes, S. Garg, X. Deng, G. Kesidis, C.R. Das, "Proxy-RED: an AQM scheme for wireless local area networks", *Proceedings of the International Conference on Computer Communications and Networks (ICCCN)*, 2004, 460-465.

[197] X. Lin, X. Chang, J. Muppala, "VQ-RED: an efficient virtual queue management approach to improve fairness in infrastructure WLAN", *Proceedings of the IEEE Conference on Local Computer Networks (LCN)*, 2005, 632-638.

[198] A. GYASI-AGYEI, "Service differentiation in wireless internet using multi-class red with drop threshold proportional scheduling", *Proceedings of the IEEE International Conference on Networks (ICN)*, 2002, 175-180.

[199] M. Heusse, F. Rousseau, G. Berger Sabbatel, A. Duda, "Performance anomaly of 802.11b", *Proceedings of the Annual Joint Conference of the IEEE Computer and Communications Societies(INFOCOM)*, 2003, 836-843.

[200] Y. Seok, J. Park, Y. Choi, "Queue management algorithm for multi-rate wireless local area networks", *Proceedings of the IEEE Conference on Personal, Indoor and Mobile Radio Communications (PIMRC)*, 2003, 2003-2008.

[201] J. Widmer, "NO Ad-Hoc Routing Agent (NOAH)", http://icapeople.epfl.ch/widmer/ uwb */ns-2 /noah/*, 2004.

[202] R. Punnoose, P. Nikitin, D. Stancil, "Efficient simulation of Ricean fading within a packet simulator", *Proceedings of the 52nd IEEE Semiannual Vehicular Technology Conference (VTC)*, 2000, 764-767.

[203] Chadi Barakat, Eitan Altman, Walid Dabbous, "On TCP Performance in a Heterogeneous Network: A Survey", *IEEE Communications Magazine*, 2000, 38(1):40-46.

[204] Yanjun Feng. "Improving TCP Performance over MANET: A Survey", *Journal of Software*, 2005, 16(3): 434-444 (in Chinese with English abstract).

[205] N.K.G, Samaraweera, "Non-Congestion Packet Loss Detection for TCP Error Recovery using Wireless Links", *Proceedings of IEE Communications,* 1999, 146(4):222-230.

[206] Y. Tobe,Y. Tamura, A.Molano, S.Ghosh, H.Tokuda, "Achieving moderate fairness for UDP flows by path-status classification", *Proceedings of IEEE Local Computer Networks(LCN)*, 2000, 252-261.

[207] S. Biaz, N. Vaidya, "Discriminating congestion losses from wireless losses using interrival times at the receiver", *Proceedings of IEEE symposium Application-Specific Systems and Software Engineering and Technology,* 1999, 10-17.

[208] Zhenghua Fu, Ben Greenstein, Xiaoqiao Meng, Songwu Lu, "Design and Implementation of TCP-Friendly Transport Protocol for Ad Hoc Wireless Networks", *Proceedings of IEEE International Conference Network Protocols (ICNP)*, 2002, 216-225.

[209] Ruy de Oliveira, Torsten Braun, "A Delay-based Approach Using Fuzzy Logic to Improve TCP Error Detection in Ad Hoc Networks", *Proceedings of IEEE Wireless Communications and Networking (WCNC)*, 2004, 1666-1671.

[210] S. Biaz, Nitin H. vaidya. "De-Randomizing Congestion Losses to Improve TCP Performance Over Wired-Wireless Networks", *IEEE/ACM Transactions on Networking*, 2005, 13(3):596-608.

[211] IETF working group on Differentiated Service. *http://www.ietf.org/charters /diffserv.html*.

[212] H. Balakrishnan, R. Katz, "Explicit loss notification and wireless web performances", *Proceedings of IEEE Global Communications Conference (GLOBECOM)*, 1998, 3483-3487.

[213] Chuang Lin, "QoS in multimedia network". *Journal of software*, 1999, 10(10): 1016-1024. (in Chinese with English abstract)

[214] Braden R, Zhang L, Berson S, "Resource Reservation Protocol (RSVP)-Version 1, Function Specification". *http://www.ietf.org /rfc/rfc2205.txt*, 1997.

[215] Baker F, Iturralde C, le Faucheur F. "RSVP reservation aggregation", *IETF Internet Draft*, 1998.

[216] K. Nichols, V. Jacobson, L. Zhang. "A two bit differentiated services architecture for the internet", *http://www.ietf.org /rfc/rfc2638*, 1999.

[217] D. Clark, W. Fang. "Explicit allocation of best effort packet delivery". *IEEE/ACM Transactions on Networking*, 1998, 6 (4): 362-373.

[218] S. Blake, D. Black, M. Carlson, E. Davies, Z. Wang, W. Weiss, "An architecture for differentiated services". *http://www.ietf.org /rfc/rfc2475.txt*, 1998.

[219] Wei Liu, Zongkai Yang, Jianhua He, Chunhui Le, Chun Tung Chou. "Analysis and Improvement on the Robustness of AQM in DiffServ Networks". *Proceedings of IEEE International Conference on Communications*, 2004, 2297-2301.

[220] W. Willinger, M. S. Taqqu, R. Sherman, D. V. Wilson. "Self-similarity through high-variability: Statistical analysis of Ethernet LAN traffic at the source level", *IEEE/ACM Transactions on Networking*, 1997, 5(1): 71–86.

[221] Y. Shu, L. Wang, L. Zhang, "Internet traffic modeling and prediction using FARIMA models", *Chinese Journal of computers*, 2001, 24(1): 46-54. (in Chinese with English abstract).

[222] S. Deb, R. Srikant, "Global stability of congestion controllers for the Internet", *IEEE Transactions on Automatic Control*, 2003, 48(6):1055-1060.

[223] L. Ying, G. E. Dullerud, R. Srikant, "Global stability of internet congestion controllers with heterogeneous delays", *IEEE/ACM Transactions on Networking*, 2006, 14(3):579-591.

[224] P. Ranjan, R. J. La, and E. H. Abed, Global stability conditions for rate control with arbitrary communication delays. *IEEE/ACM Transactions on Networking*, 2006, 14(1):94-107.

[225] D. Loguinov, H. Radha, "End-to-end rate-based congestion control: convergence properties and scalability analysis", *IEEE/ACM Transactions on Networking*, 11(5), 2003:564-577.

[226] C. V. Hollot, V. Misra, D. F. Towsley, W. Gong, "A control theoretic analysis of RED", *Proceedings of IEEE Conference on Computer Communications (INFOCOM)*, 2001, 1510-1519.

[227] Xiaomeng Huang, Chuang Lin, Fengyuan Ren, Guangwen Yang, Peter D. Ungsuman, Yuanzhuo Wang, "Improving the convergence and stability of congestion control algorithm", *Proceedings of IEEE International Conference Network Protocols (ICNP)*, 2007, 206-215.

[228] L. H. Andrew, B. P. Wydrowski, S. H. Low, "An example of instability in XCP", *http://www.cs.caltech.edu/~lanchlan/abstract/xcpInstability.pdf*.

[229] S. H. Low, L. L. H. Andrew, B. P. Wydrowski, Understanding XCP: Equilibrium and fairness, *IEEE/ACM Transactions on Networking*, 2009, 17(6):1697-1710.

[230] S. Jain, D. Loguinov, "PIQI-RCP: Design and analysis of rate-based explicit congestion control". *Proceedings of Thirteenth International Workshop on Quality of Service (IWQoS)*, 2007, 10-20.

[231] L. L. H. Andrew, K. Jacobsson, S. H. Low, M. Suchara, R. Witt, B. P. Wydrowski, "MaxNet: Theory and implementation".*http://netlab. caltech.edu/~lachlan/abstract/ maxnet/ ThAndImp.pdf*.

[232] D. X. Wei, P. Cao, S. H. Low, "TCP pacing revisited", *Proceedings of IEEE Conference on Computer Communications (INFOCOM)*, 2006, 3453-3462.

[233] J. Aweya, M. Ouellette, and D. Y. Montuno, "Design and stability analysis of a rate control algorithm using the Routh-Hurwitz stability criterion", *IEEE/ACM Transactions on Networking*, 2004, 12(4): 719-732.

[234] Francesco Vacirca, Andrea Baiocchi, Angelo Castellani, "YeAH-TCP: yet Another Highspeed TCP", *Proceedings of International Workshop on Protocols for FAST Long-Distance Networks (PFLDnet)*, 2007.

[235] Kazumi Kaneko, Jiro Katto, "TCP-Fusion: A Hybrid Congestion Control Algorithm for High-speed Networks", *Proceedings of International Workshop on Protocols for FAST Long-Distance Networks (PFLDnet)*, 2007.

[236] J Mo, RJ La, V Anantharam, J Walrand, "Analysis and Comparison of TCP Reno and Vegas," *Proceedings of IEEE Conference on Computer Communications (INFOCOM)*, 1999, 1556-1563.

[237] K. K. Ramakrishnan and S. Floyd, "The Addition of Explicit Congestion Notification (ECN) to IP", *http://www.ietf.org /rfc/rfc3168.txt*, 2001.

[238] S. H. Low, F. Paganini, J. Wang, S. Adlakha, J. C. Doyle, "Dynamics of TCP/RED and a scalable control," *Proceedings of IEEE Conference on Computer Communications (INFOCOM)*, 2002, 239-248.

[239] A. Tang, D. Wei, S. H. Low, "Heterogeneous congestion control: efficiency, fairness, and design", *Proceedings of IEEE International Conference Network Protocols (ICNP)*, 2006, 127-136.

[240] Ian F, Wang XD, Wang WL. "Wireless Mesh networks: a survey", *Elsevier Computer Networks,* 2005, 47(4):445-487.

[241] Zhang Y, Luo JJ, Hu HL. *Wireless Mesh networking: architectures, protocols and standards*. Auerbach Publications, 1st edition, 2006.

[242] IEEE 802 LAN/MAN Standards Committee. *http://www.ieee802.org*.

[243] Jun J, Sichitiu M L. "The nominal capacity of wireless Mesh networks", *IEEE Wireless Communications* 2003; 10(5):8-14.

[244] Nandiraju N, Nandiraju D, Cavalcanti D, "A novel queue management mechanism for improving performance of multihop flows in IEEE 802.11s based mesh networks",

Proceedings of IEEE International Performance, Computing, and Communications Conference, 2006, 168-174.

[245] Cao M, Ma WC, Zhang Q, "Modeling and Performance Analysis of the Distributed Scheduler in IEEE 802.16 Mesh Mode", *Proceedings of the ACM international symposium on Mobile ad hoc networking and computing (MOBIHOC)*, 2005, 78-89.

[246] Shi J, Gurewitz O, Mancuso V, "Measurement and Modeling of the Origins of Starvation in Congestion Controlled Mesh networks", *Proceedings of IEEE Conference on Computer Communications (INFOCOM)*, 2008, 1832-1845.

[247] Shi J, Gurewitz O, Mancuso V, "Starvation in operational urban mesh networks: Compounding effects of congestion control and medium access", *Rice University Technical Report TREE0709. http://www.ece.rice.edu/_jingpu/doc/tcpmeshtr.pdf*, 2007.

[248] Bianchi G., "Performance analysis of the IEEE 802.11 distributed coordination function", *IEEE Journal on Selected Areas in Communications* 2000; 18(3):535-547.

[249] Yang YL, Kravets R. "Achieving Delay Guarantees in Ad Hoc Networks Using Distributed Contention Window Adaptation", *Proceedings of IEEE Conference on Computer Communications (INFOCOM)*, 2007, 1-12.

[250] D. Kotz and K. Essien, "Analysis of a campus-wide wireless network," *Proceedings of ACM Conference on Mobile Computing and Networking (MOBICOM)*, 2002, 107-118.

[251] A. Jardosh, K. Mittal, K. Ramachandran, E. Belding, K. Almeroth, "IQU: Practical Queue-Based User Association Management for WLANs," *Proceedings of ACM Conference on Mobile Computing and Networking (MOBICOM)*, 2006, 158-169.

[252] S. Pilosof, R. Ramjee, D. Raz, Y. Shavitt, P. Sinha, "Understanding TCP fairness over wireless LAN," *Proceedings of IEEE Conference on Computer Communications (INFOCOM)*, 2003, 863-872.

[253] J. MOON and B. LEE, "Rate-Adaptive Snoop: A TCP Enhancement Scheme Over Rate-Controlled Lossy Links", *IEEE/ACM Transactions on Networking*, 2006, 14(3): 603-615.

[254] B. Sadeghi, V. Kanodia, A. Sabharwal, E. Knightly, "Opportunistic Media Access for Multirate Ad Hoc Networks," *Proceedings of ACM Conference on Mobile Computing and Networking (MOBICOM)*, 2002, 24-35.

[255] M. Heusse, F. Rousseau, G. Berge-Dabbatel, A. Duda, "Idle Sense: An Optimal Access Method for High Throughput and Fairness in Rate Diverse Wireless LANs," *Proceedings of ACM Conference of the Special Interest Group on Data Communication (SIGCOMM)*, 2005, 121-132.

[256] S. Kim, B. S. Kim, Y. Fang, "Downlink and uplink resource allocation in IEEE 802.11 wireless LANs," *IEEE Transactions on Vehicular Technology*, 2005, 54(1):320-327.

[257] Z. Fu, P. Zerfos, H. Luo, S. Lu, L. Zhang, M. Gerla, "The impact of multihop wireless channel on TCP throughput and loss," *Proceedings of IEEE Conference on Computer Communications (INFOCOM)*, 2003, 1744-1753.

[258] K. Xu, M. Gerla, L. Qi, Y. Shu, "Enhancing TCP Fairness in Ad Hoc Wireless Networks Using Neighborhood RED," *Proceedings of ACM Conference on Mobile Computing and Networking (MOBICOM)*, 2003, 16-28.

[259] R. Paulo. *http://netbsd-soc.sourceforge.net/ecn/*, 2006.

[260] IEEE WG, "Part 11: Wireless LAN Medium Access Control (MAC) and Physical Layer (PHY) Specifications, *IEEE 802.11 Standard*," 1999.

[261] J. Choi, J. Na, Y. Lim, K. Park, "Collision-aware design of rate adaptation for multi-rate 802.11 WLANs", *IEEE Journal on Selected Areas in Communications*, 2008, 26(8):1366-1375.

[262] Y. Wu, Z. Niu, J. Zheng, "Upstream/Downstream Unfairness Issue of TCP over Wireless LANs with Per-flow Queueing", *Proceedings of IEEE International Conference on Communications (ICC)*, 2005, 3543-3547.

[263] J. Ha, C. H. Choi, "TCP Fairness for Uplink and Downlink Flows in WLANs", *Proceedings of IEEE Global Communications Conference (GLOBECOM)*, 2006, 1-5.

[264] A. Ng, D. Malone, D. Leith, "Experimental Evaluation of TCP Performance and Fairness in an 802.11e Test-bed," *ACM SIGCOMM Workshop on Experimental Approaches to Wireless Network Design and Analysis*, 2005.

[265] E. C. Park, D. Y. kim, C. H. Choi, "Analysis of Unfairness between TCP Uplink and Downlink Flows in Wi-Fi Hot Spots", *Proceedings of IEEE Global Communications Conference (GLOBECOM)*, 2006, 1-5.

[266] Vivek Raghunathan and P. R. Kumar, "A Counterexample in Congestion Control of Wireless Networks", *Performance Evaluation*, 2007, 64(5):399-418.

[267] Lijun Chen, Steven H. Low and John C. Doyle, "Joint Congestion Control and Media Access Control Design for Ad Hoc Wireless Network", *Proceedings of IEEE Conference on Computer Communications (INFOCOM)*, 2005, 2212-2222.

[268] Y Su, T Gross, "WXCP: Explicit Congestion Control for Wireless Multi-Hop Networks", *Proceedings of Thirteenth International Workshop on Quality of Service (IWQoS)*, 2005,313-326

[269] Peng Yue, Bing Zhang, Zengji Liu, Weijun Zeng, "Performance Analysis and Improvement of TFRC in Ad Hoc Networks", *Journal of JiLin University*, 2006, 24(6):640-647 (in Chinese with English abstract).

[270] Dong, Y, Makrakis, D, Sullivan, T., "Network congestion control in ad hoc IEEE 802.11 wireless LAN", *Proceedings of IEEE Electrical and Computer Engineering (CCECE)*, 2003, 12-19.

[271] H.q. Zhai, X. Chen, Y.g. Fang, "Improving Transport Layer Performance in Multihop Ad Hoc Networks by Exploiting MAC Layer Information", *IEEE Transactions on Wireless Communications*, 2007, 6(5):1692-1701.

[272] YongKang Xiao, "Performance Study of MAC and TCP protocol in Ad Hoc Networks", *Ph.D. Thesis, Beijing, School of Electronic Engineering, TsingHua University*, 2004.

[273] Kitae Nahm,Ahmed Helmy,C.C.Jay Kuo, "TCP over Multihop 802.11 Networks: Issues and Performance Enhancement", *Proceedings of IEEE Conference on Computer Communications (INFOCOM)*, 2005, 277-287.

[274] Jin Ye, JianXin Wang, "A TCP protocol Based on Prediction of Congestion Probability in Hybrid Networks", *Journal of Chinese Computer Systems*, 2008, 28(10):1776-1780 (in Chinese with English abstract).

[275] G. Wu, Y. Bai, J. Lai, A. Ogielski, "Interactions between TCP and RLP in wireless Internet", *Proceedings of IEEE Global Communications Conference (GLOBECOM)*, 1999, 661-666.

[276] Kuzmanovic, "The Power of Explicit Congestion Notification", *Proceedings of ACM Conference of the Special Interest Group on Data Communication (SIGCOMM)*, 2005, 61-72.

[277] Rui Paulo,*http://netbsd-soc.sourceforge.net/projects/ecn/*, 2006.

[278] A. Gurtov, S. Floyd, "Modeling Wireless Links for Transport Protocols", *ACM SIGCOMM Computer Communications Review*, 2004, 34(2):85-96.

[279] Fei Peng. *Internet draft: draft-fpeng-wecn-03.txt.*

[280] K. Xu, Y. Tian, N. Ansari, "TCP-Jersey for Wireless IP Communications", *IEEE Journal on Selected Areas in Communications*, 2004, 22(4):747-756.

[281] S.-J. Bae, S. Chong, "TCP-friendly wireless multimedia. flow control using ECN marking", *Proceedings of IEEE Global Communications Conference (GLOBECOM)*, 2002, 1794-1799.

[282] Fei Peng, Alnuweiri, H.Leung, V.C.M., "A novel flow control scheme for improving TCP fairness and throughput over heterogeneous networks with wired and wireless links", *Proceedings of IEEE International Conference on Communications (ICC)*, 2005, 3565-3569.

[283] S. Biaz, Xia Wang, "Can ECN Be Used to Differentiate Congestion Losses from Wireless Losses?", *Technical Report CSSE04-04*, 2004.

[284] H. Bai, D. Lilja, M. Atiquzzaman, "Applying speculative technique to improve TCP throughput over lossy links", *Proceedings of IEEE Global Communications Conference (GLOBECOM)*, 2005, 3681-3687.

[285] A. Durresi, M. Sridharan, C. Liu, M. Goyal, R. Jain, "Congestion Control using Multilevel Explicit Congestion Notification in Satellite Networks", *Proceedings of IEEE International Conference on Computer Communications and Networks (ICCCN)*, 2001, 483-488.

[286] M. Sridharan, A. Durresi, C. Liu, R. Jain, "Wireless TCP Enhancements using Multi-level ECN", *Proceedings of SPIE ITCOMM*, 2003.

[287] Liu,C, Hain, R. "Improving explicit congestion notification with mark-front strategy", *Computer Networks*, 2001, 35(2):185-201.

[288] R. Jain, D. chiu, W. Hawe, "A quantitative measure of fairness and discrimination in shared computer systems", *DEC, Res.Rep.TR-301*, 1984.

INDEX

A

access, xii, 5, 54, 183, 191, 195, 201, 205, 206, 211, 217, 218, 228, 229, 230, 231, 234, 235, 246, 260, 267
accounting, 108, 109
accuracy, xi, 110, 111, 130, 131, 135, 136, 140, 179, 238
ad hoc network, 267
ad hoc networking, 267
adaptability, x, 34, 38, 45, 46, 48, 49, 58
adaptation, 112, 119, 187, 268
adjustment, 12, 15, 21, 25, 36, 39, 45, 60, 62, 131, 195, 249, 251
aggregation, 57, 139, 265
aggressiveness, 22, 48, 60, 85, 186
applications, viii, 8, 33, 37, 49, 56, 57, 63, 64, 93, 94, 139, 175, 201, 227, 253, 254
assignment, 154, 159, 161, 162, 163, 165, 173, 174
authors, 9, 25, 37, 52, 53, 54, 56, 57, 64, 81, 119, 129, 130, 140, 185, 198, 227
averaging, 109, 166
avoidance, x, 12, 14, 19, 22, 35, 56, 69, 175, 208, 246, 253, 254, 255

B

background, ix, 24, 38, 41, 44, 46, 48, 60, 183, 211
bandwidth allocation, 23, 27, 28, 185, 250, 254, 257
bandwidth resources, 25
bandwidth utilization, 22, 26, 28, 30, 34, 38, 140, 175, 177, 183
behavior, xiii, 5, 7, 10, 13, 17, 30, 70, 71, 85, 88, 90, 91, 94, 103, 113, 153, 158, 162, 170, 171, 174, 178, 181, 185, 214, 227, 237, 238, 243, 254
behaviors, 55, 81, 93, 101, 185, 251, 262
Beijing, 268
bias, 30, 131, 132, 133, 134, 136, 175
Bluetooth, ix, 191

C

caching, 58, 60
challenges, 19, 33, 175
channels, ix, 46, 196, 234
China, viii, 92
classes, 139, 183
classification, 264
clients, 87, 191
communication, x, 12, 56, 65, 91, 105, 139, 155, 168, 201, 209, 265
community, 14, 37
compatibility, 21, 36, 40, 55, 228
compensation, 91, 262
competition, 191, 194, 201, 228, 229, 230, 233, 234, 235
complement, x
complexity, 7, 21, 24, 30, 36, 51, 55, 95, 107, 117, 178, 188, 229, 256
compliance, x
components, 69, 77, 156, 220, 251
comprehension, 155
computation, 76, 110
computer science, ix
computer systems, 269
computer technology, ix
computing, vii, 3, 112, 157, 264, 267
configuration, 76, 162, 182, 183
conflict, 193, 194, 195, 234, 235
convergence, x, xi, 22, 23, 30, 43, 55, 57, 70, 80, 81, 83, 88, 90, 101, 112, 153, 154, 158, 163, 165, 170, 174, 186, 265, 266
correlation, 14, 30, 52, 70, 76, 77, 89, 129, 176, 229, 238, 241
cost, 3, 24, 49, 51, 120, 130, 140, 245
coupling, xii
cross-layer design, xii, 227, 228, 229, 230

D

damping, 72, 73, 74, 81
data analysis, 7
data rates, 119, 120, 124, 127, 217, 221
data transfer, 20, 33, 175
DCA, 20
decisions, 15, 16
deficiencies, 35, 154
deficit, 256
definition, 15, 16, 163, 165
derivatives, 97, 98
destination, 8, 12, 60, 177, 179
desynchronization, 53
detection, 22, 24, 110, 117, 153, 176, 179, 196, 254, 255, 260, 263
deviation, 71, 83, 84, 85, 86, 94, 105, 114, 115, 148, 149
differential equations, 7
differentiation, 130, 264
discipline, 122, 257
distribution, 38, 52, 53, 60, 121, 131, 134, 171, 192, 198, 200, 205, 210, 220, 238, 262
diversity, 119, 123
division, 60
downlink, xii, 119, 205, 206, 207, 208, 209, 210, 211, 212, 214, 217, 218, 221, 222, 224
draft, 259, 269
duration, 83, 129, 171
dynamics, 5, 12, 13, 52, 53, 71, 76, 79, 87, 90, 92, 95, 162, 163

E

empirical studies, 111, 140, 180
employment, 170
emptiness, 70, 85, 104
engineering, ix, 72, 253
environment, vii, 19, 24, 28, 33, 34, 39, 46, 48, 49, 52, 57, 60, 62, 63, 65, 70, 124, 185, 246
equilibrium, 26, 36, 44, 55, 158
estimating, 153, 180
evolution, ix, 70, 82, 86, 87, 88, 89, 93, 102, 156, 162, 262
external environment, 34

F

feedback, xii, 5, 7, 9, 11, 14, 15, 16, 20, 21, 22, 23, 24, 25, 28, 30, 35, 41, 43, 49, 52, 55, 60, 70, 79, 89, 90, 91, 92, 95, 96, 97, 98, 99, 133, 153, 156, 163, 170, 175, 176, 177, 185, 196, 206, 228, 235, 238, 239, 240, 243, 247, 262
flexibility, 70, 137, 191

flight, 25, 132, 133
fluctuant, 182
fluid, 6, 7, 70, 156
formula, 70, 77, 89, 90, 95, 178, 197, 208, 210
full capacity, 176

G

Georgia, viii
goals, 11, 31, 110
government, iv
GPS, 7, 8
graduate students, xiii
graph, 243
groups, x, 129
growth, ix, 20, 21, 22, 25, 35, 36, 39, 40, 41, 42, 45, 48, 60, 61, 91, 156, 176, 185
growth mechanism, 61
growth modes, 22
growth rate, 21, 25, 39, 40, 42, 45
guidance, xiii
guidelines, 70, 71, 92

H

handoff, 237
heterogeneity, ix, 76
hotels, 205, 217
hybrid, xii, 15, 87, 88, 130, 131, 137, 227, 228, 230, 232, 233, 235, 237, 238, 241, 243, 245, 246
hypothesis, 134

I

ICC, 257, 258, 259, 260, 268, 269
ideal, xi, 5, 9, 16, 87, 91, 97, 134, 163, 174
implementation, 16, 36, 51, 64, 80, 90, 99, 112, 141, 154, 156, 166, 180, 227, 266
implicit knowledge, 13
independence, 36, 45
indication, viii, 7, 11, 12, 13, 14, 35, 229
indicators, xii, 70, 206
information exchange, 30
infrastructure, 3, 264
inspiration, 31
instability, 11, 20, 108, 173, 261, 266
interaction, 56, 192, 195, 203
interface, 124, 228
interference, 46, 119, 211, 227
internet, 254, 257, 261, 264, 265
Internet, vii, viii, ix, 3, 4, 5, 6, 8, 9, 12, 19, 30, 33, 34, 35, 51, 52, 54, 55, 56, 57, 65, 69, 76, 79, 90, 91, 139, 153, 175, 176, 191, 205, 206, 216, 227, 232, 234, 237, 246, 253, 256, 257, 258, 259, 261, 262, 263, 265, 268, 269

interval, xi, 15, 21, 36, 38, 39, 48, 54, 83, 100, 110, 113, 129, 131, 132, 134, 140, 141, 142, 143, 144, 145, 155, 156, 157, 166, 167, 168, 177, 178, 179, 186, 194, 229, 234, 238, 245
inversion, 112
issues, vii, viii, x, xi, 3, 5, 14, 30, 31, 35, 48, 52, 64, 65, 70, 90, 153, 157, 206, 261

J

judgment, 49
justification, 12

L

latency, 11, 12, 38, 39, 45, 51, 65, 205
lifetime, 76, 87
links, vii, ix, 4, 5, 12, 37, 54, 57, 60, 63, 81, 86, 88, 90, 101, 104, 115, 153, 155, 162, 163, 169, 182, 183, 185, 211, 227, 255, 260, 269
local area networks, 205, 217, 264
Luo, 258, 266, 267

M

MAC protocols, 202, 226
management, ix, xi, 5, 6, 9, 11, 20, 24, 26, 27, 28, 29, 30, 31, 33, 39, 44, 48, 57, 62, 65, 69, 76, 107, 108, 110, 119, 120, 137, 139, 140, 150, 154, 156, 157, 166, 168, 173, 191, 254, 257, 262, 263, 264, 266
Markov chain, 136
matrix, 112, 141, 180, 228
measurement, 14, 52, 75, 77, 109, 110, 113, 129, 130, 145, 207
measures, x, 70, 75, 76, 89, 206
media, 56, 201, 205
membership, 156, 157, 168, 173, 174
mesh networks, 266, 267
microeconomic theory, vii
Microsoft, 237, 259
mobility, 127, 191, 237
model reduction, 95, 98
modeling, ix, x, 6, 72, 91, 153, 254, 256, 261, 263, 265
models, ix, 6, 7, 31, 52, 54, 65, 71, 81, 139, 262, 263, 265
motivation, 76, 255
multimedia, viii, 139, 256, 265, 269

N

network congestion, 3, 4, 5, 7, 8, 13, 14, 22, 33, 43, 110, 177, 178, 207, 233, 237, 240
network elements, 5

networking, ix, 14, 253, 254, 255, 256, 257, 262, 264, 266
next generation, 19, 30
nodes, vii, 3, 5, 6, 7, 9, 11, 12, 24, 28, 31, 69, 108, 119, 120, 123, 124, 126, 139, 178, 191, 192, 193, 194, 195, 198, 201, 205, 206, 207, 211, 214, 217, 218, 226, 227, 229, 232, 234, 235
noise, 7, 23, 136, 176
normal distribution, 171
numerical computations, 165

O

objectives, 64, 69, 107, 117
observations, 81, 111, 140, 160, 180, 238
optimal performance, x, 48
optimization, vii, 8, 15, 16, 49, 64, 89, 195, 227, 228
order, x, 8, 12, 13, 14, 16, 21, 28, 37, 38, 42, 49, 51, 54, 60, 70, 71, 72, 76, 77, 80, 89, 92, 95, 96, 97, 98, 100, 103, 108, 111, 112, 120, 122, 129, 139, 141, 155, 157, 177, 178, 180, 183, 194, 212, 219, 227, 232, 239, 245, 246, 263
ordinary differential equations, 71, 94
oscillation, 22, 25, 83, 87, 88, 92, 157, 185, 186
oscillations, x, 82, 84, 85, 88, 89, 90, 91, 93, 99, 102, 104, 124, 154, 162

P

pacing, 54, 157, 261, 266
packet forwarding, 57
parameter, x, 16, 22, 25, 26, 28, 39, 45, 49, 55, 60, 70, 71, 72, 73, 74, 75, 76, 77, 79, 80, 81, 89, 90, 92, 96, 98, 100, 108, 111, 113, 122, 124, 140, 160, 163, 170, 180, 210, 212, 220, 233
parameters, xi, 7, 10, 16, 21, 24, 28, 29, 36, 38, 48, 49, 65, 70, 72, 75, 76, 77, 81, 87, 90, 92, 94, 95, 97, 98, 99, 100, 107, 108, 110, 113, 124, 130, 131, 137, 140, 145, 146, 153, 161, 170, 182, 185, 195, 233, 234, 240, 246
Pareto, 87
performance indicator, 57, 63
poor, 7, 26, 28, 42, 44, 46, 88, 147
poor performance, 26, 42, 44, 46
power, 16, 124, 160
predictability, 111, 140, 150, 263
prediction, xi, 107, 110, 111, 113, 140, 141, 145, 150, 180, 257, 263, 265
predictors, 96, 97, 111, 130, 180
preferential treatment, 139
price mechanism, xii
probability, x, xi, xii, 10, 11, 52, 70, 71, 75, 76, 77, 78, 79, 89, 94, 95, 100, 102, 107, 108, 109, 110, 112, 117, 120, 121, 122, 130, 131, 135, 136, 140,

141, 143, 144, 147, 194, 195, 196, 197, 198, 199, 202, 207, 208, 209, 210, 212, 217, 218, 219, 228, 235, 240, 244, 245

propagation, 27, 35, 37, 45, 56, 63, 81, 121, 123, 124, 135, 179, 183, 209, 211

properties, xi, xii, 6, 7, 16, 52, 71, 83, 113, 128, 175, 186, 195, 216, 225, 265

punishment, xi, 107, 109, 112, 116, 117

Q

QoS, 9, 94, 119, 120, 139, 202, 254, 265
quality of service, 8, 69, 119, 139, 262
queuing theory, 198, 262

R

radio, 19, 34, 37
range, 7, 52, 58, 70, 76, 80, 81, 82, 90, 131, 140, 163, 180, 250, 256
reason, 11, 13, 26, 27, 28, 29, 30, 41, 108, 170, 173, 183, 185, 186, 193, 235
recovery, 12, 13, 14, 35, 36, 48, 255
reflection, 108, 110
region, 153, 159
regression, 111, 141, 180
relationship, 31, 52, 53, 55, 57, 76, 95
relativity, 177
reliability, 30, 33, 40, 49, 177
REM, x, 7, 11, 28, 70, 71, 81, 82, 84, 86, 87, 89, 91, 92, 93, 94, 102, 103, 104, 105, 254
replacement, 153
resource allocation, 155, 156, 228, 267
resources, ix, 5, 8, 12, 15, 25, 154, 167, 206
respect, xi, 82, 84, 90, 116, 145, 146, 147, 148, 149, 150, 237, 243
response time, 16, 45, 82
responsiveness, 9, 11, 70, 82, 87, 88
robustness, 33, 70, 81, 90, 91, 96, 257
routing, 5, 6, 52, 57, 124, 197, 199, 211, 222, 229, 237
RTS, xii, 122, 194, 195, 196, 198, 200, 201, 202, 207, 210, 211, 220, 222, 229, 230, 231, 232, 234, 235

S

sampling, 23, 133, 156
satellite, 19, 33, 34, 35, 37, 45, 46, 47, 48, 175
saturation, 22, 23, 56
scheduling, x, xii, 5, 6, 7, 8, 9, 57, 109, 217, 218, 219, 221, 224, 253, 255, 256, 257, 262, 264
searching, 132, 133
sensitivity, 28, 72, 73, 89, 208
sensor nodes, 227

shares, 25, 176, 207
sharing, 3, 7, 8, 11, 12, 108, 178, 185, 254
signals, xii, 9, 14, 23, 129, 176, 177, 179
software, 112, 141, 180, 194, 259, 265
space, 4, 5, 9, 11, 26, 28, 35, 40, 41, 51, 54, 55, 58, 144, 157, 159
speed, ix, x, 4, 5, 14, 15, 19, 21, 23, 27, 28, 29, 30, 33, 37, 39, 40, 51, 56, 60, 62, 65, 86, 90, 96, 112, 141, 153, 175, 180, 183, 185, 186, 187, 253, 256, 257, 259, 260, 263, 266
speed of response, 96
stability, x, xi, 9, 11, 20, 21, 28, 30, 36, 49, 53, 56, 57, 62, 70, 75, 76, 77, 80, 82, 87, 90, 91, 92, 98, 101, 105, 107, 112, 113, 116, 117, 153, 154, 155, 158, 159, 160, 161, 164, 170, 171, 173, 174, 185, 230, 256, 263, 265, 266
stabilization, xi, 140, 145, 146, 147, 149, 150
standard deviation, 83, 113, 115, 146, 147, 148, 149
standards, 191, 266
starvation, 57, 169, 185, 191, 192, 193, 194, 202, 203
statistics, 131, 242
storage, 3, 51, 54, 255
strategies, 23, 48, 49, 57
strategy, 21, 33, 40, 49, 57, 60, 153, 269
students, vii, ix, xiii
susceptibility, 136
switching, 12, 46, 256, 262
synchronization, 53, 56, 57, 58, 108, 120, 144

T

telephone, 253
terminals, 235
threshold, 10, 12, 21, 22, 36, 37, 39, 40, 46, 48, 54, 55, 60, 65, 119, 121, 141, 143, 145, 179, 196, 200, 201, 206, 212, 231, 232, 238, 241, 242, 245, 246, 248, 249, 264
thresholds, 60, 119, 121
tracking, 70, 77, 245
trade, 54, 56
trade-off, 54, 56
trajectory, 162, 170, 172
transformation, 159
transition, 136, 154, 243
transmits, 121, 123, 126, 231
transport, 7, 30, 55, 64, 81, 101, 153, 217, 255, 260

U

uniform, 121, 136, 198, 210, 220
updating, 100, 156, 157, 181, 187
uplink, xii, 119, 206, 207, 208, 209, 210, 214, 215, 217, 218, 221, 222, 224, 225, 267

V

validation, 254
variability, 23, 38, 263, 265
variable factor, 131
variables, 7, 76, 129, 134
variance, 16, 107, 124, 178
variations, 35, 76, 89
vector, 111, 112, 141, 180

W

weakness, 23, 28, 108

web, 56, 63, 64, 87, 89, 90, 119, 263, 265
Wi-Fi, 191, 268
windows, xii, 23, 53, 60, 129, 137, 156, 157, 175,
    177, 181, 192, 194, 201, 206, 218, 245, 255
wireless LANs, 267
wireless networks, vii, ix, xii, 15, 19, 34, 36, 44, 45,
    48, 119, 175, 191, 196, 205, 206, 214, 227, 228,
    230, 232, 237, 255, 256, 264
wireless sensor networks, 19, 33, 175

Y

Y-axis, 170